It has been well documented that American Catholics tend to be Catholics on their own terms, choosing to remain Catholic while selectively embracing official church doctrine. But why do Catholics who disagree with official church teachings on major issues such as homosexuality, women's ordination, or abortion, and who are thus institutionally marginalized, choose to remain Catholic? Why do they stay, when the cost of staying and being stigmatized would seem to be greater than the benefits they might gain from switching to religious groups whose doctrines would validate their beliefs on these issues? Michele Dillon, drawing upon interviews with Catholics who are openly gay or lesbian, advocates of women's ordination, and pro-choice, investigates why and how pro-change Catholics continue to remain actively involved in the church, despite their rejection of the Vatican's teaching on sexuality and gender.

Rather than discarding their Catholic identities, Dillon argues, pro-change Catholics remain deliberatively, reflectively, and self-conciously engaged with Catholicism, while aiming to make the church more inclusive, participatory, and pluralistic. Rather than fracturing the tradition, they seek a greater integrity between its doctrinal values and institutional practices.

While an emphasis on papal authority dominates public images and much of the literature on Catholicism, this book documents how other strands in the Catholic tradition legitimate the views of the many Catholics who disagree with the pope, and empower them to seek a Catholicism that is more closely aligned with the demands of life in the late twentieth century. Dillon identifies resources within Catholicism – the valuing of community, doctrinal reflexivity, pluralism, and a reasoned theology – that enable Catholics to carve an identity that is relatively autonomous of the church hierarchy's authority. This book demonstrates how Catholicism is defined in practice, not solely by the Vatican or the church hierarchy, b_ _ _ _ _ _ _ _ _ _ary Catholics interpret, make sense of _ _ _ _ _ _ _ _ _ _ _ on.

Michele Dillon is Associate Prof_ _ _ _ _ _ _ _ _ _ _ ty and author of *Debating Divorce: M_ _

CATHOLIC IDENTITY

BALANCING REASON, FAITH, AND POWER

MICHELE DILLON
Yale University

CAMBRIDGE
UNIVERSITY PRESS

PUBLISHED BY THE PRESS SYNDICATE OF THE UNIVERSITY OF CAMBRIDGE
The Pitt Building, Trumpington Street, Cambridge, United Kingdom

CAMBRIDGE UNIVERSITY PRESS
The Edinburgh Building, Cambridge CB2 2RU, UK www.cup.cam.ac.uk
40 West 20th Street, New York, NY 10011-4211, USA www.cup.org
10 Stamford Road, Oakleigh, Melbourne 3166, Australia
Ruiz de Alarcón 13, 28014 Madrid, Spain

First published 1999

Printed in the United States of America

Typeface Goudy 10.5/13 pt. *System* QuarkXPress [CTK]

A catalog record for this book is available from the British Library.

Library of Congress Cataloging-in-Publication data
Dillon, Michele, 1960–
Catholic identity: balancing reason, faith, and power / Michele Dillon
p. cm.
Includes bibliographical references and index.
1. Catholics – United States – Attitudes.   2. Catholic Church – United
States – Public opinion.   3. United States – Public opinion.   I. Title.
BX1406.2.D53 1999
282'.73 - dc21   98–50662
CIP

ISBN 0 521 63044 4 hardback
ISBN 0 521 63959 X paperback

For Paul,
Michael, and Andrew

CONTENTS

ACKNOWLEDGMENTS

I have enjoyed writing this book because of the cooperation and generosity of many people. First and foremost, I owe an enormous debt to all of the people who participated in this study. I deeply appreciate the openness and hospitality of members of Dignity/Boston who were happy for me, an outsider, to observe their worship and other communal activities. Most especially, I thank the Dignity women and men who consented to be personally interviewed and who during that time shared so much of the pain and joy in their lives. I also thank the members of Dignity, the Women's Ordination Conference, Catholics for a Free Choice, and the Catholic League for Religious and Civil Rights for their generosity in completing detailed questionnaires. Peggy Hayes, Ruth Fitzpatrick, Greg Lebel, Marie Baldwin, and William Donohue provided a facilitative introduction to their respective organizations. I am also greatly indebted to the theologians whom I interviewed. Special thanks are also due Chris Connors, Michelle Decoste, David Hollenbach, M. A. Ladd, Christopher Lawrence, Elizabeth Marcellino-Boisvert, Jane Powers, and Jon Schum.

I am fortunate to have benefited from conversations with Michael Hout, Gene Burns, John Coleman, Andrew Greeley, Ted Jelen, Katherine Meyer, Martin Sanchez Jankowski, Marta Vides, Ruth Wallace, and Tony Wilhelm. At Yale, I value the interest in my research shown by David Apter, Wendell Bell, Deborah Davis, Juan Linz, and Debra Minkoff. Special thanks are due to Charles Perrow, and to three anonymous reviewers for Cambridge University Press whose extensive comments on an early draft of the manuscript were very helpful and encouraging. I have also benefited from presenting my work at meetings of the American Sociological Association and the

Society for the Scientific Study of Religion, a conference sponsored by the Communitarian Network at New York University, and a Newman Hall faculty dinner at the University of California, Berkeley. I appreciate the detailed and reflective comments of Mary Child, my editor at Cambridge University Press, the copyediting provided by Russell Hahn, and Camilla Knapp for her good humor and patience in overseeing the production process.

My research was supported by Yale University's Junior Faculty Fellowship in 1995–96, which gave me time to work on this project, and by grants from the Social Science Faculty Fund, the Program on Non-Profit Organizations, and the Research Fund for Gay and Lesbian Studies. I thank Amy Gallo, Rita Melendez, Darcy Miller, and Carrie Tatum for research assistance, and Ann Fitzpatrick for expert transcribing. Quotations from *The Documents of Vatican II*, edited by Walter Abbott, are reprinted with permission of America Press Inc., 106 West 56th Street, New York, NY 10019.

While the rewards of academic life are numerous, I am happy that they are complemented by an enriching, extended family. In particular, I acknowledge my husband, Paul Wink, whose intellectual and emotional involvement is critical, and our children, Michael and Andrew, for their curiosity, exuberance, and energy unbound.

CHAPTER ONE

PRO-CHANGE CATHOLICS: FORGING COMMUNITY OUT OF DIVERSITY

Since its foundation, sociology has been concerned with the problem of the relation of the individual to the collectivity. Both Max Weber (1864–1920) and Emile Durkheim (1858–1917) were concerned with how social cohesiveness would be maintained in the face of changing institutional conditions. Weber was preoccupied with what he saw as the dehumanizing effects of an ever-expanding societal rationalization, whereas Durkheim focused on how collective solidarity might be maintained against social forces that appeared more likely to create anomie than moral order. We are still preoccupied with this long-standing sociological question. Today, the issue is whether the plurality of group identities seeking public legitimacy undermines social cohesiveness, unity, and order. There is a sense that the egalitarian advances achieved since the 1960s by women, racial minorities, and gay men and lesbian women, have been pivotal in unsettling the moral and institutional bases of social life.

While the question has been a constant one, it was raised with particular vigor in the 1960s, when diverse social movements arose and protested the idea of communality. These movements challenged the dominant culture and its inegalitarian institutional practices in the areas of family life, politics, law, and employment. The protest activity of women, gays and lesbians, and African Americans highlighted the existence of historical and sociocultural experiences that undermined the notion of a cultural universality. In so doing, they directed attention to the ways in which claims to universality are inappropriately used in practice, since rather than being inclusive, they are frequently used to restrict institutional and social participation.

Today, greater public awareness of cultural pluralism, and of the

1

ways in which some groups have been excluded from participation in various domains of public life, have sensitized people to the importance of affirming different identities. This new emphasis, however, tends to see identity differences as in tension with, rather than complementary to, participation in larger communal traditions. The tendency to draw distinctions between universalist frameworks and cultural particularism is a perspective shared both by those who lament what they see as the breakdown of community in American society as well as by those who welcome the new societal configurations as a way to revitalize democracy. Sociologists associated with the communitarian movement (e.g., Etzioni 1997: 64–73) interpret the post-1960s changes in American society as evidence of a deteriorating moral order and of social anarchy. Although concerned about the prospects for communal integration, they do not suggest a return to traditional social arrangements that fostered gender and other forms of inequality. They seek rather to establish a new balance between individual rights and social responsibilities. Grounded in the belief that, as Amitai Etzioni argues, "The greatest danger to autonomy arises when the social moorings of individuals are severed" (1997: 27), communitarians are committed to a project of moral regeneration centered on shared "commitment to a set of core values" (ibid. 13).

Etzioni observes that the sociological challenge is to develop a societal framework that allows for the "enriching particulars of autonomous subcultures and communities while sustaining the core of shared values" (ibid. 196). At the same time, Etzioni is doubtful that people committed to celebrating differences based on gender or race, for example, are willing to accept a bounded or "qualified diversity" that recognizes the necessity of core values (ibid. 197).

In contrast to the arguments advanced by communitarians, the declining impact of universal ideals is welcomed by sociologists such as Steven Seidman. He argues that foundational arguments appealing to God, reason, the laws of history, and moral or natural law, while they are not absent in America, lack public authority and moral credibility (1994: 191). In today's "culture of cynicism," he says, "claims to universality are suspected of masking particular interests" (ibid.). Seidman welcomes the cynicism towards universalism, seeing it as compatible with the pragmatism of American culture and the possibility of achieving a more democratic public culture which affirms "more local styles of moral legitimation" (ibid. 192).

Ideologically divergent analyses of contemporary American society thus concur in implying a tension between the realization of particular identities and integration with a broader communal tradition. For social conservatives, "too much" diversity is seen as breeding cultural relativism, fragmentation, and social anomie. For those with a post-modern inclination, on the other hand, the celebration of diverse identities tends to be posited as necessarily marginalizing the appeal of what they consider to be repressive universal traditions. To argue either for a universalism that suppresses differences, or for the prolifer-ation of subcultural groupings that dissociate identity from larger com-munal connections, is a tempting response to the challenges posed by cultural diversity. Yet this dichotomized approach does not allow for the forging of new social patterns that creatively encompass the inte-grative aspects of a broadly shared tradition with the uniqueness of par-ticular group experiences. As Jane Mansbridge observes (1993: 359), "community, in most cases, entails particularity."

Craig Calhoun (1995: xii) argues that it is possible theoretically to find a way out of the dualistic opposition represented by the tension between universality and difference. He calls for a critical theory that while focusing on power and cultural differences also pays attention to the general principles that underlie social relationships and social inte-gration. Similarly, Steven Seidman, notwithstanding his critique of universal or foundationalist arguments (1994: 191), also recognizes that local struggles over the politics of cultural difference do not neces-sitate the disavowal of "broader forms of social solidarity" (Nicholson and Seidman 1995: 35). But can this nondualistic theoretical approach work in practice? That is the question underpinning this book. I will show that the contestation of universal claims can be integrated in practice with participation in a more global moral community.

FOCUS OF THIS STUDY

I address the relation between diversity and community in the institu-tional context of the Catholic Church. Catholicism is not a universal tradition, in the sense that it is clearly not the religious tradition to which all people adhere but is instead one of many diverse communal traditions in modern society. As a transnational and transgenerational doctrinal and institutional tradition, however, the Catholic Church comprises a more universal than local community. I focus on institu-tionally marginalized American Catholics. These are Catholics who choose to stay Catholic even though their understanding of

Catholicism is denounced in official church teaching. Catholics who are gay or lesbian, advocates of women's ordination, or pro-choice on abortion are the primary subjects of my investigation. These Catholics occupy a cultural space that challenges the assumption of a dichotomized opposition between the affirmation of difference and the maintenance of solidarity with a broader tradition. Professional Catholic theologians are also a focus of this study. I include them in order to explore how from their institutional location as experts within the tradition but outside the church hierarchy, they view the possibilities that exist for forging a broader understanding of Catholic identity than that allowed by official church teaching.

In a time when identity is considered an individual "design project" (Berger, Berger, and Kellner 1973: 71–74), and when the politics of lifestyle (Giddens 1991: 214) and of difference (cf. Calhoun 1995: 214; Fuss 1989: 97–112) are making difference a source of subcultural celebration rather than social stigma, the Catholics in my study choose to maintain links with the institutional church and to work from within to effect change. To be openly gay or lesbian and Catholic, to be Catholic and committed to women's ordination, or pro-choice and Catholic, explicitly engages the tension between holding a particular identity and simultaneously maintaining connection to a more global community in which these identities are officially defined as contradictory. In writing this book I was thus interested in understanding the subjective meanings (cf. Weber 1978: 399) that Catholics inject into and derive from Catholicism as they affirm their plural identities, and how these meanings in turn act as resources for change in the church.

This book will show that the articulation of differences does not demand the sacrificing of commitment to a more global communal tradition. I will argue, in fact, that rather than leading to fragmentation and anomie, differences can constitute a source of change and redefinition of the larger community. The concern that differences may fragment community is a valid one. Clearly, the narcissistic celebration of differences can, on the surface at least, undermine the commonalities shared by diverse groups in society. Yet, differences and community invariably coexist. In the Catholic Church, dissent from what are purported to be core doctrines does not necessarily fracture the tradition and unity of the church. Similarly, in the political sphere, protest is inextricably intertwined with the institutional practices and traditions against which it is aimed. Whether differences are ignored, acknowledged and denigrated, or acknowledged and affirmed, it is evident that differences comprise community and are an essential ingredient in the process of communal change, vibrancy, and adaptability.

DATA SOURCES

In order to investigate how institutionally marginalized Catholics negotiate their multiple identities, my research has focused primarily on members of organizations committed to change in the Catholic Church: members of Dignity, a national association of gay and lesbian Catholics,[1] members of the Women's Ordination Conference (WOC), an organization committed to the ordination of women, and volunteer regional activists for Catholics for a Free Choice (CFFC), an organization advocating official church recognition of moral pluralism on abortion. Although each organization has a primary focus on issue-specific concerns, Dignity, WOC, and CFFC are participants in the broad-based Call to Action movement for change in the Catholic Church. Call to Action (CTA) was established by laypeople following an initiative by the U.S. bishops, who held a Call to Action conference of the laity in 1976 to devise a program for Catholic institutional renewal and social justice. Call to Action holds an annual conference which has evolved into "a national congress of persons, communities, and organizations working to give birth to" a transformed church (CTA organizational literature).[2]

The study used a variety of data-gathering methods. I combined content analysis of archival data, ethnographic research, self-administered questionnaire surveys, and personal in-depth interviews. At the outset I conducted a content analysis of the organizational literature (promotional materials and newsletters/journals) of Dignity, WOC, and CFFC in order to establish a strong firsthand knowledge of each group's historical origins and evolution, and of the various issues and tensions that had emerged as salient to each group's organizational id-

---

1. Recognizing that sexuality is pliable, Dignity/USA's formal mission and membership also includes bisexual and transgendered Catholics. While I do not wish to be disrespectful to people who are bisexual or transgendered, I use the summarized "gay and lesbian" phrasing in this book for ease of presentation, even though I recognize that to do so may be seen by some readers as collusion in the use of disempowering language categories.
2. CTA also coordinates Catholic Organizations for Renewal (COR), which is a network of over thirty national and regional pro-change Catholic groups, including Dignity, WOC, and CFFC.

entity. I conducted an ethnographic study of Dignity/Boston, a local chapter of gay and lesbian Catholics, in order to identify the routine practices that they use in building an identity that affirms their sexuality and their Catholicism. The Dignity data comes from a five-month observation study of community activities. In addition, I surveyed participants in Dignity/Boston using a self-administered questionnaire, and conducted in-depth, face-to-face interviews with twenty-six active members of the chapter. This triangulated research approach to the study of Dignity provides a vivid representation of the ways in which talk and action combine into the collective reworking and integration of multiple identity affiliations.

In addition to the Dignity study, I also surveyed members of the Women's Ordination Conference (WOC) and regional volunteer activists for Catholics for a Free Choice (CFFC). I sent a self-administered mail questionnaire to randomly selected members of WOC chosen from its membership mailing list, and to a smaller targeted group of CFFC regional volunteers. The surveys provide extensive data concerning the arguments Catholics use to legitimate views of Catholic identity alternative to those delineated in official church teaching.

I supplement the data gathered from pro-change Catholics (Dignity, WOC, and CFFC) with mail questionnaire survey data from a sample of members of the Catholic League for Religious and Civil Rights, a national organization committed to publicly defending official church teaching. I incorporate this data in order to probe the cultural commonalities among Catholics whose views of church doctrine differ quite considerably. Finally, my study included in-depth, face-to-face interviews with faculty members in theology sampled from two geographical centers of theological inquiry in the United States: the Boston Theological Institute, a consortium of universities, colleges, and seminaries in the greater Boston area, and the Graduate Theological Union at Berkeley, California.[3] As professional experts deeply immersed in the Catholic tradition but relatively marginal to the church hierarchy, theologians offer a distinctive understanding of the range of institutionally legitimate options available to Catholics who selectively disagree with the Vatican. Although theologians are not collectively engaged in any publicly organized pro-change project,

---

3. Of the twenty theological faculty members interviewed, some were moral theologians and others were specialists in ethics or church history. For ease of reference, I use the more general category of "theologians."

they constitute a significant voice in the articulation of Catholicism and the extent to which its official boundaries can be shifted. (I provide a more detailed description of the research methods used, sample selection procedures, and pro-change respondents' sociodemographic data in the Appendix.)

This book clearly is not a study of American Catholics as a whole. Nor is it a study of the individual antecedents of institutional loyalty among Catholics. I do not, for example, examine how different life experiences or patterns of religious socialization, respondents' experiences of Catholicism in their families of origin, schools, and in other domains impact upon their commitment to Catholicism. These variables, as other studies document (D'Antonio et al. 1996; Davidson et al. 1997), are significant in influencing long-term commitment to, and subjective understandings of, Catholicism. Not all Catholics, of course, stay Catholic; many switch to other denominations or refrain from participating in any public or institutionalized form of religious expression.[4] To understand why Catholics leave or disengage from participation in the church would comprise a different study.

THE SOCIAL AND INSTITUTIONAL CONTEXT OF IDENTITY

The object of this book is to illuminate the identity construction mechanisms used by institutionally marginalized Catholics. In sociology, there is a long theoretical tradition starting with Karl Marx, developed by Karl Mannheim (1936: 79–83, 264–311), and used more recently by some feminist theorists (e.g., Harding 1991; Collins 1990; D. Smith 1990a), that the experiences of those on the margins provide a critical standpoint from which to discern the ways in which inequality is perpetuated. Institutionally marginalized people have less invested in maintaining the status quo and having experienced collective action against their marginality may be more likely to be aware of and to see beneath the appearances that maintain unjust practices (Harding 1991: 123–132). The standpoint of marginalized individuals and groups, just as any other position, should not be thought of as mo-

4. In his study of spirituality among American baby boomers, Wade Clark Roof (1993: 175) found that 81 percent of those who grew up Catholic still identified themselves as Catholic. Mainline Protestants had a retention rate of 65 percent, and conservative Protestants had a rate of 80 percent.

nolithic (see Flax 1990: 141; Harding 1991: 121 n.19). Further, there is always the possibility that those who are on the margins may distort institutional processes or fail to act on their own perceived interests. Nevertheless, self-conscious holders of objectively contradictory identities continuously confront the routine dilemmas associated with negotiating difference and maintaining multiple loyalties (cf. Calhoun 1995: 185–187).

How this study's pro-change Catholics, as people with multiple overt loyalties, construct identities that are relatively autonomous of official church teaching may point to the processes that are also available to and/or tacitly engaged by other Catholics. Although it is well documented that the majority of Catholics are Catholics "on their own terms," whereby they compartmentalize the teaching of the church hierarchy from participation in the doctrinal and communal tradition (Greeley 1977; 1985; Hout and Greeley 1987), we do not know how they validate their Catholicism. The strategies adopted by other Catholics who remain involved in the church may differ from those used by this study's respondents. The ways in which pro-change Catholics use and reinterpret Catholicism, however, may, I believe, illuminate what other American and Western Catholics do in an attenuated and relatively unself-conscious way. Furthermore, the mechanisms employed by pro-change Catholics may suggest useful strategies for people in general as they confront the identity dilemmas associated with the globalism and fragmentation of late modern society. With social life increasingly disconnected from the "external referents" supplied by family and local communal attachments and obligations (cf. Giddens 1991: 146–148), and characterized by networks whose participants tend to share a common technological rather than cultural vocabulary (cf. Castells 1997: 1–4), pro-change Catholics may illuminate how it is possible to use external communal traditions as anchors for an identity grounded in multiple bases.

How pro-change Catholics express their Catholicism addresses important theoretical debates in sociology. In the late 1960s, the sociologists Peter Berger and Thomas Luckmann (1966) introduced the concept of the social construction of reality. Highlighting the paramount reality of everyday life and practical commonsense knowledge, Berger and Luckmann (ibid. 19–27) emphasized that society and culture are the products of people's own activity. Although people experience institutions as external to them and as having a reality of their own (ibid. 29–32), Berger and Luckmann stressed that institutions, including religious institutions, are themselves the products of social activity. In short, while society is an objective reality, it is simultaneously a human product. Berger and Luckmann's emphasis on the social context in which meanings are produced focused attention on the human agency that inheres in institutional reproduction. Social processes, therefore, while still external to people, were no longer assumed to be the result of anonymous social, historical, natural, or divine forces.

The publication of Berger and Luckmann's book coincided, moreover, with the emergence of the new social movements of the 1960s and 1970s, and their creation of what Steven Seidman (1994: 235) refers to as "new subjects of knowledge (African-Americans, women, lesbians and gay men) and new knowledges." These movements thus provided a public and practical demonstration of the various ways in which the taken-for-granted commonsense knowledge about what is "normal" could be overturned and transformed.

Once attention is directed to the context in which knowledge is produced, it inevitably leads to a probing of who and what defines knowledge, and of how it is organized in institutional practices (see, for example, Foucault 1978: 18–20). This interrogation begins the process of unveiling the power interests behind what used to appear as the "natural," taken-for-granted assumptions of social life. If commonsense knowledge really is paramount in social life, then the everyday experiences of ordinary people become valid sources of knowledge production. Recognition of the multiplicity of valid standpoints thus challenges the idea that there is a single locus of interpretive authority. It is this transformation in the sense of ownership of interpretive authority that empowers individuals and groups to engage in action against inequality, and to build "new" identities that challenge the traditional view of identity as pre-given and immutable. In this new understanding, as Stuart Hall emphasizes, identity is processual and fluid. It is a never-ending "production" which because it is "always in process . . . belongs to the future as much as to the past" (1992: 222, 225).

I will argue that the contestation of official church teaching by Catholics who are gay or lesbian, advocates of women's ordination, or pro-choice on abortion reflects their appreciation for the fact that doctrine is, in part, a social construct contingent on the specific historical, cultural, and institutional contexts in which it emerges. Pro-change Catholics' sense of Catholicism is grounded in the view that interpretive authority is diffuse. In this understanding, interpretive power in the Catholic Church is not located solely in the official hierarchical power structure, but is dispersed, seen in the everyday interpretive activities of ordinary Catholics. It is this democratic understanding of interpretive authority that enables pro-change Catholics to make Catholic doctrine a site of what Steven Seidman (1994) would call "contested knowledge." They are thereby able to produce relatively autonomous interpretations of Catholicism that make sense in light of their diverse experiences, including their experiences of Catholicism.

It is not just pro-change Catholics who are sensitive to social context in their approach to Catholic doctrine. An analysis based on the social construction of meaning also needs to be applied to the official church. As I will document, it is important to recognize that as an institution, the church's organizational structure, doctrines, and practices are, in part, products of the social and historical context in which the church has evolved. In this view, the accent on the church hierarchy's authority, no matter how "natural" or divinely prescribed it may seem, is the result of particular social and political contingencies. The church hierarchy itself, moreover, as the official collective voice of the church, constructs doctrine and is not simply the mediator or transmitter of divinely willed meanings.[5] In Catholicism, a core of doctrinal

5. In this book, when I refer to the church hierarchy I will be referring to those who hold sacred office in the church — that is, the Pope and the college of bishops (the magisterium), and the various Vatican congregations and councils (such as the Congregation for the Doctrine of the Faith, headed by Cardinal Ratzinger) whose work informs and disseminates papal teaching and that are central to the "governance of the universal church" (Reese 1996a: 106). In short, to talk about the church hierarchy is to variously and somewhat interchangeably include the Pope, collectivities of bishops (such as, in America, the National Conference of Catholic Bishops [NCCB]), and the Vatican (referring to the Pope and/or the Congregation for the Doctrine of the Faith, for example). In using such terms as the church hierarchy or the Vatican, my intent is not to reify official church processes but simply to communicate in shorthand the empirical fact that the organizational structure of the church is hierarchical and its official doctrines and practices are controlled by a governing hierarchy (Pope, cardinals, bishops). The church hierarchy speaks as a collectivity even though clearly not all bishops necessarily agree with the Pope or with their confreres on any given issue. Moreover, the Pope, national conferences of bishops, and the diverse Vatican bureaucracies all enjoy various degrees of autonomy from one another. For clarifications on the complexities of the church's organizational structure see Reese (1996a). In this book, for ease of reference I cite collective statements issued by the NCCB or by any of its committees by using the general label "U.S. Bishops."

beliefs (e.g., the divinity, incarnation, and resurrection of Christ, the Trinity) comprise the "essentials" of Catholic faith. It is nonetheless the case that dogma is not pre-given but is extrapolated and developed over time by church leaders as they come to achieve a clearer theological understanding of redemption, and equally important, respond to the political and social context in which faith is articulated.[6] The contextual nature of doctrine is, as we would expect, even more pronounced in the case of official church teaching regarding institutional practices and individual morality. The argument that the meanings of Catholic doctrine are context-dependent is further supported by the findings from the theologians whom I interviewed.

EMANCIPATORY PROJECTS

The redrawing of the boundaries of Catholic identity by pro-change Catholics may be seen as an emancipatory project. An emancipatory project, as discussed by Anthony Giddens, seeks to shed the constraining "shackles of the past" with a view toward achieving a transformative future wherein inequality between people based, for instance, on class, gender, or sexual orientation is eliminated (1991: 210–211). The institutional mechanisms of modernity (e.g., democracy, capitalism, law), including post-Enlightenment religion (F. Schüssler Fiorenza 1992: 74–75), marginalize and exclude people even while they hold out the possibility of emancipation. In this view, modernity "has become the threat *and* the promise of emancipation from the threat that it creates itself" (Beck 1992: 183, emphasis in original). To engage in an emancipatory project therefore is to prioritize "the imperatives of justice, equality, and participation" (Giddens 1991:

6. To recognize that doctrine develops over time (see, for example, Noonan 1993) is not to suggest that it is therefore somehow invalid. Distinctive to Catholicism is an appreciation that theology, rather than being derived from a biblical fundamentalism or literalism, is a "living tradition" (Curran 1992: 3–6). Doctrine thus unfolds and changes, and its articulation can be prompted by various challenges from within and outside the church. Thus, for example, although from Apostolic times the church has insisted on the human incarnation of Christ, early church councils (Antioch and Nicaea) affirmed and elaborated on Christ's humanity in response to Gnostic and other heresies. See *Catechism of the Catholic Church* (1994: 104–105). Further demonstrating the processual development of dogma, although belief in the Immaculate Conception of Mary the Mother of God is a core tenet of Catholic faith, this was not formally proclaimed until 1854 by Pope Pius IX.

6, 212).[7] Although there is variation in the practical interpretation given to these values by pro-change Catholics, Dignity, WOC, and CFFC respondents all aim toward achieving a more inclusive church. Their push for institutional change is processual. Their projects necessarily evolve while they explore the boundaries and possibilities of an emancipatory agenda itself, and calibrate this with their commitment to maintaining participation in the Catholic doctrinal and communal tradition.

Instead of being motivated by subcultural resistance, emancipatory projects have an "offensive" impetus that drives them toward "conquering new territory" (Habermas 1987: 393). The new territory sought by this study's participants is the institutional legitimacy of a Catholic identity that recognizes the variety of differences that are inherent in everyday life. Pro-change Catholics seek not only to overturn official church teaching delegitimating Catholics who are gay or lesbian, or advocates of women's ordination, or pro-choice on abortion. In addition, they seek to reconstruct an inclusive, egalitarian, and pluralist church wherein these identities are validated. Clearly, the identity issues associated with this study's pro-change Catholics differ in their salience for the individuals involved. They are, moreover, not the only identity politics pervading American society or the Catholic Church today. As emphasized by Craig Calhoun (1995: 215), identity politics should not be considered the prerogative of those on the ideological "left." Ideologically and/or doctrinally conservative people are also involved in identity politics, involving in their case, for example, the reaffirmation of traditional gender and family roles (see Davidman 1991; Weaver and Appleby 1995).

Appropriating the concept of emancipatory politics (Giddens 1991: 212) provides a useful analytical device by which both to cluster and to restrict the identity concerns relevant to this study. Participants in

7. Giddens distinguishes between emancipatory politics and life politics. He argues that while the former is a politics of life chances, the latter is a politics of choices and of lifestyle and life decisions (1991: 214–215). Giddens notes that "virtually all questions of life politics also raise problems of an emancipatory sort" (ibid. 228). Since in practice, I believe, the politics of choice is inextricably linked to an emancipatory politics, I refer to the identity projects of this study's Catholics as emancipatory rather than life projects even though of course the identity negotiation of this study's participants is clearly about life choices. It may be more accurate, then, to call their projects "emancipatory life projects," but this is a cumbersome phrase.

Dignity, WOC, and CFFC are variously engaged in pushing for the elimination of institutional impediments to diversity and simultaneously pushing for the expansion of interpretive and participative equality in the church. Unlike conservative Catholics who support the maintenance of distinctions restricting the intrachurch participation of their coreligionists, pro-change Catholics are committed to remodeling the church as a more inclusively pluralistic community. In thus differentiating between emancipatory and non-emancipatory visions, (Giddens 1991: 212; Habermas 1987: 393), I am endorsing the view that the Enlightenment ethic of participative equality is an objectively defensible moral value, one which ought to be judged preferentially over inequality (Bell 1994).

Although socially constructed, new interpretations and new identities are not created in a vacuum. They are always influenced and bounded by a particular historical, cultural, and institutional context. As many sociologists emphasize, specific institutional contexts provide resources that both constrain and enhance the opportunities for institutional change (cf. Friedland and Alford 1991: 254–256; Powell 1991: 188; Sewell 1992; Swidler 1995: 34–36). This study's investigation of the negotiation of identity is anchored in the institutional context of the Catholic Church and its confluence with American culture. It is the church's institutional history, with its rich tradition and symbolic resources, that limits and expands the possibilities for forging doctrinal and institutional change. Just as the church's hierarchical structure should be understood in terms of the church's history, this study's pro-change Catholics should be situated in the context of the church in American society. To be an American gay Catholic, for example, may be very different from what it means to be a Brazilian or English gay Catholic. Both Catholicism and being gay have different meanings in different cultural settings, and this is of course true within America as well as cross-nationally. American Catholicism, nonetheless, is the relatively bounded context in which rituals, ideas, symbols, and traditions are dynamically used by this study's pro-change Catholics to articulate identity and effect institutional change.

This study will show that pro-change Catholics' identity negotiation is informed and empowered by the institutional context in which it takes place. On the one hand, pro-change Catholics have to engage with official church arguments (relating, for example, to the immorality of same-sex sexual relations or of abortion) and institutional practices (e.g., the ban on women's ordination) with which they disagree.

At the same time, the symbolic resources they use are in large part provided by the church's own doctrinal and institutional history. Importantly, it is these doctrinal rather than nondoctrinal cultural resources that pro-change Catholics use to legitimate their pro-change projects. Rather than using distinctively American arguments, such as appeals to individual or group rights (cf. Glendon 1991), the respondents in this study reflexively engage the Catholic tradition. They reflect on and use existing Catholic doctrine to support the doctrinal and institutional changes they advocate. Thus WOC respondents, for example, rather than asserting that it is their right as women or as Americans to be ordained, draw instead on Christ-centered theological themes (e.g., the universality of redemption and of Christ's ministry, baptismal equality) to support their claims for ordination.

Distinctive to the Catholic theological tradition since at least the Middle Ages is a strong emphasis on the coupling of "faith and reason" in contrast to either a biblical literalism or a "blind leap" approach to faith (McCool 1977). Consequently, while the Pope and the bishops (the magisterium) comprise the official "teaching authority," there are, as the Catholic theologian Charles Curran (1992: 11) emphasizes, "strains in the Catholic tradition that strongly oppose any authoritarian understanding of either teaching or ruling." Today an emphasis on a historically and culturally contextualized "faith and reason" means that there is a theological expectation in Catholicism that church doctrine should "make sense." Despite the image of a monolithic and immutable tradition, church doctrine and institutional practices are open to change and do change. As demonstrated most recently by the Second Vatican Council (1962–1965), equality, pluralism, doctrinal reflexivity, and historical consciousness are practical values central to the church's identity. The Catholic tradition, therefore, is not homogeneous but contains diverse symbolic resources that can be variously interpreted and used to transform the church while maintaining continuity with the tradition. Whether as an intended or unintended consequence, Catholic history and theology provide emancipatory ideals that pro-change Catholics can use in forging an identity and a church that validates many options.

In this regard I should note that the authority of practical reason and individual conscience has long been recognized in Catholic thought, going back to Saint Augustine (d. 430) and elaborated in more recent times by Vatican II. Assent to official church teaching is a cognitive process. As emphasized by the distinguished Jesuit ecclesiologist Francis A. Sullivan, decisions of the magisterium call for "religious submission of mind and will," in other words, "sincere assent," which is an act of judgment (1983: 162). Sincere assent to papal decisions, therefore, cannot be coerced. Since assent is a cognitive process, Sullivan argues that the church hierarchy cannot rely on its formal authority alone but must provide Catholics with reasoned arguments that validate the official interpretation of the question at issue. The process of evaluative reasoning involved in giving assent thus suggests that Catholics who fail to assent to official church teaching should be characterized not as "dissenting" but more accurately as "non-assenting" Catholics.[8]

REVALUING CULTURAL PLURALISM

One of the criticisms of universal arguments is that their categorical divisions (e.g., male versus female, East versus West) essentialize individuals and groups in ways that homogenize and, in some sense, dehumanize people (Said 1978: 27). Iris Young argues that representing a dominant group's experiences as the norm is a form of cultural imperialism whereby other perspectives are rendered invisible and simultaneously stereotyped as the exotic Other (1990: 58–59; see also Said

---

8. Francis A. Sullivan offers specific guidelines as to how a Catholic should respond to a magisterial decision which contravenes a view the person holds to be true (as, for example, on birth control). Sullivan argues that free will requires that the person dutifully and sincerely examine the papal opinion, and honestly reexamine her or his own opinion in light of the views expressed by the magisterium. There must be, in short, an "honest and sustained effort to overcome any contrary opinion" that the person holds (Sullivan 1983: 163–164). At the same time, as Sullivan elaborates: "The magisterium cannot be content to appeal to the will of the faithful, it must also appeal to their mind, by presenting its teaching with reasons that are clear and convincing. . . . if the magisterium fails to offer convincing arguments for its teaching, and relies too heavily on merely formal authority, it will not be offering to the faithful the help that many of them will need to rid themselves of their doubts about the truth of the official teaching, and achieve a sincere assent to it" (ibid. 165). Sullivan explains further that: "If in a particular instance, Catholics have offered their religious submission and will to the authority of the magisterium, by making an honest and sustained effort to achieve internal assent to its teaching, and still find that doubts about its truth remain so strong in their minds that they cannot actually give their sincere intellectual assent to it, I do not see how one could judge such non-assent, or internal dissent, to involve any lack of obedience to the magisterium" (ibid. 165–166).

1978: 39–42). The deployment of monolithic categories tends toward polarization, counterposing undifferentiated groups against one another. Yet, as Craig Calhoun (1995: 221) points out, tension between identities at both the individual and the collective levels is inescapable.

I argue that cultural differences are not necessarily polarizing or threatening to communal integration, but are constitutive of what it means today to live in a moral society. Pluralism is a defining characteristic of modern democratic societies. As the political philosopher Chantal Mouffe (1996: 246) argues, acceptance of pluralism is part of the conceptual definition of modern democracy and not simply a function of its size. Pluralism is not a prerequisite solely of modern democracy. The Catholic theologian David Tracy argues that "an insistence on the plurality of ways within every great religion is an ethical and religious responsibility" (1987: 95–96). Accordingly, the pluralism that comprises modern society, and members' and institutions' obligatory openness to those differences, means that the recognition of difference is necessary to protect social life "against any attempts of closure" and the suppression of differences (Mouffe 1996: 255). In this view, communal integration is served by institutional procedures and values that enable differences to be expressed and integrated into ongoing communal conversations whose negotiated outcomes do not silence differences.[9]

Cultural and theological pluralism is intrinsic to Catholicism and, as I will document, is evident among contemporary Catholics. I will highlight two manifestations of Catholic pluralism. First, I will show that even though this study's Catholics are members of organizations that are jointly committed to institutional change, there are specific

9. The Catholic Church not only affirms the importance of ongoing dialogue in the church as a way to resolve disagreements (Abbott 1966: 244) but has also formalized in canon law the consensual collegial basis of the church hierarchy's teaching authority (F. Sullivan 1991: 59). It is thus noteworthy, for example, that the exercise of papal infallibility is constrained by the "consensus" that exists within the church on a particular issue. Francis Sullivan (1995: 5) explains that ". . . the whole body of Catholic bishops, in union with the bishop of Rome, speaks infallibly not only in an ecumenical council, when they solemnly define a doctrine, but also when, without being gathered in council, in their "ordinary" teaching they are in agreement in proposing a particular judgment to be held definitively." In the absence of such consensus, theologians may query, for instance, the infallible nature of Vatican teaching on women's ordination.

cultural and theological differences among them that reflect their respective projects. Second, just as there are differences among pro-change Catholics, it is also the case that there are commonalities between them and Catholics who oppose change. To illustrate this second point, I draw on the supplementary data gathered from doctrinally conservative Catholics who are members of the Catholic League for Religious and Civil Rights. This comparison shows that even though pro-change respondents differ in substantial ways from conservative Catholics, they share with them an attachment to specific ideas and symbols that are part of a collective Catholic memory. Although these symbols (e.g., the Eucharist) are neither static or uniformly understood, they objectively integrate doctrinally diverse Catholics and are subjectively used by them to distinguish themselves from non-Catholics. In addition, as I will suggest, commitment to the meanings embodied by these shared symbols may simultaneously be a significant resource in legitimating change in the church. Recasting pluralism in a positive light against its negative framing as a threat to social cohesion thus directs attention toward the "symbolic universes" (Berger and Luckmann 1966) that link people who occupy different identities, and toward the possibilities that exist for forging community out of diversity.

EMANCIPATORY DISCOURSE

This study's focus on Catholic identity engages important questions in social theory, culture, and the sociology of religion. One of the dominant themes in contemporary sociology revolves around the question of how to free ourselves from inegalitarian structures and traditions. Discussion of this issue inevitably focuses on whether change can be achieved by recasting existing social structures, or whether it is necessary to create new structures that make a radical break with existing institutional frameworks. Not surprisingly, this question is implicit in much of the writing of two dominant contemporary thinkers, the late French philosopher Michel Foucault (1926–1984) and the German philosopher and sociologist Jürgen Habermas (b. 1929).

Although both Foucault and Habermas are critical of the dominance of technological and scientific rationality in social life (see McCarthy 1991: 43–53), they each offer different prescriptions for the achievement of emancipatory social relations. Foucault favors the inventiveness of noninstitutionalized "manners of being" over "ready-made formulas" (1981/1997: 137–139) that restrict the creativity of social relations. He also emphasizes the superiority of actual practices ("ways of living") over talk and knowledge in their transformative potential (1982/1997: 130–131). Foucault is thus skeptical that social change can be achieved by arguing from within existing institutional structures and conceptual categories because he sees these mechanisms as the very tools that perpetuate domination and inequality. For example, the language we use to reason about and categorize the world is itself, according to Foucault, the product of a social-institutional context arbitrarily organized to produce and regulate power, so that language itself restricts our ability to argue against power and inequality. For Foucault, power is everywhere, and since resistance against power is itself part of a power relation, "there is no escaping [power]" (1978: 93, 95–96). All attempts to "get at the truth" and its power-infused classifications of the world, are themselves part of the circular power relations which maintain "regimes of truth" (1977/1984: 72–75).[10]

Foucault offers the Catholic confession as an example of how power relations work in practice. As Foucault observes, "one does not confess without the presence (or virtual presence) of a partner who is not simply the interlocutor but the authority who requires the confession, prescribes and appreciates it, and intervenes in order to judge, punish, forgive, console, and reconcile" (1978: 61–62). Notwithstanding the presence of an external authority figure, however, the truth of the confessional discourse is not guaranteed "from above" by the power inequalities that exist between the priest and the penitent. The truth is guaranteed, rather, from within, by the internalization of the process and categories of self-interrogation (examination of conscience) and the "basic intimacy in discourse between the one who speaks and what he is speaking about" (ibid. 62). For Foucault, therefore, a person who confesses is not liberated but is further disempowered, since he or she colludes in institutional rituals whose categories of self-interrogation and self-expression are devised to maintain domination and inequality (e.g., the identity of "sinner"). Moreover, even if we reject confession, its power to dominate continues because we cannot escape from think-

---

10. Although emphasizing that situations can never be free from power, Foucault recognizes that there are always possibilities for changing the particulars of any specific situation. He thus acknowledges the innovative impact of social movements that are "outside the normal or ordinary" political institutional processes in effecting change (1984b/1997: 172–173).

ing in terms of the familiar, self-disciplining and guilt-inducing categories that it has ingrained in us.

In short, because he argues that to talk is to engage in subjugation of the self, Foucault rejects the possibility that language and other institutional procedures, such as voting in the political domain (see Apter 1995 for a critique), can be used to transform attitudes and practices. He instead values the option of silence,[11] and noninstitutionalized, experimental ways of living. In Foucault's framing, with power constitutive of social life, it is futile to try to use reason to cut through power and establish new forms of social organization grounded in equality and justice. Since for Foucault, the idea of reasoned argumentation free from power is utopian, the only practical morality that we can aim toward is to play the ubiquitous "games of power with as little domination as possible" (1984a/1997: 298). Here I will argue that Foucault's theoretical analysis of social relations and power is too pessimistic and does not allow for the complexity of everyday life. People experience and act within institutional frameworks in more complicated and multifaceted ways. Specifically, this study's findings will show that the institutional and doctrinal tradition of Catholicism provides pro-change Catholics with emancipatory resources that they use to argue for and build a more inclusive church.

Jürgen Habermas, like Foucault, is suspicious of reason. In particular he is critical of the ways in which reason has been used for strategic purposes of domination, exploitation, and control. Habermas (1975: 33–94) regards the institutionalization of criteria of economic, scientific, and technical rationality by the state and other bureaucracies as dehumanizing. Unlike Foucault, however, Habermas (1975: 142–143; 1984: 94–101) argues that reason is the means by which people can resist the colonization of their everyday world by an all-pervasive technical rationality. Habermas thus calls not for the abandonment of reason but for a reasoned critique of reason (McCarthy 1984: v–vi) as he seeks to restore a noninstrumental, communicative rationality to social life. Distinctive to Habermas is the view that people can interact with one another nonstrategically, "without making each

---

11. On Foucault's appreciation of the importance of silence in friendship and as a way of resisting the obligation to speak that he experienced growing up in the Catholic, petit bourgeois, provincial culture of France, see Foucault (1982/1997: 121–122). Foucault laments that "silence unfortunately has been dropped from our culture."

other into means for achieving individually predetermined ends" (Joas 1993: 127).

Thus Habermas's understanding of the practical use of language is very different from Foucault's. For Habermas (1984: 95), language is the mechanism facilitating the achievement of social relations grounded in and reproduced by reasoned argumentation. Central to Habermas's thesis is what he calls an "ideal speech situation." In this idealistic context of communicative action, participants seek to reach a common understanding of the situation at issue and of plans for future mutually agreed action (ibid. 86). Participants use language to raise validity claims about the sincerity, propositional truth, and normative rightness of each other's statements (ibid. 75). The purpose of this reciprocal deliberation is to achieve a reasoned consensus or negotiated understanding that in turn becomes the basis for action. Communicative action is a cooperative process of reasoned interpretive negotiation "in which no participant has a monopoly on correct interpretation" (ibid. 100). In other words, to use language is to be able to ask questions about the world and about one's own and other people's experiences in it, and this reflexivity carries with it the potential for emancipation.

Habermas elaborates that:

> Communicatively achieved agreement must be based in the end on reasons. And the rationality of those who participate in this communicative practice is determined by whether, if necessary, they could under suitable circumstances, provide reasons for their expressions. . . . The "strength" of an argument is measured in a given context by the soundness of the reasons; that can be seen in, among other things, whether or not an argument is able to convince the participants in a discourse, that is, to motivate them to accept the validity claim in question. (1984: 17–18)

Habermas's concept of an ideal speech situation ruled by reason has been criticized for marginalizing the importance of power in social interaction and the different interests, identities, and language capabilities of participants attempting to engage in a noncoercive conversation (see, for example, Frazer and Lacey 1993: 19–21, 144–147; Gould 1996; I. Young 1996). Several critics point out that the emphasis on reason negates the importance of emotion and the affective attachments that are part of people's experiences and communicative styles (e.g., Calhoun 1995; I. Young 1996). Habermas's embrace of what Iris Young calls the "disembodied coldness of modern reason" underemphasizes the metaphorical, rhetorical, playful, storytelling, and nonlingustic aspects of everyday communication (1990: 125, 118; 1996: 129–132). Moreover, as Patricia Hill Collins (1990: 212) observes, "new knowledge claims are rarely worked out in isolation from other individuals and are developed through dialogue with other members of a community." Yet the implications of individuals' participation in specific social contexts are ignored by Habermas.

An interesting shortcoming of particular relevance to this study is Habermas's view of the limits of religiously grounded arguments (cf. 1975: 120). Because the truth claims of religious redemption are grounded in dogma and tradition, and therefore cannot be rationally defended, Habermas sees religion as undermining reason and a source of distorted and coercive communication. With the "authority of the holy" displaced in modern societies by the "authority of an achieved consensus" (1987: 77), a "religious discourse . . . is limited in the degree of its freedom of communication . . ." (1992: 233). In essence for Habermas, a reasoned religious argument necessarily sheds its religious component, since it "is no longer borrowed from the language of a specific religious tradition, but from the universe of argumentative discourse that is uncoupled from the event of revelation" (ibid. 233).

It is of course true that just as one cannot defend one's aesthetic, political, or cultural preferences using reasons that can be objectively validated, neither is it possible to mount a reasoned defense of the validity of particular faith beliefs. Yet just because religious faith cannot be rationally defended does not mean that all aspects of a religious tradition are closed to reason. Treating religion as a premodern, undifferentiated belief system, Habermas fails to see the diverse strands that exist within a given religious tradition. As the Harvard Catholic theologian Francis Schüssler Fiorenza argues, Habermas overlooks how transformations in religion and theology have brought "the critical principles of Enlightenment into religion itself and into theological reflection" (1992: 74). Post-Enlightenment religion, rather, is increasingly independent of cosmology, and elaborates historically and culturally specific ethical principles pertaining to the "common good" of society (ibid. 74–77). Religious participation, moreover, rests in many instances on personal convictions rather than on unreflective submission to dogma, tradition, or official authority (see, for example, D'Antonio et al. 1996; Greeley 1985).

Notwithstanding the various shortcomings in Habermas's theory, I will argue that his model may ultimately offer us the best means for developing new forms of social organization grounded in participative equality. My claim is based on two reasons. First, when reason is used with an awareness of how shifts in historical and cultural consciousness moderate the practical interpretation of values such as equality, it can expand the institutional possibilities for creating more egalitarian and reciprocal social relations (in families, the church, public policy making, etc.). While it is utopian to believe that we can evaluate the soundness of a reasoned argument outside of our own sociohistorical context, it is also the case that there is nothing "instant" or self-evident about rationality or the process of emancipation or progress in any domain of social life.

Second, Foucault's analysis, though valuable in alerting us to the pervasiveness of power in social and institutional practices, is defeatist. Remaining silent, or responding to social inequality with inventive practices that are "outside" the ordinary institutional channels, may be necessary strategies as a last resort. But, in the meantime, because social relations are processual, we can push toward achieving greater equality by using reason to inquire into our various traditions and institutional practices (see Delanty 1997; Tracy 1994: 198; 1987: 20). Such a critique may lead to finding creative ways within those traditions that validate participative equality. My findings will show that pro-change Catholics use reason to inquire into the Catholic tradition and in doing so, find resources that demonstrate the doctrinal reasonableness of their claims for a more inclusive and deliberative church. This study, therefore, will highlight the emancipatory power of reason, and it will also underscore that in people's lives, reason and faith are interlinked, and are experienced and appropriated within specific power relations.

AMERICAN CULTURAL VOCABULARIES

This study's exploration of Catholic identity also engages sociological debate over the language that dominates American culture. Several scholars suggest that the moral vocabulary Americans use is antithetical to sustaining community participation and integration. Mary Ann Glendon (1991) argues that an absolutist and hyperindividualistic rights dialect dominates American public debate. "Rights language," she argues, "not only seems to filter out other discourses; it simultaneously infiltrates them" (1991: 177). In particular, Glendon is critical of the ways in which law and public policy do not provide the linguistic and conceptual categories that facilitate the expression of social responsibility, duty, and obligation. Glendon thus worries that a strong consciousness of individual and group rights militates against sustaining a deliberative democracy and its civil institutions.

From a communitarian perspective, the problem of maintaining social order and solidarity in the absence of a core communal vocabulary is accentuated by the diversity of contemporary society. "Multicommunity membership," Amitai Etzioni contends, protects individuals from "moral oppression and ostracism," but it also "mutes the moral voice to some extent" (1997: 128). In particular, Etzioni (ibid.) argues, the moral voice is substantially weakened when there is "incongruity among the values of a person's multiple communities."

In *Habits of the Heart*, Robert Bellah and his coauthors (1985) emphasize how the primacy of a self-oriented language of therapeutic individualism undercuts communal attachments. Their interviews with white middle-class Americans found that despite respondents' engagement in other-oriented committed relationships, they were frequently unable to access America's languages of biblical religion or civic republicanism. These communal languages of tradition and commitment, Bellah and his colleagues argue, would expand how people think about and engage in community. Bellah and his coauthors emphasize the importance of what they call "practices of commitment" — the ritual, aesthetic, and ethical practices that define the patterns of loyalty and obligation that keep "communities of memory" alive (1985: 154). They suggest that in the absence of such practices, a culture of separation and fragmentation threatens to erode the meaning and coherence of social life, and the collective will to build a just society (ibid. 282–287).

The primacy of a language of sentiment in how Americans talk about moral values is also noted by James Hunter (1994: 122–149). Focusing on the abortion debate, he finds that the authority of personal experiences and emotions displaces people's ability to ground their views in a language of conviction, derived from either a shared theology or secular philosophy. Hunter argues that what he sees as the inaccessibility of a shared cultural vision lessens the possibility for finding common ground where debate about public goods can be sustained (1994: 12).

These criticisms of American moral language lead to the expectation that this study's sample of pro-change Catholics, comprised primarily of well educated, middle-class white Americans, might similarly rely on arguments accentuating individualistic, rights-oriented, and personal themes to support their claims for a more participative church. My findings will show, in fact, that this is not the case. Although pro-change Catholics have access to the rhetoric of individual and group rights, they defend their vision of Catholicism using arguments squarely grounded in the Catholic doctrinal tradition. They reflexively engage doctrine to substantiate a Catholic identity that validates differences while simultaneously maintaining continuity with the Catholic tradition. Pro-change Catholics want a transformed church that is inclusive in practice, but they want to integrate this with what they consider to be core aspects of Catholicism as their community of memory. As I will show, their interpretation of Catholicism is one that in the present seeks to cohesively link the past with the future.[12]

CATHOLICISM AS CULTURAL PRODUCTION

As the preceding discussion has elaborated, this study investigates sociological questions that transcend religion. Nevertheless, since the research focuses on Catholics and the institutional context of American Catholicism, the arguments of this book have implications for theorizing in the sociology of religion. Specifically, this book offers an empirical perspective on the production of religious meanings. In particular it emphasizes the impact of doctrinal reflexivity and how the interpretive autonomy of religious believers is central to their continuing commitment to a religious tradition.

Conflicts over doctrine and interpretive authority are, of course, not new. Within the Catholic Church diverse intra-church movements have protested the church hierarchy's authority since at least the twelfth century (Congar 1967: 138). The challenge posed to the monopolization of interpretive authority was highlighted most vividly with the schismatic Protestant Reformation in the sixteenth century (see Elton 1963: 15–22). But while interpretive conflict is not new, the reflexivity associated with modern times opens up new possibilities for

12. While this book emphasizes the anchoring and mobilizing resources provided by Catholicism as a communal tradition, Lichterman (1995) emphasizes the significance of personalist values in mobilizing collective action.

dealing with it. The individual and institutional reflexivity of the contemporary era (Berger, Berger, and Kellner 1973: 74; Giddens 1991: 20), including the reflexivity of religious institutions themselves, emphasizes awareness of the social as opposed to the natural or divine construction of doctrine. One result of this reflexivity is that individuals and institutions are empowered to interrogate traditions for clues, symbols, and ideas that might legitimate an emancipatory agenda.

Institutional reflexivity is an inherently risky project insofar as critical investigation of the institutional tradition may yield no reasonable grounds for the reconstruction of alternative practices. On the other hand, it also offers the possibility of change from within the institution itself. In the case of the Catholic Church, for example, Vatican II endorsed a wide array of specific institutional and doctrinal reforms. More far-reachingly significant, Vatican II publicly validated the principle that doctrinal and institutional change was a necessary process attendant on the church's own historical consciousness. As a boundary-shifting event in its own right, and as an event that demonstrated the permeability of apparently fixed boundaries, Vatican II compelled new understandings both of the church as an institution and of Catholic identity. In particular, it displaced the supremacy of the church hierarchy as the "producer" of Catholicism and offered a more egalitarian and culturally dynamic understanding of the production of religious meanings.

Emphasizing religion's cultural dimensions, Robert Wuthnow points out that religion is not solely institutionalized through its organizational characteristics but also in "customary manners of speaking" (1992a: 50). Thinking of religion as culture underscores the fact that it is "something tangible, explicit and overtly produced" (ibid. 52). We thus become cognizant that religion is a socially contextualized human product that "must be continuously produced and reproduced" by people (Berger 1967: 6). Since religion "derives its objective and subjective reality from human beings" (Berger 1967: 48), religious meanings and the structure of religious authority are contingent on the social context in which they take form.

Accordingly, the study of the production of religious meanings can benefit from empirical and theoretical insights provided by the sociology of culture more broadly. Attention to the sociohistorical context in which cultural categories are institutionalized underscores the fact that the taken-for-granted hierarchies of everyday life are neither inevitable or immutable. As sociologists have documented, the bound-

aries between high culture and popular culture that are institutionalized in art museums (DiMaggio 1986), for example, and the social class
distinctions in personal habits, tastes (Bourdieu 1984), and values
(Lamont 1992), represent the conjoint influence of social, economic,
and cultural forces at critical points in history. Similarly, the diverse
ways in which ideas are interpreted underscore the relative open-endedness of all symbols and how they can be appropriated for different
purposes depending on the social contexts of their users (see, for example, Hall and Jefferson 1976; Hebdige 1979; Press 1991; Radway 1984).

Thinking of religion as a cultural product thus directs attention to
the processes of its mediation; in other words, to how the content of
religion is produced, transmitted, and received. Since the transmission
of religion or any other symbolic form involves the packaging of meanings, the mediation process is a thoroughly interpretive activity (Hall
1973). Interpretive activity, as we know from scholars of the mass
media, is an active and creative process, one that is socially, historically, and locally contextualized (Thompson 1990: 145–147). In this
sense, as Dorothy Smith (1990b: 197) observes, "all texts are indexi-
cal" since "their meaning is not fully contained in them but completed in the setting of their reading." In making sense of the meanings
packaged by a producer, the interpreter creates new meanings.
Accordingly, the "reception" or interpretation of meaning is itself part
of the meaning production process (cf. Thompson 1990: 316–317). In
practice, therefore, a sharp dividing line cannot be drawn between the
production and reception of symbolic content, and this includes religious doctrine.

Taking a culturally dynamic view of the interpretive production of
religion offers us a new way to understand the relevance of religion in
contemporary society. I argue in this book that while institutionally
bounded, the "reception" of doctrine, as is true of any symbolic content, is itself an important and analytically autonomous moment in the
production of meaning. By contrast to perspectives that stress a structural view of ideology production (e.g., Burns 1992; 1996), the findings
of this book will highlight that religious meanings are in part produced
deliberatively, reflexively, and self-consciously by participants in a religious tradition.

While the construction of religious meaning takes place within a
relatively bounded institutional context, this context is both constraining and empowering (cf. Powell 1991; Sewell 1992). There is, as
David Tracy (1987: 36–37) reminds us, "no such thing as an unam-

biguous tradition." The institutional context of Catholicism enables its participants to draw on and rework elements within the tradition in ways that broaden the meanings of Catholicism and the possibilities for their institutional expression. The vibrancy of "being Catholic" is empowered by the institutional and symbolic resources available to and creatively appropriated by participants in the tradition. Unless we consider the relatively autonomous interpretive authority of Catholics as producers of doctrinal meanings, we are hard pressed to make sense of their religious involvement.

Religion as cultural production raises questions about the supply-side religious economy model currently dominating the sociology of religion. Roger Finke and Rodney Stark (1992), for example, argue that in a pluralistic religious economy, religious firms (denominations, sects) compete against one another to maximize the appeal of their "product" to distinct market segments. The most successful firms are those who respond to the costly (strict doctrinal) demands of their current and potential customers, thus neutralizing their tendency to switch to an alternative firm and product. In the supply-side model, demand for religious goods is not something that is pre-given or that shifts in response to changing tastes and preferences. Rather, "demand must be *stimulated*" by vigorous suppliers (Finke, Guest and Stark 1996: 204, emphasis in original).

Although Finke, Stark and their collaborators (e.g., Finke and Stark 1992; Finke et al. 1996; Stark and McCann 1993) emphasize the salience of doctrinal content for believers, they nonetheless takes a one-sided view of who produces doctrine. Doctrine is produced by the supplier firms. The relative autonomy of consumers to produce their own interpretations of doctrine independent of the "objective" content of the producing firm or religious organization is not considered. For Finke and Stark (1992), the mediation of religion seems to constitute a clear-cut transaction rather than a dynamic interpretive process in which the meanings of doctrine are diversely understood, negotiated, and frequently contested. Believers have authority as consumers but not as producers; they can only influence the production process by the ever-present threat that inheres in their freedom to switch to a different supplier.

Laurence Iannaccone takes a more complex view of the religious production process. He observes that "most Western religions rely on collective, congregational production" and "deal in . . . commodities that blur the line between producer and consumer" (1995a: 288–289).

Yet since Iannaccone's analytical focus is primarily directed toward addressing opportunity costs, stigma, free rider problems (e.g., 1992; 1995a; 1995b) and other features of the religious production environment (1997), he does not consider the inherently cultured nature of religious commodities and the relative open-endedness of their interpretation. For Iannaccone, automobiles and absolution are commensurable commodities (1995b: 77). It is thus cost differences — that is, differences in the level of sacrifice and stigma that are imposed — and not differences in the theology, history, and organization of different religious groups that drive religious demand (1992: 283). These costs, moreover, for Iannaccone as for Finke and Stark, are assumed to be objective and straightforward in the "price" they exact. In other words, there is no attempt to uncover how consumers differentially construe supplier-imposed sacrifices and stigma.

The tendency therefore of the religious economy model either to emphasize a supply-side approach to religious production (e.g., Finke and Stark 1992), or while recognizing religion as a collective production process (e.g., Iannaccone 1995a), to marginalize the fact that religious commodities are cultural commodities, attenuates its influence in explaining why, for example, American Catholics who disagree with official church teaching on sexuality, women's ordination, or abortion choose to remain Catholic. Why in a pluralistic religious economy do these pro-change Catholics act as if the church were in fact a monopoly church? Why do they stay Catholic when, on the surface at least, the costs of staying and being stigmatized within the church would seem to be greater than the benefits they might accrue from switching to another religion whose doctrines would appear to validate their particular views?

Whereas the religious economy model legitimates the agency of religious believers primarily as consumers who are responsive to competing suppliers (but less so as autonomous cultural producers), the cultural agency of believers is discounted, for example, in Mark Chaves's definition of secularization. He proposes that "we abandon religion as an analytical category when studying secularization" (1994: 750). Suggesting that secularization is best understood as the declining scope of official religious authority, Chaves argues that at the individual level, "religious authority redirects attention away from religious ideas, sentiments, and affiliations and towards religious control/influence over actions of individuals" (ibid. 768). Accordingly, for Chaves, the disjuncture in the Catholic Church between official church teaching and Catholics' attitudes is explained as an indication that "there is religion, but there is little effective religious authority" among American Catholics (ibid. 769). By employing a narrow understanding of religious authority that equates authority with the formal authority of church office, Chaves negates the interpretive authority of believers and the symbolic content of doctrine. A sociological interest in why Catholicism continues to have "authority" and meaning for the majority of Catholics who reject "the religious authority" of the church hierarchy is outside the purview of his definition.

Gene Burns (1996), by contrast, advocates a cultural approach to understanding religion. But, because he is interested in probing the structural constraints on the exercise of power (1992: 16; 1996: 49), Burns tends to privilege the interpretive power of the church hierarchy in a church where "the laity are more acted on than they are actors" (1992: 16). Yet it is also true that Catholic laity across space and time have lived (and continue to live) a Catholicism which in many important respects was (and is) quite autonomous of the church hierarchy. Burns acknowledges the varieties of Catholicism that exist within the church, but, understandably, given his structural focus, views the doctrinal autonomy demonstrated by certain groups (e.g., nuns) as a "negative autonomy" vis-à-vis the church hierarchy (1992: 131).

Although the church is a hierarchically structured organization (see Reese 1996a), the church hierarchy itself, notwithstanding its power, is only one important part of a doctrinal, institutional, and communal tradition that comprises many strands. While it would be naïve to understate the structural power of the church hierarchy, it is also the case that since participation in a religious tradition is a voluntary and an interpretive activity, believers enjoy a certain autonomy of meaning construction that transcends and is beyond the control of church officials. Burns (1996) clearly recognizes that there may be resistance to the doctrinal meanings transmitted by church officials, but he does not value interpretive resistance as doctrinal production in its own right. In short, his focus on power structures does not facilitate recognition of the fact that there are multiple "micro" producers and multiple sites of doctrinal production.

I will argue that the richness and dynamism of Catholicism today, while clearly not independent of the church hierarchy's structural power to produce doctrine, is relatively autonomous from it. The interpretive autonomy of pro-change Catholics to construct meanings that are at odds with official church teaching enables them to maintain their participation in the church and simultaneously actualize their commitment to being Catholic and gay or lesbian, Catholic and an advocate of women's ordination, or Catholic and pro-choice. Equally important, the meanings that pro-change Catholics generate to make sense of religious doctrine are not privatized or depoliticized products (cf. Bellah et al. 1985; Berger 1967; Schluchter 1990). To the contrary, they are publicly enacted in how they live out the emancipatory ethics of Catholicism (e.g., equality, justice, community) and engage in collective action aimed toward making the church more inclusive. Thus, for example, gay and lesbian Catholics establish unique worship communities, autonomous of the church hierarchy, in which they work at integrating what it means to be gay and Catholic or lesbian and Catholic. By the same token, pro-choice Catholics' political activism on abortion is informed, in part, by their interpretations of Catholic theology.

More broadly, the interpretive autonomy of pro-change Catholics has practical consequences for how the church as a whole talks about and understands Catholicism and thus for the institutionalization of new doctrinal meanings. This is a dimension of religion that is as significant as its formal rules (Wuthnow 1992a: 50). The circulation of new ideas and meanings provides redefined conceptual frameworks (see Sewell 1990) legitimating shifts in personal, collective, and institutional identities and practices. Through forging new ways of talking about and practicing Catholicism, pro-change Catholics open up future transformative possibilities for the church as a whole. It is significant, moreover, that they do so from within the institutional bounds of Catholicism and using the symbolic resources of the church rather than appealing to arguments based on individual rights, for instance, to articulate the possibilities for doctrinal and institutional change.

In short, although pro-change Catholics do not have the formal authority to change the officially defined doctrines and practices of the church, their presence in the church matters. They are transforming the church's institutional conversations and destabilizing some of the taken-for-granted meanings of Catholicism. The alternative interpretations of Catholic identity articulated by pro-change Catholics thus carry the potential to play a crucial role in hindering the reproduction of some existing church practices and facilitating the institutionalization of new doctrines and practices that reflect a more participative church. Although the church is a hierarchically structured organization that emphasizes institutional routines derived from a putatively "constant" tradition, it is clearly evident that Catholic doctrine and practices change. Since, as I noted earlier, the church is a reflexively self-critical institution, the doctrinal engagement of pro-change Catholics offers a public articulation of Catholicism that the church hierarchy and other Catholics must respond to, even if they ultimately reject the validity of some or all of pro-change Catholics' claims.

The interpretive autonomy of this study's participants has a postmodern charge to it insofar as the practical meanings pro-change Catholics generate challenge the "grand narratives" in official church teaching. Rather than accepting official church definitions that there is one universal way of being Catholic, pro-change Catholics demonstrate the multiplicity of ways within Catholicism. At the same time it is evident that the new understandings of identity that pro-change Catholics forge are not privatized, subjective or idiosyncratic articulations (cf. Berger 1967: 152-153; Wuthnow 1989a: 116), but are objectively integrated with the Catholic doctrinal tradition itself. As I will document, pro-change Catholics' doctrinal reflexivity facilitates their finding in the Catholic tradition the emancipatory elements that legitimate both their demands for a more egalitarian, inclusive and deliberative church, and their choice to affirm an identity that maintains solidarity with the larger Catholic community.

OVERVIEW

This study explores the emancipatory projects of institutionally marginalized Catholics – Catholics whose understanding of the doctrinal and institutional possibilities of Catholicism is rejected by church officials. The book will illuminate some of the resources that enable prochange Catholics to negotiate identity and build a more inclusive and participative church. I begin in Chapter 2 by using historical accounts documenting how official church teaching on the issues of interest to this study (homosexuality, priesthood, and abortion) have developed and shifted in response to changing social and cultural circumstances. This overview will underscore that the church's institutional practices and doctrines are not invariant, a point highlighted most recently by the doctrinal deliberations and decisions of the Second Vatican Council. I conclude this chapter by arguing that Vatican II, in particular, provides Catholics with the symbolic resources supporting the construction of an emancipatory church.

Chapter 3 focuses on the arguments used by the Vatican to expli-
cate its stance on the doctrinal issues contested by this study's participants (homosexuality, women's ordination, and abortion) and its view
of the role of theologians in the church. I highlight the Vatican's assertion of its magisterial authority, and discuss how its representation of
categorical differences among Catholics negates certain voices and
theological positions within the church. In the Vatican's understanding, women's natural-symbolic differences from men, for example,
make their ordination as priests impossible, and the essentially different nature of homosexual acts renders them objectively disordered as
compared to heterosexual acts, which are in principle life-giving. In
parallel fashion, interpretive differences on issues such as abortion
crystallize for the Vatican the moral relativism that it sees as undermining universal moral principles.

Chapter 4 begins by summarizing post–Vatican II trends in
American Catholic attitudes, demonstrating their autonomy from official church teaching. I then focus on Catholics' collective mobilization
against the church hierarchy's authority as seen in the emergence of
groups committed to change in the church. This chapter traces the
evolution, agenda, and tensions within the three pro-change groups of
central interest to this study, namely Dignity, a national association of
gay and lesbian Catholics, the Women's Ordination Conference
(WOC), and Catholics for a Free Choice (CFFC).

The next three chapters use empirical findings from Dignity, WOC,
and CFFC respondents. Chapter 5 presents ethnographic data from
Dignity/Boston, in-depth interviews with select participants, and data
from a survey of Dignity members to illustrate the routine community
practices and tensions associated with enacting a reconstructed
Catholic identity. I focus in particular on how gay and lesbian
Catholics negotiate the specificity of their situational context while
maintaining continuity with the church's more universal tradition.

Doctrinal reflexivity is the theme of Chapter 6, which provides further illustration of the interpretive authority demonstrated by pro-
change Catholics. This chapter draws on surveys of WOC and CFFC
respondents to elaborate the arguments they use to support their
respective agendas. The data indicates that respondents ground their
projects primarily in the Catholic tradition, using existing doctrine to
critique doctrine and transform the church. In addition, many respondents also incorporate a power-based critique of the church hierarchy,
and discuss women's de facto and possible future contributions to the

church. In discussing pro-change Catholics' reasoning, I emphasize the emancipatory resources available within Catholicism (contrary to Foucault's view of the negative impact of institutions on social change) and focus on the evident interrelation between religion and reasoned argumentation (contrary to Habermas's disavowal of religion).

Internal communal pluralism is the theme of Chapter 7. This chapter presents findings underscoring the fact that cultural differences characterize collectivities and that they do so without necessarily fragmenting communal solidarity. I present data showing attitudinal differences among Dignity, WOC, and CFFC respondents on issues of faith, morality, sexuality, gender, and politics. I also introduce survey data from doctrinally conservative Catholics, respondents from the Catholic League for Religious and Civil Rights. These data underscore major differences between pro-change and conservative Catholics over interpretive authority and doctrine. Yet, of particular significance, the comparative analyses also point to several commonalities between the two doctrinally opposed groups. Shared commitments and memories, I argue, provide symbolic resources that can be harnessed in the service of building a Catholic communality that recognizes differences in a more inclusive and pluralistic church.

Chapter 8 explores the links between the identity constructions of pro-change Catholics and those offered by the Catholic theologians whom I interviewed. The opinions the theologians offer about Catholicism, interpretive authority, and the demands of Catholic identity present a remarkable parallel to the views articulated by the respondents in the preceding three chapters. Crystallized by the theologians' emphasis on a reasoned and reasonable theology, I conclude this chapter by noting how differences in institutional position may account for the disparate interpretations of Catholicism offered by the theologians relative to the church hierarchy. Chapter 9, the final chapter, synthesizes the preceding chapters by drawing out the theoretical and practical implications of the study's findings. In broad terms, I discuss communal connectedness and pluralism, the importance of reason as an emancipatory resource, and conclude by emphasizing a dynamic view of personal and institutional identity, including Catholic identity.

CHAPTER TWO

DOCTRINAL CHANGE IN THE CATHOLIC CHURCH

The efforts of pro-change Catholics in moving the church toward a greater affirmation of diversity inevitably dispute some of the taken-for-granted doctrines and practices that appear as core to the church's public identity. In particular, the Catholic Church presents an image of a divinely prescribed hierarchical institution whose teaching is constant and immutable. Yet from an historical perspective it is evident that change in doctrines and practices has been a feature of the church since earliest times. Accordingly, the boundaries of Catholicism and what is core to the tradition, are less rigid than might be assumed from the image of an immutable church that is presented in official church accounts and frequently perceived as such by Catholics and non-Catholics alike (cf. O'Malley 1989: 15–16).

The Catholic theologian Yves Congar argued that there is a tendency for the church hierarchy "to regard itself as a source" of revelation and to present itself as identical to rather than an interpreter of the Catholic faith tradition (1967: 336–337). The church hierarchy's tendency to identify itself as a "source" of doctrine makes it difficult for it to explicitly acknowledge that doctrine changes and that church structures, including official understandings of the church hierarchy's authority, are mutable. The church hierarchy seeks to bolster its own authority and what it considers to be the essential structure of the church by appealing to a "constant" tradition which has "always taught" that certain doctrines and organizational forms are fundamental to the identity and functioning of the church.[1] The church hierar-

---

1. It is instructive in this regard to note that Cardinal Ratzinger, head of the Vatican Congregation for the Doctrine of the Faith, has stated that "Catholic

hy's emphasis on an immutable tradition obscures the fact that the church hierarchy redraws the boundaries of Catholicism in response to changing historical, political, and cultural contexts, and that in this process it is responsive not only to political elites and anonymous social forces (e.g., the Enlightenment) but to the circumstances and traditions of the communities (the laity) that comprise the church.

The history of the Catholic Church contains many diverse strands that contribute to its multifaceted identity. This chapter draws on historical accounts of the church to highlight the origins of official teaching on the substantive issues of concern to this study's pro-change Catholics, namely homosexuality, the priesthood, and abortion. It does not provide an exhaustive historical analysis of the development of official church teaching on the specific doctrinal questions. Such a task clearly is beyond the scope of any one study and as is ably demonstrated by the existing historical scholarship, the relevant issues have been well researched by scholars with expertise in particular areas.

Since the purpose of this chapter is to emphasize that church doctrines and practices are not invariant or immutable, the second part of the chapter offers a selective consideration of the doctrinal and institutional changes formalized by the church at Vatican II (1962–1965). I will discuss those aspects of Vatican II that legitimated a new understanding of interpretive authority in the church. This contextualist perspective on the church will suggest that Vatican II, with its emphasis on an egalitarian and communicative model of the church, is as viable and as representative of the Catholic ethos as was Vatican I's institutionalization almost one hundred years earlier (1869–1870) of the dogma of papal infallibility.

It is important to note here that despite its centrality in the contemporary church, the formalization of papal infallibility is a relatively recent phenomenon. Its enactment at Vatican I was an initiative designed to bolster papal power against the advance of democracy, on the one hand, and of science and reason on the other (see McSweeney 1980: 22–32; Rude 1964). The claim of papal infallibility has been present in the church since the eleventh century. In 1075, Pope Gregory VII (1073–1085) formulated a set of principles asserting the divine source, supremacy, and universality of papal authority and the irrevocability of papal pronouncements (Laurentin 1973: 101–102). Congar

teaching develops by building on past affirmations rather than on overturning them." Reported in *Origins* 24 (April 6, 1995): 690.

(1967: 179, 181) identifies these initiatives as critical to the subsequently enduring hierarchical character of the church, especially the idea that papal pronouncements should be given privileged authority by virtue of the sanctity of the papal office and not based upon their substantive content.[2]

The theological rationale for formalizing infallibility at Vatican I (1869–1870) was the belief among the majority of bishops present that the claim was legitimated by the Pope's status as the successor to Peter and the apostles. Rather than seeing the articulation of papal infallibility as a socially and historically constructed response to the political pressures of Modernity, those who endorsed the dogma saw it as developing and institutionalizing meanings that were "revealed" during Christ's life. As the Catholic theologian Gustave Thils points out, the bishops deliberating at Vatican I believed that they "were in continuity with the twelve apostles who received from the Lord, together with their mission to found and rule the Church, the promise of his help till the end of time" (1973: 31).

Yet evidently not all of the bishops shared the view that infallibility, irrespective of its framing in divine source, was an appropriate claim for the Vatican to make in the late nineteenth century. The proposal was strongly contested by several bishops attending the council who challenged both its theological legitimacy and its political wisdom. American bishops, in particular, were concerned about the implications of an official declaration of infallibility for church-state and Protestant-Catholic relations (Hennesey 1963: 139, 194–195, 198). Arguing that the timing was inopportune, some bishops maintained that all Catholics commonly understood the Pope to be infallible, so it was not necessary to make this a dogma of faith (Hennesey 1963: 191, 196–198). Nevertheless, despite their reservations, all the bishops who opposed papal infallibility during the debates at Vatican I eventually gave their adherence to the proclamation after it was endorsed by the majority in attendance (Hennesey 1967).

The medieval historian Brian Tierney emphasizes that the institutionalization of papal infallibility was driven by sociopolitical forces rather than being the explication of a doctrine that was "received from the beginning of the Christian faith" (Tierney 1971: 862–863). He

---

2. For comprehensive historical overviews of the organizational development of the early church and the emergence of the primacy of Rome, see Blank (1973), Dulles (1985), Grant (1970), Hollister (1982), and Wagner (1994).

argues that although "[a]ll the standard Catholic discussions of infallibility emphasize continuity rather than change in the church's teaching on this matter . . . it is very hard for a historian to see the emergence of the doctrine of papal infallibility as the slow unfolding of a truth that the church has always held" (ibid. 863).

This chapter's illustrative overview will underscore the fact that Catholic doctrine is not scripturally predetermined or the expression of some reified Tradition but is formulated and modified by the church hierarchy in response to the press of changing social and cultural conditions. A social constructionist perspective toward Catholic doctrine suggests that the official interpretations used to validate doctrine and institutional practices in part derive from, and are contingent on, the historical, political, and cultural context in which the church operates. The church hierarchy is not a source but an interpreter of revelation. Thus while doctrine and the disclosure of the meanings of revelation develop over time, a social constructionist view points to the historical and cultural discontinuities in the church hierarchy's presentation of Catholic doctrine and to the contextual influences that may account for its favoring some interpretations over others.

HISTORICAL ORIGINS OF OFFICIAL CHURCH TEACHING ON HOMOSEXUALITY, PRIESTHOOD, AND ABORTION

HOMOSEXUALITY

The archival research of the Yale historian John Boswell challenges the popular misconception that Christianity was the cause of intolerance toward gay people (1980: 6). Boswell acknowledges that his and other scholars' research does not adequately explain what accounted for the "rabid and obsessive negative preoccupation with homosexuality as the most horrible of sins" starting in the fourteenth century (1994: 262). His arguments, however, point to the complex societal origins of intolerance toward gays rather than locating the source of intolerance in Christian theology.

Boswell notes that as the only institution to survive the disintegration of the Roman Empire following the barbarian invasions of the fifth century, Christianity was the "conduit" for, but not the "author" of, the narrower views of sexual freedom including homosexuality that characterized later European society (1980: 127–128). He observes that although Christianity became the state religion in the fourth century, it was not until the sixth century that the empire introduced "legislation flatly outlawing homosexual behavior" (1980: 171). Boswell suggests that those theologians who condemned homosexuality as unnatural (such as Augustine) did so in large part because they were from the rural provinces where homosexuality was more clandestine and "bizarre" than it was in the urban areas, where it was daily visible (1980: 151–152).

Boswell also discusses evidence indicating the popular acceptance of "passionate friendships" among women martyrs and the veneration of paired same-sex saints who had "intense" friendships in the early church (1980: 135; 1994: 135–140). Boswell identifies the late third/early fourth century same-sex pair of Bacchus and Serge as "by far the most influential" (1994: 146–147). Bacchus and Serge were Christians and Roman soldiers with close ties to the emperor. The pair apparently shared a single household and they were "usually referred to and often pictorially depicted together (sometimes rubbing halos together and with their horses' noses touching)" (1994: 153). According to Boswell, "in what is by far the most common version of their lives, Serge is referred to as the 'sweet companion and lover' of Bacchus" (1994: 154).

Boswell argues that early medieval Christians were relatively indifferent toward homosexual behavior (1980: 200), and that "passionate friendships" were common among the monastic clergy as late as the Middle Ages (1980: 202). Pointing to the greater relevance of other theological questions for the church, Boswell notes that the first church synod to deal with homosexuality was the Third Lateran Council in 1179 (1980: 128).

Boswell thus maintains that the negative attitude subsequently adopted by the late medieval church was culturally rather than either scripturally or theologically grounded. In particular, Boswell argues that Thomas Aquinas's categorization of homosexual acts as "unnatural" appears to "have been a response more to the pressures of popular antipathy than to the weight of the Christian tradition" (1980: 329). Boswell does not exonerate Aquinas for making such concessions to popular prejudice, and he notes the enduring influence of Aquinas's theological categorization on solidifying attitudes of intolerance toward gays. He emphasizes, nevertheless, that "intellectual responses to homosexuality generally reflected rather than caused intolerance" (1980: 330).

While not marginalizing the medieval church's role in the domination and stigmatization of marginal groups, Boswell argues that the status of homosexuality was not in and of itself sufficient grounds for the invocation of church-imposed penalties. Boswell claims it was unlikely that "many people were prosecuted by the Inquisition simply for homosexual behavior, which by the thirteenth century had come to be regarded by much of the church as a carnal sin but not a heresy per se . . . few if any cases are known in which . . . homosexuality was the sole offense of a heretic" (1980: 285).

Further documenting what might be interpreted as church tolerance of gay relationships, Boswell (1994) claims to have uncovered archival manuscripts suggesting the existence of Christian liturgical ceremonies solemnizing same-sex unions in premodern Europe. Boswell finds the earliest same-sex union ceremony in an eighth-century manuscript, which, he argues, represents a much older tradition, as suggested by its use of prayers invoking the fourth-century paired saints Bacchus and Serge (1994: 147, n.172). By the twelfth century when, according to Boswell, liturgical marriage ceremonies were more developed and formalized, so too was the service for same-sex unions. The same-sex union liturgy involved among other features the burning of candles, the placing of the two parties' hands on the Gospel, the joining of their right hands, an introductory litany, the Lord's Prayer, communion, and a kiss (1994: 185). Boswell clearly recognizes that the meanings and purposes of what we understand as friendship, love, and marriage vary across cultures and across time. His careful and painstaking documentary analysis leads him to conclude, nonetheless, that these unions functioned in fact as "gay marriages" (1994: 280–281).

Boswell's scholarship is not without controversy. Several reviewers challenge, for example, the basis of Boswell's thesis that the liturgical unions he discusses were in fact celebrations of gay relationships rather than of nonerotic friendships based on "brotherhood" (e.g., Bray 1994; Reynolds 1995). In light both of the Vatican's condemnation of gay relationships and the civic politics surrounding the question of legalizing same-sex relationships as marriages, it is not surprising that Boswell's research is seen by some reviewers as having "a contemporary social agenda," and has been rejected as a misrepresentation and historical distortion of Christian practices (e.g., Wilken 1994: 25–26).

However valid some of the criticisms of Boswell's research may be, his work as a whole provides an alternative way of thinking about commonly accepted notions of what counts as normal and constant in

everyday practices. As one comparatively sympathetic reviewer of
Boswell's work suggests, the research he presents may eventually give
scholars "more cause to question their assumptions" concerning the
historical origins of same-sex marriages (M. Young 1995: 165–166).
Equally important for the purposes of this study, Boswell's reconstruction of the origins of official church teaching on homosexuality raises
the possibility that what influences the articulation and interpretation
of religious doctrine is not some "orthodox" or pre-given theology but
the sociocultural context in which it occurs.

PRIESTHOOD

The socially contextualized nature of official church teaching on who
can be priests is also apparent from historical accounts. In contrast to
the church hierarchy's exclusion of women from ordination and thus
from sacramental and hierarchical roles in the church, several theologians point to the prominence of women both in Christ's revelatory
actions and during the founding decades of Christianity. The Irish theologian Dermot Lane, for example, offers many illustrations of
women's scriptural presence. He observes that women "are active as
witnesses to the resurrection, as deaconesses of the Church, as
prophetesses in the Assembly, as catechists in the community and as
evangelists of the good news" (1985: 672). Lane concludes that "one
cannot fail to be impressed by the extraordinary visibility of women in
the mission and ministry of Jesus, especially when one bears in mind
the predominantly patriarchal culture that existed in first-century
Palestine" (ibid. 670). Lane also points to the importance of house
churches as public places of communal worship in the development of
the early church and he argues that women "played a significant leadership role" in their founding (ibid. 672–673).[3]

Lane attributes the decline of women's leadership in the church to
a number of societal factors. He highlights the influence of the patriarchal culture of Judaism and Greek philosophy on Christianity, the

---

3. In the first three centuries or so of early Christianity there were no distinct
   institutions or specifically designed "churches." Followers of Jesus continued to
   meet communally after his death in the households of various people where
   family members, friends, extended kin, and workers associated with the household would gather for fellowship. These house-churches served as the core
   communal organizational units for early Christianity and "diversity was likely
   in both worship and group organization" (White 1997: 546).

early church's strong opposition to the Gnostic movement in which women were prominent, and what he calls the "ambiguous alliance" between church and state that began with Constantine (ibid. 673). Church leaders denounced the Gnostic practice of allowing women priests as incompatible with Christianity (see Grant 1970: 120–131). In response to Gnosticism and other heretical interpretations, the church established a specially commissioned ministry so that by the end of the third century, ministerial functions showed a high degree of hierarchical organization from the Pope down to bishops, priests, deacons, acolytes, and readers (Bokenkotter 1990: 31, 49; Wagner 1994: 121–122).[4] The ordination of priests was one of the most important spiritual duties of bishops, and although priests unlike bishops tended to come from the lower but nonservile classes, by the end of the fourth century, with Christianity the official religion of the empire, the clergy had taken on the character of a "sacred caste" (Bokenkotter 1990: 129, 40).

Recognizing the social and cultural context in which church practices evolve, Dermot Lane notes that "the original vision and praxis of Jesus became overlaid with social and cultural accretions that were unready to accept the unity and equality of *all* human beings before God and in the service of the Church of Christ" (1985: 673, emphasis in original). Elisabeth Schüssler Fiorenza similarly stresses that the adaptation of the church to Greco-Roman culture meant that the leadership roles women had in the early Christian movement were either eliminated or, as in the case of deaconesses, relegated to the inferior ministry of serving only women (1993: 86).

As in the case of the development of official church doctrine on homosexuality, the prevailing cultural understandings of women's "nature" and social status were similarly woven into the articulation of a theological argument against women priests. Again, the medieval period was critical in influencing future thinking on the issue. Medieval theologians, most notably Thomas Aquinas, argued that women's "defective" rationality prevented them from becoming priests. Yet it is also noteworthy that the medieval theologian Duns

4. Gnosticism was an early sect whose adherents denied divine providence, and the incarnation and resurrection of Christ, and who claimed a secret and privileged knowledge (gnosis) of divine will unavailable to others (Grant 1970: 120–131). Another early heretical movement was Montanism. It combined prophecy and apocalyptic predictions and emphasized asceticism, martyrdom, and ecstatic utterances (ibid. 132–135).

Scotus viewed women's exclusion from ordination as constituting a great injustice. According to Thomas Shannon, Duns Scotus believed that the categorical exclusion of women from being priests was so unfair that it could be comprehended only if understood as a direct command from Christ (1995a: 354).

Despite official opposition to women priests in the early and medieval church, there is historical evidence suggesting that women continued to exercise authoritative roles within the church. Ladislaus Orsy (1996), a Jesuit professor of canon law, provides documentary evidence that from the thirteenth until the late nineteenth century, "lady abbesses" in Europe exercised "quasi-episcopal" jurisdiction in particular territories. The abbesses controlled practices "ordinarily reserved to bishops" such as the convocation of synods and the authorization of when and where priests could celebrate Mass and hear confessions.

One such abbess was Lady Maria-Benedicta, who identified herself in 1868 as the "Prelate, Mother and legitimate Administrator of spiritual things of the Royal Monastery" of Las Huelgas in Spain, and of its "dependent convents, churches, adjunct hermitages." In the document translated by Orsy, the abbess expresses her satisfaction with the qualifications of a presbyter applicant, and gives permission to him to "celebrate, properly robed, in this church of the monastery, and in all other churches, hospitals, and hermitages within our District, Dependencies, and Jurisdictions" and also to preach and hear confessions (quoted in Orsy 1996: 11). Orsy asks why, if such quasi-episcopal practices were "abuses," the jurisdictions of abbesses were recognized by the Vatican for centuries without being condemned until Pius IX abolished their privileges in 1873. While Pius IX judged the jurisdictional role of the abbesses as "unsuitable for modern times," he nonetheless recognized the past validity and contributions of abbesses to the church (Orsy 1996: 11–12).

The development of official teaching requiring celibacy was also influenced by sociohistorical considerations. Beginning in the fourth century, the church enforced the expectation that priests would be celibate, a ruling that in contemporary times has been affirmed by Vatican II (see Cahill 1996: 168–169). Historically, the celibacy requirement was driven primarily by the assumption that "sexual intercourse was incompatible with the sacred character of the clerical state" (Bokenkotter 1990: 50). According to church historian Thomas Bokenkotter, elevating the clergy above the laity was seen as a necessary polarization to revive the distinction between the sacred and the profane that had collapsed with Constantine and the alliance of church and state (ibid.).

Despite the theoretically sacred status of the clergy, historical accounts of European peasant societies depict priests as integrated with, rather than segregated from, the communities in which they executed their priestly duties. Although priests were more likely than their neighbors to be literate, they nonetheless shared in the same farm work and trades of the other men in the community, and they also engaged in sexual relations (Carroll 1996: 203; Greeley 1995: 73). Contrary therefore to the official church teaching and the voiding of all clerical marriages at the Second Lateran Council in 1139 (Bokenkotter 1990: 129), married priests, and in some instances married bishops, were common at least until the Council of Trent (1545–1563), when the practice was denounced (Carroll 1996: 203; Greeley 1995: 73; Hollister 1982: 216).

ABORTION

The influence of historical and cultural context on the formulation of doctrine is also demonstrated by the development of the church's stance on abortion. Although abortion was condemned by early Christian writers, the Jesuit historian John Connery finds no trace of any official church legislation against abortion during the first three centuries (1977: 46). Punitive legislation was first sanctioned at the Council of Elvira (305) but less than ten years later the Council of Ancyra (314) weakened the severity of the earlier penalties. Rather than imposing Elvira's penalty of life-long excommunication on adulterous women who had abortions, Ancyra took a more forgiving attitude and received them back into the church after a period of ten years' penance (Connery 1977: 46–48). Although both Elvira and Ancyra were local councils, the Ancyra understanding of abortion became the official norm for the church during the subsequent few centuries (ibid. 48–49; Noonan 1970).

Abortion nonetheless continued to be a subject of theological controversy. In particular, leading Christian writers disagreed over distinctions between the "unformed" and the "formed" fetus (as fetuses that were forty days old were called), and over whether the time of animation or ensoulment should be identified only with the formed fetus. According to Connery, a tradition developed in which only the abortion of a formed fetus was considered homicide (1977: 63). Whether animation and formation should be considered synchronous developments was left an open question by Saint Augustine (ibid. 56–58). The canon law decrees compiled (between 1139 and 1150) by the twelfth-century monk and legal scholar Gratian, restricted ensoulment to the formed fetus and categorized such abortions as homicides (ibid. 90–91). This teaching was given official recognition during the papacy of Innocent III (1198–1216) (ibid. 96–97).

From the early fourteenth century, abortion of the unanimated fetus to save the life of the mother found "considerable support" among theologians (ibid. 124). Nonetheless, the increasing prevalence of abortion during Renaissance times and popular disregard for official church penalties led the church hierarchy to restore its earlier practice of treating abortion as a sin deserving of excommunication. In 1588, Pope Sixtus V mandated excommunication as the universal Catholic penalty for abortion (ibid. 147–148).

The new position departed from the church's officially sanctioned previous teaching in significant ways. It no longer differentiated between the animated and the unanimated fetus, and it restricted the giving of absolution to the penitent following confession. By 1591 however, the impracticalities associated with the policy led Pope Gregory XIV to modify the official church stance. Unlike his predecessor, he restricted excommunication only to cases of abortion of the animated fetus. This remained official church teaching until 1869 when Pope Pius IX reintroduced excommunication as the penalty for the principals involved in an abortion irrespective of the stage of embyronic development (Connery 1977: 148). The new Code of Canon Law enacted in 1917 explicated that excommunication applied to "mothers" who had abortions. This clarified ambiguities associated with the 1588 papal decree on excommunication, which had led some people to argue that excommunication applied only to the doctors and others involved in carrying out the procedure and not to the woman receiving the abortion (Noonan 1970: 41).

The preceding discussion directs attention to the historical variability in the church's disposition toward particular groups and specific doctrinal questions. Illustrative examples of the development of official church teaching on homosexuality, the ordination of women, celibacy, and abortion, indicate that the substance of church doctrine is not removed from the context in which it is expressed. No matter how absolute the church hierarchy may be in its representation of doctrine, these examples suggest that church teaching does not follow a

constant doctrinal stance uncontaminated by the press of sociocultural concerns.

VATICAN II AND DOCTRINAL CHANGE

In more recent times, the idea that Catholic doctrine and church practices are immutable was radically undermined by the church hierarchy
itself at Vatican II. In church history, Vatican II is widely considered a
revolutionary event (O'Malley 1989: 19). Although monumental, as
Helen Rose Ebaugh emphasizes, it was "one event in a much broader
historical process that had its roots in centuries of church history, in
particular, the nearly 100 years of strain and struggle that had gripped
parts of the church since the First Vatican Council" (1991: 3), when
papal infallibility was formalized. Most important, as John Seidler and
Katherine Meyer (1989: 38) discuss, the issue of the church hierarchy's
authority and the church's relationship to the contemporary world
were enduring sources of tension after Vatican I.

Both of these issues had surfaced particularly during the late nineteenth and early twentieth centuries as laity and church elites articulated understandings of Catholicism that challenged the dominance of
the Vatican (see Seidler and Meyer 1989: 37–50). Since the mid
1800s, the lay movement in the Catholic Church had steadily gained
prominence and greater autonomy from Rome (Vaillancourt 1980),
and liturgical changes had introduced an increased role for the laity in
the Mass (Sheppard 1967). Theologically, the turn of the century witnessed Americanist and Modernist ideas arguing for a church that was
less wedded to a monarchical model and instead more culturally
engaged and pragmatic.[5]

5. Americanism is associated with the ideas of Isaac Hecker, a converted Catholic
    priest and founder of the religious order popularly known as the Paulists, and a
    few leading American bishops of the time (see Fogerty 1985; McAvoy 1957).
    Americanists articulated a liberal understanding of the legitimacy of religious
    pluralism and emphasized the strength derived for the church from the auton-
    omy of church and state (McAvoy 1957). Although distinct from American-
    ism, the Modernist movement in European Catholic theology was driven by a
    similar concern that the church should be open to the modern world.
    Modernists challenged the church hierarchy's interpretive authority by advo-
    cating the embrace of science and reasoned criticism as legitimate means of
    biblical scholarship and Catholic doctrinal knowledge (Kurtz 1986).
    Modernists also challenged the idea of an immutable, ahistorical and unre-
    visable epistemology as articulated by Thomas Aquinas's thesis of a "single,

In addition to these antecedents, Vatican II was also motivated by global events outside the church, especially by the impact of the First and Second World Wars. As expressed by Pope John XXIII, who convened the council, his decision was both a response to the dark instrumentality of the Enlightenment, and a visionary expression of optimism regarding the reflexivity of reason, science, and history made possible by the Enlightenment. John XXIII lamented the negative consequences of scientific and technological progress demonstrated most clearly in what he considered the tragic destruction caused by war. Yet despite his sensitivity to the darkness caused by "scientific conquests," he was optimistic about the fate of humanity. John XXIII affirmed the critical importance for church and society of learning from history, which as he noted is "the teacher of life" (1962/1966: 712). In John XXIII's view: "Scientific progress itself, which gave man the possibility of creating catastrophic instruments for his destruction, has raised questions. It has obliged human beings to become thoughtful, more conscious of their own limitations, desirous of peace, and attentive to the importance of spiritual values" (1961/1966: 704). Papal confidence in the emancipatory possibilities of human reflexivity thus underpinned the task given to the bishops at Vatican II in their charge to remedy some of the problems associated with the "spiritual ruins" of the modern age (ibid.).

Vatican II was distinguished by the openness of its deliberative process, its clear affirmation of historical consciousness and doctrinal development, and the breadth of its focus on all aspects of Catholic institutional and personal life (O'Malley 1989: 15). As Jesuit church historian John O'Malley remarks, "The very breadth of the issues which the Council chose to review and reformulate and the all-inclusive [global] audience that the Council finally chose to address would

changeless conceptual framework" (McCool 1977: 247), and which had been officially restored as the centerpiece of Catholic education by Pope Leo XII in 1879 (McCool 1977: 227–228). The Vatican denounced both Americanism (Leo XIII, 1899) and Modernism (Pius X, 1907). Most noteworthy, the Modernist challenge to official church authority was resolved by the Vatican's decision to excommunicate the leading theologians identified with the movement (Kurtz 1986: 159). The Vatican's response to the new ideas associated with Americanism and Modernism had the effect of severely stifling theological creativity in the church and driving it underground (Sanks 1974: 145).

seem to suggest that we are facing a major turning point in the history of Catholicism, at least in intent" (1989: 24).[6]

The strong consensus among sociologists, historians, and theologians is that Vatican II redefined the church from a rigidly hierarchical, authoritarian, imperialist, antimodern institution to one that has become more relevant to and engaged in the modern world. The reforms of Vatican II were critical in laying the groundwork for the pro-change projects of contemporary Catholics. Focusing on the church's ideological struggle with political liberalism, Gene Burns (1992: 49) highlights Vatican II's partial embrace of a liberal approach to church-state relations, and its engagement with sociopolitical issues. j34 Casanova argues that Vatican II's doctrinal and institutional reforms transformed the church from a state-centered to a society-centered institution, which allowed it to reenter the public sphere in order to "defend the institutionalization of modern universal rights" (1994: 71, 220).

Helen Rose Ebaugh emphasizes the council's role as "a major resource in the movement toward greater liberalization and modernization of the church" (1991: 12). While some sociologists (e.g., McSweeney 1980) focus on the impact of Vatican II in delegitimating the church hierarchy's authority, Seidler and Meyer rightly argue that "the concept of delegitimation is much too limited and negative" since it neglects "the increased emphasis on other forms of authority within the Church" (1989: 27–28). Seidler and Meyer interpret Vatican II and the subsequent contested struggle over authority as giving rise to a new paradigm of the church as "participatory," one which "emphasizes the human side without abandoning its link with the divine." In this new understanding of the church, according to Seidler and Meyer, people's participation depends on the extent to which they are accorded "dignity and respect" and their interests are represented (ibid. 161). Central to the emphasis on a participative church, the council, as I will discuss below, recognized the importance of making the church a more dialogically engaged community.

6. As a qualification to the radical nature of Vatican II's deliberative process, women were not participants. The sociologist Ruth Wallace, who was one of four American women involved in organizing a series of discussions during the fourth session of the council, observes that "there was only a few instances where any attention was given to the contribution of women to the church" (1991: 125).

VATICAN II'S INSTITUTIONALIZATION OF
COMMUNAL INTERPRETIVE AUTHORITY

The argument of this book is that the doctrinal synthesis articulated at Vatican II can be seen as the church's formal affirmation of the communality and interpretive openness that were variously present throughout church history. The new framework sought to balance the supreme authority of the church hierarchy with an emphasis on respect for lay competence and reasoned dialogue among all church members (and between Catholics and non-Catholics). Vatican II thereby shifted, whether intentionally or not, the system of power relations in the church. The redrawing of interpretive authority validated an understanding of religious identity derived from a more egalitarian, communal sense of church ownership rather than from the church hierarchy's universal definitions alone.

The rhetorical style of the council documents themselves provides a template for the church's institutional shift from hierarchical decree toward an engaged deliberative communality. John O'Malley argues that Vatican II forged a new nonjuridical style that "attempted to . . . reconcile opposing viewpoints rather than vindicate one of them," adopting an approach that was "calculated not so much to judge and legislate as to prepare individuals for a new mind-set with which to approach all aspects of their religious lives" (1989: 26).

Vatican II acknowledged the church as a divinely constituted "hierarchically structured society" and stated without explication that there were "essential" differences between the laity and the church hierarchy (Abbott 1966: 39, 27). Yet the motif of communal equality and its practical interpretive implications are evident throughout Vatican II's "text." As I will elaborate, Vatican II institutionalized the doctrinal-intellectual resources for an emancipatory agenda grounded in rational-critical discussion. Vatican II affirmed the values of equality, religious freedom, and diversity; recognized the importance of social movements in achieving change; emphasized culture as a human and social product; validated the legitimacy of diverse interpretive stances; stated explicitly that disagreements were to be resolved by dialogue rather than official authority; and argued for consistency between egalitarian values and institutional practices.

EQUALITY AND PLURALISM
Vatican II acknowledged the equality of membership in the church conferred by baptism and stated that both the laity and the ordained

are interrelated participants in "the one priesthood of Christ" (Abbott 1966: 27). The council stated that "there is in Christ and in the Church no inequality on the basis of race or nationality, social condition or sex" (ibid. 58). There is, therefore "but one People of God," whose diversity and catholicity contribute to the good of the whole church (ibid. 31).

Emphasizing the important role of conscience in both church and societal matters, Vatican II upheld the authority of individual moral reasoning long recognized in Catholic theology. Since, as the council stated, conscience is a person's "most secret core and sanctuary" (ibid. 213), religious freedom must be accorded to the individual in order that he or she not be prevented from acting according to conscience. In other words, a person, whether acting as an individual or in community, cannot be coerced into behavior that is contrary to what he or she believes (ibid. 678-682). Further acknowledging the practical reality of cultural pluralism, the council affirmed the legitimacy of diversity in values and lifestyles. It exhorted people that they have an obligation to "respect and love . . . those who think or act differently than we do in social, political, and religious matters." It was the council's view, moreover, that a commitment to understanding "differences" would facilitate communication with those who are different (ibid. 227).

EMANCIPATION

Vatican II did not just provide Catholics with arguments validating equality and pluralism in the church. Equally significant for the mobilization of collective action, it also invited Catholics to engage in emancipatory politics and provided them with the rationales for such action. Using the liberal democratic language associated with political revolution, the council stated that "the Church proclaims the rights of man." While cautioning that emancipatory movements should be "penetrated by the spirit of the gospel," it praised "the dynamic movements of today by which these rights are everywhere fostered" (ibid. 241).

Suggesting that identities cannot be fragmented or compartmentalized but should constitute "one vital synthesis," the council observed that there cannot be a "false opposition between professional and social activities on the one part, and religious life on the other" (ibid. 243). In this reading, because identities cannot be compartmentalized, the movement toward enacting identity and human rights in society cannot be split from the obligation to realize human rights in the church. It is not clear whether the council participants intended this interpretation. However, in a footnote to the "rights of man" paragraph, Walter Abbott comments that "the Council now makes it unequivocally clear that the Church intends to play its true historic role as a champion of human rights and to align itself with those who fight for these rights" (ibid. 241).

The scope of the emancipatory agenda envisioned by the council was given further expression in its insistence that the laity be given "every opportunity" to "participate in the saving work of the Church," and that lay people be permitted and obliged to express informed opinions on issues pertaining to "the good of the Church" (ibid. 60, 64). This would seem to suggest that lay participation extends to saving the church from inegalitarian practices that contravene the church's own admonition that greater recognition be given to the "just freedom" and "basic equality" of all (ibid. 64–65, 227).

The interpretation that Vatican II obligated the formation of intra-church movements to reconstruct a more egalitarian church is also supported by Vatican II's understanding of culture. The council affirmed that men and women are the conscious "artisans and authors" of their culture, a development it regarded as having "paramount importance for the spiritual and moral maturity of the human race." Since people are responsible for "the progress of culture," the council noted that this may lead them to look "anxiously upon many contradictions which [they] will have to resolve" (ibid. 261).

It was evidently the council's intent that contradictions within the church should be the object of collective action. The council stated that "by their combined efforts" lay people should "remedy any institutions and conditions of the world which are customarily an inducement to sin, so that all such things may be conformed to the norms of justice" (ibid. 63). Significantly, the council acknowledged the gap between theory and practice in the church's institutional life and argued that it should be redeemed. It stated: ". . . it does not escape the Church how great a distance lies between the message she offers and the human failings of those to whom the gospel is entrusted" (ibid. 245).

DELIBERATIVE DIALOGUE

The council advised that cultural change should be guided by the extent to which it enables the development of "the whole human person harmoniously" (ibid. 261–262). Recognizing the essential importance of communication to individual and communal growth, the council observed that people must "be free to search for the truth, voice [their] mind, and publicize it" (ibid. 265). Demonstrating further openness to principles of reason, the council noted that freedom of inquiry and of expression would be assisted by developments in theology, the social and natural sciences, and other branches of knowledge (ibid. 268–269).

While Vatican II reminded the laity that they should give "close attention to the teaching authority of the Church" (ibid. 244), it also explicitly affirmed the reasoned interpretive equality of all church members. Anticipating disagreements within the church, the council rejected the authority of sacred office in favor of the authority of communicative reason. It stated:

> it is necessary for people to remember that no one is allowed . . . to appropriate the Church's authority for his opinion. They should always try to enlighten one another through honest discussion, preserving mutual charity and caring above all for the common good. . . . all the faithful, clerical and lay, possess a lawful freedom of inquiry and of thought, and the freedom to express their minds humbly and courageously about those matters in which they enjoy competence." (Ibid. 244, 269–270)

Since Vatican II also aspired for lay people to "develop and deepen" their understanding of the "sacred sciences" (ibid. 270), it is apparent that the council did not intend a narrow view of lay competence that was limited to nonreligious issues. The council clarified in fact that it would be through dialogue with the laity that pastors would "more clearly and more suitably come to decisions regarding spiritual and temporal matters" (ibid. 65). In short, the council recognized the importance of engaged critical dialogue as central both to the church's mission of global communality and to the obligation to bridge the gap between theory and practice in its own institutional life. As the council elaborated: "Such a mission requires in the first place that we foster within the Church herself mutual esteem, reverence, and harmony, through the full recognition of lawful diversity" and a common dialogue that recognizes "freedom in what is unsettled" (ibid. 305–306).

As the above discussion indicates, Vatican II can be interpreted as providing Catholics with the symbolic resources necessary to support institutional transformation aimed at establishing greater correspondence between a Catholic ethic of equality and the church's own practices. Although Vatican II reaffirmed the authority of the church hierarchy, it wedded this to a dynamic understanding of the church as a deliberative community. In this vision, "honest discussion" informed by reasoned reflection was recognized as the means for dealing with conflicting interpretations of Catholic identity. The authority of hierarchical office per se, therefore, did not confer expertise; as the council stressed, "no one is allowed to appropriate the Church's authority for his opinion" (ibid. 244). Vatican II accordingly legitimated the creation of a deliberative church, wherein participants' interpretations of Catholicism would be compelled by communal, practical reason, rather than the power of magisterial office alone.

The communally deliberative model of the church validated by Vatican II should not be seen as some sort of aberration in the church's history. It could be argued that Vatican II's reforms reflected a unique response by church leaders to the destructive and authoritarian human impulses evidenced by the successive wars of the twentieth century, or that they were crafted as a necessary counterpoint to the church hierarchy's authority consolidated at Vatican I. A longer view of church history, however, suggests that Vatican II was well in tune with the Catholic tradition. Historical accounts argue that the early church in particular was communal, with the exercise of official authority locally diffused (e.g., E. Schüssler Fiorenza 1983/1994; Grant 1970). Moreover, even as the church became increasingly bureaucratized the universal claims of the papacy were restricted in practice by political officials and local church synods (Bianchi and Ruether 1992: 8; Grant 1970: 157–159, 194; Hollister 1982: 216, 223).

The church's tradition of communal responsiveness was demonstrated by the shifts already highlighted in the evolution of Catholic doctrine on the questions of sexuality, priesthood, and abortion. This discussion indicated that rather than being divinely ordained and immutable, the substance of official church teaching on the respective issues derived in part from the church's openness to the historical and cultural context in which it formulated doctrine. In this reading, the model of communally diffused interpretive authority formalized by Vatican II strikes one as thoroughly Catholic. It is in keeping with the origins and doctrinal development of Catholicism and with the Catholic theological emphasis on the necessary coupling of faith and reason at both the individual and the institutional levels.

Notwithstanding Vatican II's emphasis on communal deliberation, post–Vatican II papal teaching on the issues of interest to this study (homosexuality, the priesthood, abortion, and the role of the theologian), shows a more restricted understanding of doctrine and its interpretation. That is the subject of the next chapter.

OFFICIAL CHURCH TEACHING ON HOMOSEXUALITY, WOMEN'S ORDINATION, ABORTION, AND THE ROLE OF THE THEOLOGIAN

Pro-change Catholics' understanding of Catholic identity is at odds with the official Catholic view on such issues as homosexuality, women's ordination, and abortion. It is important, therefore, to consider the origins and basis for the Vatican's position on these controversial issues. This chapter provides an encapsulated outline of the church hierarchy's teaching, and of the Vatican's disposition toward Catholic theologians. Theologians' institutional position as professional experts within the church is clearly very different from the status of gay, lesbian, feminist, and pro-choice Catholics. Nonetheless, theologians' calls for the church hierarchy to recognize their intellectual autonomy similarly challenge the Vatican's interpretive authority. The "proper" role of the theologian, therefore, has also become a focus of Vatican concern. This chapter's review will illustrate the firmness of Vatican opposition to homosexual relations, women's ordination, abortion, and theological pluralism, and the clarity with which it denounces interpretations of Catholicism that deviate from this.

VATICAN TEACHING ON SEX, GENDER, ABORTION, AND THEOLOGICAL EXPERTISE

HOMOSEXUALITY

The Vatican's stance on homosexuality derives from its view of natural law. The Catholic Church differentiates between natural law, the law of the Gospel, and civil and ecclesiastical law (all of which have their source in divine law). Independent of scripture and church law, the Catholic moral theological tradition emphasizes "the goodness of the human and of human reason in arriving at moral wisdom and knowledge" (Curran 1992: 45). Catholic teaching thus understands morality and ethics to be divinely prescribed and rationally ordered in ways that enable the common good. In natural law theory "reason reflecting on nature" points to what is morally correct. In other words, "the human mind reflecting on human experience" discovers which moral rules are appropriate or inappropriate (Hannon 1992: 22; see also Cahill 1996: 46–50). Natural law thus assumes that there are certain self-evident, eternal, and immutable truths which can be discerned by a reasoning adult (or which a reasoning adult can be helped to discern with moral guidance).

Natural law theory has a prominent place in Catholic moral theology. Saint Augustine argued that truth and every just law are inscribed in the human heart. More notably, Thomas Aquinas elaborated that natural law is "nothing other than the light of understanding placed in us by God . . . at the creation" (*Catechism of the Catholic Church* 1994: 426). Aquinas argued that while the application of the natural moral law varies depending on the particular circumstances of people's existence, the precepts grounding it are historically constant, immutable, and universal. In Catholic theology, natural law is the overarching basis for civil law since it emphasizes the dignity of the individual and people's social rights and obligations.

In official church teaching, homosexuality is contrary to the natural law. As stated by Thomas Aquinas, "certain special sins are said to be against nature; thus, contrary to heterosexual intercourse, which is natural to all animals, is male homosexual union, which has received the special name of the unnatural vice" (1948/1991: 107). Natural law informs the church hierarchy's understanding not just of homosexuality but of sexual morality as a whole. As clarified by Pope Paul VI in his 1968 encyclical *Humanae Vitae*, Catholic teaching on sexuality asserts that in "observance of the norms of the natural law . . . each and every marriage act must remain open to the transmission of life" (Paul VI 1968: 11). By extension, any sexual activity that deviates from divinely ordained and "wisely arranged natural laws" (ibid.) and which is not open to the transmission of life is morally wrong. This is the logic that leads the Vatican to condemn homosexual, premarital, and extramarital sexual relations, and the use of artificial contraception in any sexual relation including marriage.

The Vatican's opposition to gay and lesbian relationships is elaborated in two major statements on homosexuality issued within ten years of one another.[1] In a 1976 "Declaration on Homosexuality," the Vatican's Congregation for the Doctrine of the Faith (CDF) emphasized that "immutable principles" stemming from the "essential order of [man's] nature . . . transcend historical contingency." Reiterating traditional Catholic teaching on sexual morality, the declaration stressed that "every genital act must be within the framework of marriage" (CDF 1976: 488). Upholding the universality and objectivity of this teaching, the Vatican rejected arguments suggesting that the morality of sexual relations should be based on subjective motives or "sincere intentions," stating instead that morality "must be determined by objective standards" (ibid: 488).

The declaration distinguished between "constitutional" homosexuality derived from "some kind of innate instinct or a pathological constitution judged to be incurable," and "transitory" homosexuality based on environmental factors which it identified as "false education," the lack of "normal sexual development," habit or bad example. Since according to the Vatican, constitutional homosexuality unlike its transitory counterpart is innate, the CDF advocated that constitutional homosexuals be treated with pastoral understanding so that they may be "sustained in the hope of overcoming their personal difficulties and their inability to fit into society" (ibid. 489). The Vatican is unequivocal, nonetheless, in condemning all "homosexual acts" as "objectively disordered" regardless of their innate basis. The CDF stated: "According to the objective moral order, homosexual relations are acts which lack an essential and indispensable finality. In sacred scripture they are condemned as a serious depravity and even presented as the sad consequence of rejecting God. . . . homosexual acts are intrinsically disordered and can in no case be approved of" (ibid.).

Subsequent Vatican concerns that the immorality of homosexual acts was "a subject of debate" among Catholics caused the Vatican to issue a second position statement on homosexuality. The CDF's second statement (CDF 1986) noted that despite the condemnation of homosexual relations in its first statement (CDF 1976), in public debate an "overly benign interpretation was given to the homosexual condition

1. The documents' formal titles are Declaration on Sexual Ethics, issued by the Congregation for the Doctrine of the Faith (CDF) in December 1975, but published in America in January 1976. Thus throughout this book I refer to the Declaration as CDF 1976. The title of the second document is Letter on Homosexuality (CDF 1986).

itself, some going so far as to call it neutral or even good" (CDF 1986: 379). Although the Vatican did not identify the sources of "false" interpretation, the first declaration's (1976) publication in America occurred in the context of renewed debate on sexual morality among theologians.

Two publishing events stand out as challenges to the Vatican's stance on homosexuality. In 1976, John McNeil, a Jesuit priest and founding member of Dignity, the national association of gay and lesbian Catholics (see Chapter 4 for a more detailed discussion of the group's origins and mission), published a book in which he argued for the morality of homosexuality.[2] The second event was the publication in June 1977 of a major collective Catholic theological study on sexuality (Kosnik et al. 1977). Given its source and substance, this second book undermined official teaching more significantly than McNeil's. The study was commissioned in 1972 by the Catholic Theological Society of America (CTSA), the largest and oldest association of Catholic theologians in the U.S., as a theological response to the declining adherence of Catholics to official church teaching on sexuality (Kosnik et al. 1977: 78). The authors emphasized that the findings, while based on consultation with a broad range of CTSA members, were not to be taken as the CTSA's official position (ibid. xi–xv). Notwithstanding the authors' qualifications about the study's significance, it clearly enjoyed high credibility among American Catholic theologians.

The theology of sexuality elaborated in the CTSA study broadened the Vatican II emphasis on the procreative and unitive purposes of marital sexuality to emphasize sexuality's "creative and integrative" purposes (ibid. 86). The authors stressed that contrary to the act-cen-

2. The title of McNeil's book is *The Church and the Homosexual*. In August 1977 the CDF issued a directive against McNeil prohibiting him from publicly lecturing on or discussing the ethics of homosexuality. In explaining the reasons for its silencing of McNeil, the congregation stated: "We find it extraordinary that a book so clearly contradicting the moral teaching of the church would be published a few days after the publication of Persona humana [CDF 1976]. . . . no reasonable person could imagine that time for serious study and evaluation had been given to the declaration of the authentic magisterium of the church in this case." See *Origins* 7 (March 16, 1978): 612–615. McNeil adhered to the directive but, canceling his scheduled public address at that year's Dignity convention, noted in a letter to Dignity that the Vatican "did not demand a retraction or repudiation of my ideas or judgments in the book." See *Origins* 7 (September 22, 1977): 218–219.

tered understanding of sexuality derived from an "oversimplification of the natural law theory of St. Thomas" (ibid. 88), a person-centered approach that paid attention to the cognitive, emotional, social, and moral development of the whole person was faithful to both the biblical understanding of human nature and core values in the Christian tradition (ibid. 86). Rejecting a dual moral standard in evaluating sexuality, the authors stressed that "homosexuals enjoy the same rights [to love and intimacy] and incur the same obligations as the heterosexual majority" (ibid. 214). Arguing that "all sexual behavior draws its meaning and significance from the intention or motivation of the person or persons involved" (ibid. 89–90), the authors identified several values which they argued should be constitutive of "wholesome and moral sexual conduct." Among the values identified as morally important were whether the relationship was self-liberating, other-enriching, honest, faithful, socially responsible, life-serving, and joyous (ibid. 92–95). The authors' views of sexual morality thus clearly rejected the narrow emphasis on physical sexual acts elaborated in both *Humanae Vitae* and the CDF's position on homosexuality.

In light of what the Vatican interpreted as "grave disregard" for its teaching on sexuality, it is not surprising that its 1986 letter was more authoritarian than its earlier declaration (CDF 1976). The Vatican defended its teaching, stating that it was not based on "facile theological argument, but on the solid foundation of a constant biblical testimony" and the church's "own constant tradition" (CDF 1986: 379, 380). Whereas the 1976 letter distinguished between "constitutional" and "transitory" homosexuality, the 1986 letter focused more specifically on the nonsinful but nonetheless "objectively disordered" nature of the innate or constitutional homosexual orientation. It clarified that "[a]lthough the particular inclination of the homosexual person is not a sin, it is a more or less strong tendency ordered toward an intrinsic moral evil and thus the inclination itself must be seen as an objective disorder" (ibid. 379). Once again, the CDF stressed the sinfulness and selfishness of homosexual acts, stating: "Homosexual activity is not a complementary union able to transmit life; . . . when [homosexual persons] engage in homosexual activity they confirm within themselves a disordered sexual inclination which is essentially self-indulgent" (CDF 1986: 380).

The Vatican focused much of its discussion on criticizing what it called the "pro-homosexual movement in the church." It argued that the movement is comprised of "homosexual persons who have no intention of abandoning their homosexual behavior," and who "either ignore the teaching of the church or seek somehow to undermine it." Reasserting the church hierarchy's authority, the letter asserted that the "contradictory action" of homosexual Catholics who reject Christ's teaching while claiming a desire to conform to it "should not have the support of the bishops in any way." The CDF thus instructed bishops to sever church ties with groups representing "contradictory" Catholics, stating that "[a]ll support should be withdrawn from any organizations which seek to undermine the teaching of the church, which are ambiguous about it or which neglect it entirely" (ibid. 382).[3]

The new *Catechism of the Catholic Church* (1994: 505) affirms that "homosexual acts are intrinsically disordered" but it also condemns "unjust discrimination" against homosexuals whom it states "must be accepted with respect, compassion, and sensitivity." In the fall of 1997, the U.S. Catholic bishops (United States Catholic Conference) collectively issued a statement, "Always Our Children," as a pastoral message to parents of homosexual children. In their statement, the bishops stressed that parents should continue to demonstrate their love for a son or daughter who has a "homosexual orientation" even if they do not approve all "related attitudes and behavioral choices" (1997: 290). While reaffirming official church teaching asserting the human rights of homosexuals, the bishops also reiterated that "homogenital behavior is objectively immoral" even though the orientation is not im-

---

3. Of particular note, making an implicit reference to the AIDS epidemic and its association as a "gay disease," the Vatican argued that "[e]ven when the practice of homosexuality may seriously threaten the lives and well-being of a large number of people, its advocates remain undeterred and refuse to consider the magnitude of the risks involved." The Vatican presented the church hierarchy, by contrast, as concerned for those not represented by "the pro-homosexual movement" and those who might be influenced by its "deceitful propaganda." Although the letter condemned violent speech and action against homosexuals, it nonetheless contextualized violence against gays as part of the larger problem of moral breakdown that it attributed implicitly to the gay rights movement. The Vatican argued that "when civil legislation is introduced to protect behavior to which no one has any conceivable right, neither the church nor society at large should be surprised when other distorted notions and practices gain ground, and irrational and violent reactions increase" (CDF 1986: 380-381). In general, however, and in accord with Catholic teaching on the inherent goodness of the human person, a punitive attitude toward people with AIDS does not characterize official Catholic statements. The U.S. Bishops (1989a) have emphasized that AIDS should not be seen as a punishment from God.

moral in itself (ibid.). With the exception of the 1997 statement, the American bishops have not commented extensively, either individually or collectively, on the morality of homosexual behavior. They have instead focused their intellectual and pastoral energy on responding to AIDS and affirming the civil rights of gays and lesbians (e.g., Quinn 1992).[4]

WOMEN'S ORDINATION

Women's exclusion from ordination in the Catholic Church is presented by the Vatican as a doctrine "belonging to the deposit of faith" (CDF 1995: 405). Unlike homosexuality and abortion, it is not seen by the church hierarchy as a transreligious issue of individual morality, and unlike the ban on married priests, it is not simply a church law. The question of women's ordination became a public issue in the church in the mid 1970s, prompted by the decision of the Anglican Church in England to ordain women. Since that time, the Vatican has been unequivocally clear that women cannot be priests. It has steadfastly maintained this position notwithstanding the scriptural, historical, and theological ambiguities surrounding the question. These ambiguities were noted, for example, in 1976 by a special Vatican-appointed commission that concluded that it was not possible to settle the question on the basis of scripture alone. [5]

The Vatican's opposition to women priests does not mean that it denies the visibility and prominence of women in scripture, in the early church, or in the contemporary church. Quite the contrary, although the Vatican rejects the scriptural and historical evidence as validating women priests, all of its major statements on ordination acknowledge women's contributions to the church. It also recognizes

4. While the bishops have stated that "[c]ampaigns advocating safe/safer sex rest on false assumptions about sexuality and intercourse" (U.S. Bishops 1989a: 429), they also emphasize the importance of medical research, the need to protect the rights of those with HIV/AIDS, and the importance of compassion, social justice, and parish and community networks in order to help people suffering on account of AIDS. Also in keeping with Catholic teaching, the bishops have stated that "we must reject the idea that this illness is a direct punishment by God" (ibid. 431). For detailed studies of the Catholic Church and AIDS, see Kowalewski (1994) and R. Smith (1994).

5. See "Women's Ordination: Letters Exchanged by Pope and Anglican Leader," *Origins* 6 (August 12, 1976): 129, 131–132; and "Biblical Commission Report," *Origins* 6 (July 1, 1976): 92–96.

that the arguments posited by medieval theologians denying women's rational ability to be priests were presented in a way that "modern thought would have difficulty in admitting or would even rightly reject" (CDF 1977: 519).

The Vatican presents three main reasons for its ban on women's ordination. It argues first that to ordain women would contravene the will and intention of Christ, who did not call women to be apostles; second, that since women do not physically resemble Christ, they cannot mimic the role of Christ in the sacramental consecration of the Eucharist; and third, that an exclusively male priesthood is part of the church's constant and essential hierarchical tradition. What is interesting about the church hierarchy's opposition to women priests is that the Vatican presents church doctrine as being outside its authority. The Vatican therefore has to maintain two somewhat contradictory claims simultaneously. On the one hand, using the thesis of apostolic succession, it claims a sacred power to know divine intentions. On the other hand, it also argues that the institutional arrangements that were configured by the will and example of Christ are beyond its interpretive authority. Thus in the Vatican's own construction (e.g., John Paul 1994: 51), even if it wanted to ordain women, it would not be empowered to do so because of its obligation to maintain what it regards as the institutional blueprint demonstrated by Christ's intentions.

For the Vatican, the validity of an exclusively male priesthood is grounded in the example of Christ's having had only male apostles. The Vatican argues that the significance of Jesus's not choosing women apostles is rendered "all the more remarkable" in light of the fact that Jesus acted contrary to the cultural norms of his time and was antidiscriminatory in his attitude toward women in all other domains (CDF 1977: 520). Since, as the Vatican argues, "the church has no power over the substance of the sacraments" but is constrained by "the supreme event of the history of salvation" and thus "bound by Christ's manner of acting" (CDF 1977: 521), "the church, in fidelity to the example of the Lord does not consider herself authorized to admit women to priestly ordination" (CDF 1977: 519). Pope John Paul II reiterated this view in a major statement on women's ordination issued in 1994 ("Ordinatio Sacerdotalis"). John Paul further defends what he frames as the givenness of women's exclusion from ordination by stressing its immutable link to "Christ's free and sovereign choice" in entrusting "only to men the task of being an 'icon' of his countenance" (1995b: 142).

The iconic significance of male priests was initially outlined by the Vatican in its 1977 declaration on women's ordination. The Vatican stressed that the physical "ability to represent Christ" is essentially gender-based. Since the priest acts "in persona Christi, taking the role of Christ, to the point of being his very image, when he pronounces the words of [eucharistic] consecration [Do this in memory of me] . . . The priest is a sign . . . that must be perceptible and which the faithful must be able to recognize with ease . . . " (CDF 1977: 522). Accordingly, women cannot be priests taking the role of Christ because "there would not be this 'natural resemblance' which must exist between Christ and his minister if the role of Christ were not taken by a man" (ibid.). The U.S. bishops have similarly affirmed the sacramental-sign rationale that women cannot be priests on account of their physical-symbolic inability to represent Christ (1992: 502). In official church teaching, therefore, naturally visible gender differences – but not differences associated with ethnicity, social class, or personality, for example – are the distinguishing markers of who can and who cannot represent Christ.

Although the Vatican stresses what it regards as divinely prescribed essential differences between women and men, it is unequivocal in asserting women's equality with men. The Vatican's 1977 declaration underscored that a male priesthood is not related to men's "personal superiority." Elaborating traditional Catholic social teaching on the complementarity of gender relations, the declaration distinguished between "equality" and "identity" and argued that the differentiation of roles does "not favor the superiority of some vis-à-vis the others." Implicitly arguing against feminist demands for equality of role opportunity, the declaration emphasized that "the priestly office cannot become the goal of social advancement." According to the Vatican, since the priesthood has its origins in divine revelation, the priesthood is "of another order" and thus cannot be considered a "human right" (CDF 1977: 523).

The argument that an exclusively male priesthood is essential to the church was underscored by John Paul II. In his 1994 statement on women's ordination, John Paul defended the church's male priesthood and hierarchical structure, claiming that "it is to the holiness of the faithful that the hierarchical structure of the church is totally ordered." In addition to reiterating previously stated reasons for women's exclusion from ordination, John Paul concluded his letter authoritatively stressing that ordination was to be considered a settled question not open to further debate. He stated:

> Although the teaching that priestly ordination is to be reserved to men alone has been preserved by the constant and universal tradition of the church and firmly taught by the magisterium in its more recent documents, at the present time in some places it is nonetheless considered still open to debate . . .Wherefore, in order that all doubt may be removed regarding a matter of great importance, a matter which pertains to the church's divine constitution itself . . . I declare that the church has no authority whatsoever to confer priestly ordination on women and that this judgment is to be definitively held by all the church's faithful. (1994: 51)

The majority of individual American bishops responded to John Paul's statement by taking a generally positive view (see, for example, *Origins*, June 4, 1994: 53–58). Archbishop Rembert Weakland of Milwaukee, however, commented on the pastoral difficulties he expected to encounter in trying to defend John Paul's closure of debate on the issue (ibid. 55–56); and another bishop, Michael Kenny of Juneau, Alaska, pointedly observed that John Paul's statement "was much more about authority than it is about ordination" (Kenny 1994: 16). Speaking as a collectivity, the U.S. bishops acknowledged a diversity of opinions on women's ordination and the pain caused to women because of "persistent sexism" (U.S. Bishops 1994: 421). They nonetheless affirmed that John Paul's position was "to be definitively held by all the faithful" (ibid. 417). Somewhat curiously in light of John Paul's insistence on the closure of debate, the bishops emphasized that in both church and society "dialogue is indispensable for bringing about genuine peace." They offered their pastoral reflection – recognizing sexism but accepting women's exclusion from ordination – "as one moment in a developing dialogue, with the hope that all women and men of the church will receive it as such and continue as participants in what can be a sacred conversation for all of us" (ibid. 419).[6] The possibility that a "sacred conversation" might be feasible was

---

6. As is their pattern regarding all questions of gender equality and discrimination, the bishops also affirmed "the fundamental equality of women and men" (U.S.

quickly dampened by the Vatican. In the fall of 1995, coinciding with the Women's Ordination Conference's celebration of the twentieth anniversary of its founding, the Vatican's Congregation for the Doctrine of the Faith affirmed that John Paul's earlier declaration on ordination was infallible and immutable. The CDF asserted that the validity of women's nonordination "is a matter of full definitive assent, that is to say, irrevocable, to a doctrine taught infallibly by the church . . . It is to be held always, everywhere, and by all, as belonging to the deposit of faith" (CDF 1995: 405).

ABORTION

Since the prevalence of abortion in contemporary society is seen by the church hierarchy as the preeminent human rights issue of our time (U.S. bishops 1989b), it is not surprising that Pope John Paul has made abortion a major focus of his papacy and has used his authority to define the absolute immorality of abortion. John Paul's most extensive discussion of abortion is in two major encyclicals which he issued within two years of one another, "Veritatis Splendor" (1993) and *Evangelium Vitae, The Gospel of Life* (1995a). Both of these encyclicals discuss abortion in the context of the Vatican's more broadly encompassing concern with moral relativism, and especially with what John Paul diagnoses as today's "culture of death." In John Paul's evaluation, contemporary culture is an emergent "veritable culture of death" characterized by abortion, contraception, sterilization, reproductive technologies, euthanasia, and capital punishment. These practices and the institutions promoting them constitute a "war of the powerful against the weak," a "conspiracy against life" (1995a: 22, 30).[7] At a time when the public proclamation of human rights is politically acceptable, John Paul comments on the significant and "surprising contradiction" that

Bishops 1994: 420). The bishops' condemnation of sexism in society (ibid. 421) was first stated in the first draft of a proposed pastoral letter on women (U.S. Bishops 1988), that after successive drafts subsequently failed to receive the necessary two-thirds support from the American bishops, thus precluding it from having the "teaching authority" of a pastoral letter.

7. "Signs of hope" are observed by John Paul, that a "culture of life" is emerging to counteract the culture of death, evidenced by growing opposition to war and to capital punishment, and a new sensitivity to ecological and quality of life issues (1995a: 49–50). For John Paul, the conflict between life and death compels each person to accept their share of responsibility and to redress the values conflict by "choosing to be unconditionally pro-life" (ibid. 50).

the right to life at birth and at death is being denied or endangered (ibid. 31).

In particular, John Paul uses "Veritatis Splendor" to reaffirm "fundamental truths of Catholic doctrine" that "risk being distorted or denied" in today's culture of "overall and systematic" dissent (1993: 299). According to John Paul, these circumstances have arisen, in part, on account of a disregard for the church hierarchy's teaching authority in favor of the moral autonomy of the individual (ibid. 300). The roots of the problem also lie in secularism and cultural pluralism, and especially stem from the fact that even among church members there has been a break between faith and morality (ibid. 300, 323–324).[8] While John Paul welcomes modern culture's "heightened sense" of the dignity, uniqueness, and conscience of the human person (ibid. 308), he argues that this has led to an individualistic ethic and an exalted and unconstrained understanding of personal freedom. Consequently, the authority of individual conscience informed by self-interest is pitted against the authority of the church hierarchy to interpret what is objectively correct.

In John Paul's view: "the individual conscience is accorded the status of a supreme tribunal of moral judgment which hands down categorical and infallible decisions about good and evil. . . . the inescapable claims of truth disappear, yielding their place to a criterion of sincerity, authenticity and 'being at peace with oneself' " (ibid. 308). In other words, there is a disregard for human reason's dependence on "divine wisdom," and by extension the "specific doctrinal competence on the part of the church and her magisterium is denied" (ibid. 309).

In a bow to historical consciousness, John Paul acknowledges that the "truth of the moral law," like the "deposit of faith" develops over time. He is firm, however, that it is the task of the magisterium to specify and determine the enduring substantive validity of "the norms expressing that truth" (ibid. 314). Moreover, he contends that while individuals' reasoning and theological reflection contribute to this interpretive task, a " 'creative' understanding of moral conscience" that diverges from the magisterium cannot be allowed (ibid. 314).

It is the culture's "self-indulgent" rejection of the precepts of natural law, and an attendant moral relativism, that John Paul regards as

---

8. John Paul's most recent encyclical, "Fides et Ratio" (Faith and Reason), issued in October 1998, further elaborates on the breakdown between reason and morality, and in particular focuses on how post-Enlightenment rationalism is unable to integrate issues of faith and redemption.

central to what he judges to be a contradictory culture of death (ibid. 300). By contrast to secular trends, John Paul argues that "the moral truths derived from natural law . . . are universally valid. They oblige each and every individual, always and in every circumstance" (ibid. 313). Thus John Paul rejects various theological "positions" including personalism, moral proportionality, and critiques of physicalism/biologism that seek to attenuate the objective immorality of intrinsically evil acts (ibid. 303, 309, 312). In the concrete application of natural law, John Paul argues that although circumstances and intentions influence the morality of an act, there are independently, because of their consequences, "intrinsically evil acts." Offering examples of such acts, he lists those delineated by Vatican II, including homicide, genocide, abortion, euthanasia, subhuman living conditions, and degrading conditions of work. In addition, much like his predecessors since the 1930s, John Paul categorizes "contraceptive practices" as intrinsically evil (ibid. 321).[9]

John Paul engages views maintaining that abortion (or homosexuality or artificial contraception) may be valid moral judgments depending on the circumstances involved. He observes that the church hierarchy's uncompromising stance prohibiting intrinsically evil acts is often regarded as evidence of intransigence and lack of compassion. John Paul counters this claim by arguing that "genuine compassion" derives from a concern with the person's "authentic freedom," and not from a "concealing or weakening [of] moral truth" (ibid. 325); true freedom, from this perspective, is found not in self-indulgence, but in the "gift of self" (ibid. 323).

John Paul recognizes that "intentions may be good, and circumstances frequently difficult" (ibid. 326), but he insists that ethical guarantees can make no exceptions. Thus in a 1985 "Letter to Women," John Paul discussed the "atrocities" of rape but noted that even in these circumstances "the choice to have an abortion always remains a grave sin" (1995b: 140). Importantly, however, John Paul partially exonerated rape victims' recourse to abortion. Pointing to sociocultural conditions (e.g., gender inequality, "hedonistic permissiveness") which encourage "aggressive male behavior," he stated that "before

9. John Paul emphasizes the responsibility of an individual to disobey "intrinsically unjust" laws that permit abortion or euthanasia. Since it is "never licit to cooperate formally in evil" (1995a: 136), it is also illicit to participate in campaigns favoring, or to vote for, such laws (ibid. 134), regardless of the reasons that might be invoked in defense of one's cooperation (ibid. 136).

being something to blame on the woman, [abortion] is a crime for which guilt needs to be attributed to men and to the complicity of the general social environment" (ibid. 140). Nevertheless, despite his sensitivity to women's situation, John Paul is uncompromising in his condemnation of abortion. The Vatican thus resists the "modern totalitarianism" (John Paul II 1993: 326) ethical relativism represents by upholding clear-cut and what it understands as universally applicable moral truths.

Accordingly, John Paul has invoked his power to confirm that abortion and other forms of "direct killing" including euthanasia and capital punishment are grave moral evils. In *Evangelium Vitae* he declared: "by the authority which Christ conferred upon Peter and his Successors, and in communion with the Bishops of the Catholic Church . . . I confirm that the direct and voluntary killing of an innocent human being is always gravely immoral. . . . I declare that direct abortion, that is, abortion willed as an end or a means, always constitutes a grave moral disorder. . . . I confirm that euthanasia is a grave violation of the law of God" (1995a: 101, 112, 119). Unlike the church hierarchy's focus on abortion, however, capital punishment receives comparatively less attention in Vatican statements and in the public policy engagement of Catholic bishops in different national contexts.[10] This is so even though official church teaching regards opposition to both abortion and the death penalty as being necessitated by adherence to a consistent ethic of life (e.g., John Paul 1995a: 155–156).

The greater willingness of church officials to vigorously engage in national policy debates on abortion (see Dillon 1995; 1996a) while being more equivocal on the death penalty reflects a somewhat artifi-

10. In 1980, in America, the National Conference of Catholic Bishops issued a statement on capital punishment in which they argued against the use of the death penalty. Since the publication of Pope John Paul II's *Gospel of Life*, many American bishops have individually and collectively reiterated church opposition to the use of the death penalty. For example, the New Mexico bishops (*Origins* 26 [February 27, 1997]: 585, 587–588) and the Colorado bishops have issued public statements opposing capital punishment. Individual bishops of Denver, Oklahoma City, and St. Louis, and a representative of the United States Catholic Conference, have issued statements affirming their opposition to the death penalty following the death penalty jury verdict in the case of Timothy McVeigh, who was found guilty of the Oklahoma City Federal Building bombing. See *Origins* 27 (June 26, 1997): 81, 83–86. The U.S. bishops' Statement on Political Responsibility for the 1996 presidential election

cial division in official church teaching between sexual as opposed to sociopolitical morality, and the church's prioritization of its authority over the former (cf. Burns 1992: 50). Although both abortion and the death penalty are politically controversial questions (in the United States and elsewhere), the greater immediacy of abortion to the domain of individual/sexual morality means that the church hierarchy believes that it has a greater responsibility and competence to intervene in such debates, while remaining tacitly more willing to yield to the demands of the political environment (e.g., public opinion) on capital punishment.

THE ROLE OF THE THEOLOGIAN

The supremacy of the church hierarchy's authority is the primary substantive theme in Vatican pronouncements on the role of the professional theologian. The Revised Code of Canon Law promulgated by John Paul in 1983 contains a new canon (Canon 812) requiring that theological faculty "should have a mandate from the competent ecclesiastical authority" (Euart 1993: 465). Canon 812, which clearly defines the subsidiary relation of the theologian to the magisterium, was also incorporated into a major Vatican document on Catholic universities. This statement declared that "Catholic theologians, aware that they fulfill a mandate received from the Church, are to be faithful to the Magisterium of the Church as the authentic interpreter of Sacred Scripture and Sacred Tradition" (Langan 1993: 246).[11] The supreme interpretive authority of the magisterium and theologians'

also stressed the church's opposition to capital punishment (*Origins* 25 [November 16, 1995]: 377). Nonetheless, highlighting the ambiguous moral status given by church officials to the death penalty as opposed to abortion, Cardinal O'Connor of New York, a vocal opponent of abortion and a strong critic of politicians who favor legal abortion, has stated that while he opposes the death penalty, "a good Catholic can responsibly be for or against use of the death penalty under certain restricted conditions." Reported in *Origins* 25 (April 4, 1996).

11. The relevant document is the Vatican's Apostolic Constitution on Catholic Universities, Ex Corde Ecclesiae, issued in August 1990 (see Euart 1993). Although the Vatican's document raised concerns among theologians that bishops would become more directly involved in monitoring the theological course curricula in Catholic colleges and universities, the National Conference of Catholic Bishops, following a deliberative process of investigation of the issues involved, voted at its November 1996 meeting to allow Catholic educational institutions to follow their own procedures in the hiring and retention of

subservience to the "church," interpreted as the church hierarchy, is also reaffirmed in the Vatican's Instruction on the Ecclesial Vocation of the Theologian (CDF 1990). The instruction acknowledges that the theologian's task obliges engagement in the surrounding culture in order that, as Vatican II discussed, the theologian will be enabled to "better illumine" different aspects of faith (ibid. 120). The instruction argues that while theological-cultural openness is "an arduous task" that has "risks," the nature of which are unspecified by the Vatican, it is "legitimate in itself and should be encouraged" (ibid.) The instruction is clear, nonetheless, that theology's pursuit is driven not by culture, but by scripture and scripture's faithful interpretation through the church's living tradition "under the guidance of the magisterium" (ibid. 122).

Theologians are reminded that like the church hierarchy, they have an obligation to respect the general faithful of the church. The Vatican exhorts theologians not to think of themselves as superior to their coreligionists, but it also assumes that the laity, as nonprofessional theologians, may easily be led into doctrinal error. As the Vatican stated: "Never forgetting that he is also a member of the people of God, the theologian must foster respect for them and be committed to offering them a teaching which in no way does harm to the doctrine of the faith" (ibid. 120).

Most noteworthy is the instruction's condescension toward the critical and the innovative theologian.[12] Echoing Pope Pius XII's stress on the danger of ideas that are motivated by theologians who, "desirous of novelty," distance themselves from the church's "sacred Teaching Authority" (1950: 176), the instruction urges theologians to monitor

professionally qualified faculty (see U.S. Bishops 1996b). Subsequently, the Vatican Congregation for Catholic Education requested that the bishops draw up a second draft of their ordinances in order to clarify some ambiguities. For instance, where the U.S. bishops stated ". . . That the [Catholic] institution . . . makes serious effort to appoint individuals who are committed to the Catholic faith tradition or, if not Catholic, who are aware and respectful of that faith tradition," the congregation suggested the wording "shall ensure the appointment of." See "Vatican Observations on U.S. Bishops' Ex Corde Ecclesiae," *Origins* 27 (June 12, 1997): 53–55.

12. In "Veritatis Splendor," which is also very critical of the "lack of harmony" between several theological positions and magisterial teaching (1993: 300, 309, 312, 314, 328-330), John Paul quotes directly from several passages in the *Instruction on the Ecclesial Vocation of the Theologian* (CDF 1990) concerning dissent, and theologians' relationship to the magisterium.

their intellectual motivations. It thus asserts that: "The obligation to be critical . . . should not be identified with the critical spirit which is born of feeling or prejudice. The theologian must discern in himself the origin of and motivation for his critical attitude. . . . while the theologian might often feel the urge to be 'daring' in his work, this will not bear fruit . . . unless it is accompanied by the patience which permits maturation to grow" (CDF 1990: 120).

In the Vatican's view, the maturation of new ideas is a process in which it should be actively engaged. This process, however, entails the Vatican less as a partner in conversation with theologians, and more as an authoritative voice. Although the instruction states that new ideas may necessitate "many corrections" within the "context of fraternal dialogue" before they are acceptable to the "whole church" (CDF 1990: 120), it clarifies the definitive role of the magisterium in the dialogue. With echoes, once again, of Pius XII's stress on magisterial authority, the instruction states: "in order to serve the people of God as well as possible, in particular by warning them of dangerous opinions which could lead to error, the magisterium can intervene in questions under discussion which involve . . . certain contingent and conjectural elements" (ibid. 122).

The instruction acknowledges the remote possibility of magisterial "deficiency," stating that "it could happen that some magisterial documents might not be free from all deficiencies." The Vatican insists nonetheless on the overall superiority of its judgment. Thus the instruction states: "It would be contrary to the truth if, preceding from some particular cases, one were to conclude that the church's magisterium can be habitually mistaken in its prudential judgments or that it does not enjoy divine assistance in the integral exercise of its mission" (ibid. 123).

The instruction also provides detailed guidelines as to how theological dissent should be appropriately handled. It sees the magisterium as the sole channel through which dissent should be mediated. The Vatican requires that the individual theologian make a "loyal effort" to revise opinions which are contrary to the magisterium. If the theologian continues to hold the contrary opinion, he or she is then obliged to communicate the personal difficulty to the "magisterial authorities." The instruction, underscoring the Vatican's abhorrence of Catholic public debate and the challenge it poses to its authority, warns theologians against making their dissent public. It states that theologians "should avoid turning to the 'mass media'. . . for it is not by seeking to exert the pressure of public opinion that one contributes to the clarification of doctrinal issues and renders service to the truth. . . . Indeed, when dissent succeeds in extending its influence to the point of shaping a common opinion, it tends to become a rule of conduct. This cannot but seriously trouble the people of God and lead to contempt for true authority" (CDF 1990: 123–125).

The instruction highlights, moreover, the fundamental difference between the Vatican's view of the church and a more democratic model wherein cooperative dialogue might occur. It argues that "standards of conduct appropriate to civil society or the workings of a democracy, cannot be purely and simply applied to the church" (ibid. 125). The legitimacy of the Vatican's nondemocratic attitude toward dissent is reiterated by John Paul in "Veritatis Splendor." He states categorically:

> While exchanges and conflicts of opinion may constitute normal expressions of public life in a representative democracy, moral teaching cannot depend simply upon respect for a process . . . Dissent, in the form of carefully orchestrated protests and polemics carried on in the media, is opposed to ecclesial communion and to a correct understanding of the hierarchical constitution of the people of God. . . . the right of the faithful to receive Catholic doctrine in its purity and integrity must always be respected. (1993: 330)

John Paul acknowledges the valuable assistance of theologians in the work of the church (ibid. 329). He points out, nonetheless, that "theological opinions constitute neither the rule nor the norm of our teaching" (ibid. 331). In *Evangelium Vitae*, John Paul further highlights the ultimate dispensability of theologians and also notes the threat that they can pose to the reproduction of Catholic doctrine. He thus reminds his fellow bishops of their privileged teaching authority, and exhorts them to be vigilant in ensuring that "sound doctrine" is taught by theologians and others in the educational institutions within their jurisdiction (1995a: 147).

In sum, statements issued by the Vatican during John Paul's papacy on the role of the theologian, much like its positions on homosexuality, women's ordination, and abortion, reclaim the superiority of papal interpretation. Eschewing the idea of a dialogical church, John Paul rejects the validity of doctrinal pluralism. In the Vatican's view, theological opinions that are contrary to those which it endorses betray the truth in a grievously irresponsible manner (John Paul 1995a: 147). The Vatican thus requires that its doctrinal interpretations be accepted by theologians and other Catholics on account of the sacred and structurally essential authority underpinning them.

TENSION BETWEEN MAGISTERIAL AUTHORITY AND OPENNESS TO REASON

The above overview of official church teachings on homosexuality, women's ordination, abortion, and the role of the theologian shows that Vatican arguments clearly vary depending on the question being addressed. Independent of the specific issue, however, two overarching themes dominate the Vatican's teachings. One is the assertion of magisterial authority, and the second is the use of that authority to demarcate an authentic Catholicism. Both point to tensions associated with the church hierarchy's appropriation of the natural law in the legitimation of doctrine.

MAGISTERIAL AUTHORITY

I will first consider the issue of natural law and the church hierarchy's authority. As noted at the beginning of this chapter, natural law theory presupposes that reason reflecting on nature will ascertain the correct rules of conduct in a given situation. If we take this idea seriously, the embrace of natural law should lead to a deemphasis on the church hierarchy's interpretive authority. If it is self-evident to reflective human beings what behavior is morally appropriate, then it should not be necessary for some other authority to delineate universally valid behavior. While people may need guidance to help them reflect upon the morality of a particular course of action, the Vatican's construal of this task focuses more on the authority of those making the moral proclamation than on the substance and implications of the course of action at issue. Consequently, as used by the Vatican, it may sometimes seem that is not natural law but law by fiat that drives its moral pronouncements.

On homosexuality, women's ordination, abortion, and the role of the theologian, John Paul has made the church's magisterial authority an explicit concern. As highlighted in the discussion of the Vatican's arguments, John Paul frames Catholic dissent as evidence of disregard for the interpretive authority of his office, and he uses his statements, in part, to reassert papal authority. There is nothing veiled about this. On the contrary, as documented here, the Pope emphasizes the prevalence of moral dissent and theological pluralism in motivating the substantive addresses of his papacy. John Paul continues, moreover, to formally consolidate the supremacy of the Vatican's interpretive authority. Most recently, John Paul's apostolic letter "Ad Tudendum Fidem" (1998) adds "new norms" to the Code of Canon Law in order to "impose expressly the duty to preserve the truths proposed definitively by the magisterium of the church and to institute canonical sanctions concerning the same matter" (John Paul 1998: 114). In essence, the new strictures mean that anyone who rejects official church teaching on homosexuality, women's ordination, or abortion, among other issues, "would be in the position of rejecting a truth of Catholic doctrine and would therefore no longer be in full communion with the Catholic Church" (Ratzinger 1998: 118).

Contrary to Vatican II's affirmation of intrachurch dialogue and the relevance of informed lay opinions to the common good (Abbott 1966: 244), John Paul does not recognize the validity of any views that differ from official church teaching. He insists on the noncontestibility of doctrinal claims that a majority of the laity (cf. D'Antonio et al. 1996; Greeley and Hout 1996) and many theologians (e.g., CTSA 1997) regard as unsettled or in need of revision. Common to John Paul's statements is the contention that any understanding of Catholicism that is at odds with the Vatican is erroneous. In short, the Vatican presents itself as the supreme interpreter of the natural law and also of the law of the Gospel and of Catholic tradition. In this view, there is little scope for the autonomy of individual reason to reflect on nature or on the church's doctrinal tradition. The Vatican's accent on official authority thus contravenes the emphasis in Catholic theology on the coupling of faith and reason and the reasonableness of the assent of faith (cf. McCool 1977; F. Sullivan 1983). At the present time, the reclaiming of papal interpretive authority appears to override the Vatican's openness to practical, communal reason. One manifestation of this is the Vatican's tendency to defend its teaching by reiterating previous papal statements on the contested question and to ignore counterarguments. For example, in his 1994 statement on ordination, John Paul defended the rationale that Christ did not intend women to be priests by quoting what both Paul VI and he himself had said on the subject in earlier statements.[13] Despite the theological and cultural arguments favoring women's ordination that have emerged since it was first broached in the 1970s, John Paul did not engage those ideas or offer new theological or cultural reasons that would bolster the Vatican's unchanged position.

This institutional strategy of legitimation-by-reiteration, coupled with an emphasis on the supremacy of papal authority, overshadows, and from the Vatican's perspective renders virtually irrelevant, the substantive validity of any counterarguments that might be presented. Accordingly, official church teaching may be thought of as an instance of "form masquerading as content" (Spence 1988: 82) as the church hierarchy seeks to maintain the primacy of its power. The accent on magisterial authority as a source rather than a mediator of divine revelation that developed after the Council of Trent (1545–1563) (cf. Congar 1967: 179, 181) thus finds renewed expression today in the Vatican's delineation of Catholic identity.

THE VATICAN'S "DISCOURSE OF DIFFERENCE"

A second theme in official church statements concerns the Vatican's presentation of what might be called its "discourse of difference." The Vatican draws clear lines demarcating who and what is legitimate in what it presents as the correct understanding of Catholic doctrine. Thus official church teaching on gays and lesbians emphasizes essential differences in sexual orientation between homosexuals and heterosexuals; women's exclusion from ordination is justified by the natural difference between women and men; views on abortion distinguish moral relativists from universalists; and theologians' intellectual creativity is counterposed against the sacred authority of bishops.

What is striking about the Vatican's discourse of difference is the end to which it is employed. Whereas the invocation of difference is commonly invoked today to celebrate specific identities, the church hierarchy emphasizes differences in ways that, intended or not, delegitimate the carriers of difference. Vatican statements thus provide an example of how, as Craig Calhoun observes, "the rhetoric of difference

13. This Vatican strategy provides an illustration of how once something is institutionalized, it "exists as a fact, as part of objective reality, and can be transmitted on that basis" (Zucker 1991: 83).

can be turned to the repression of differences" (1995: xiv). Let me illustrate this with the Vatican's teaching on women. As already indicated, in arguing against women priests, John Paul (1994; 1995b), like Paul VI (1976) before him, emphasizes the different but equal genius (or character) of women and men. Yet this drawing of gender distinctions is used by the Vatican to ban women from participating as priests in the church. Acknowledging that women "have often been relegated to the margins of society," John Paul (1995b) argues against inequality while elaborating what the church hierarchy regards as the naturally ordered basis of gender roles. According to John Paul, "the presence of a certain diversity of roles is in no way prejudicial to women, provided that this diversity is not the result of an arbitrary imposition, but is rather an expression of what is specific to being male and female" (1995b: 142).

Notwithstanding the church hierarchy's emphasis on the equality of complementary gender roles, the categorical exclusion of women from certain roles by virtue of their different genius as in the case of ordination, is seen from a social constructivist perspective as both arbitrary and prejudicial. As the sociologist Cynthia Fuchs Epstein has demonstrated, distinctions tend to be invidious in their practical consequences. As she elaborates: "Dichotomous distinctions rarely avoid creating ranked comparisons, and in the case of female-male, whatever characteristics are ascribed to each gender, those associated with men rank higher" (1988: 233). Independent therefore of whether or not the demarcation of differences is intended to be discriminatory, it invariably is.

While the church hierarchy sees natural gender differences as benign even as it uses those differences to exclude women from being priests, it pathologizes natural differences in sexual orientation. In the case of homosexuality, the Vatican explicitly upholds a two-tiered distinction. One, it defines homosexuality as unnatural and thus as "objectively disordered" relative to heterosexuality. Second, among the "objectively disordered," the Vatican differentiates "transitory" from "constitutional" homosexuals, although it also holds the latter "morally culpable" if they "act" on their unnatural natural differences.

The Vatican's contrasting interpretations of natural gender and natural sexual differences suggest that what is natural and unnatural, benign and pathological may have more to do with who construes human nature than with a divine and objectively ordered plan. Overall, by using dichotomous categories to highlight and invalidate

differences, whether they pertain to sexuality, gender, abortion or theology, the church hierarchy seeks to reproduce the apparent normalcy
of the divisions upheld in official church teaching. Once again, as
Cynthia Fuchs Epstein argues, "Dichotomous categories are especially
effective as an ideological mechanism to preserve advantage.
Dichotomous systems of thought serve the existing power structures
and organization of society by reinforcing the notion of the 'we' and
the 'not-we,' the deserving and the undeserving" (1988: 233).

Therefore, although John Paul II advocates the promotion of a "new
feminism" which transforms culture by rejecting "male" models of
domination (1995a: 176), in practice his vision excludes the possibility of a transformed church wherein gender and other distinctions are
not used against those who are "different." By emphasizing differences
in order to repress the intrachurch participation of the carriers of difference, the Vatican reproduces the "male" model of domination that
it so unequivocally condemns. In the Vatican's schema of differences,
to be heterosexual rather than homosexual, male rather than female, a
moral universalist rather than a moral proportionalist, a bishop rather
than a theologian, is to be closer to the truth of divine revelation and
to being an authentic Catholic. In this interpretation it is not surprising, perhaps, that consonant with the church hierarchy's accent on its
own authority, the dice are loaded in favor of the church hierarchy
itself. As I shall demonstrate in subsequent chapters, however, the
Vatican's delegitimation of difference does not mean that it has the
"last word" on what constitutes Catholic identity. Despite the weight
of the church hierarchy's authority, the Vatican's positions on homosexuality, women's ordination, and abortion, for example, have not
inhibited pro-change Catholics in this study from reclaiming what
they see as the authenticity of their Catholicism.

Pro-Change Groups in the Contemporary Church: Dignity, the Women's Ordination Conference, and Catholics for a Free Choice

Support for lay autonomy in the church has historically been a prominent feature of American Catholicism. In continuity with the pluralistic tradition set in place by colonial Catholicism and expanded during the republican period (1780–1820), nineteenth-century American Catholicism emphasized a democratic approach to church governance, stressed the values of religious freedom and intelligibility, and argued for a vernacular liturgy (Dolan 1985: 111; see also Ahlstrom 1972: 330–335, 540–547). Thus in the mid-nineteenth century several immigrant communities fought over whether to establish a European monarchical or an American democratic model of the church. These rifts continued into the twentieth century and during the pre–World War II period contributed to the split of hundreds of thousands of East European immigrants from what they regarded as an overly controlling hierarchical church (Dolan 1985: 184–189). Systematic attempts by the Vatican to restrain democratic tendencies and to uphold the primacy of the church hierarchy's authority were especially evident with Vatican I (1869–1870) and the Vatican's subsequent condemnation of Americanism (Leo XIII, 1899) and Modernism (Pius X, 1907). Nonetheless, the tension between the church hierarchy's authority and personal autonomy was a continuing, if at times subdued, feature of American Catholicism from the late nineteenth century until Vatican II, when it became more public and pronounced (Seidler and Meyer 1989; Vaillancourt 1980).

OVERVIEW OF POST–VATICAN II CATHOLIC ATTITUDES

The post–Vatican II period witnessed a broad-based and qualitative shift in American Catholics' disposition toward the church hierarchy's authority over faith and (sexual) morals. Three major interrelated developments stand out. One is the impact of the publication of *Humanae Vitae* (Paul VI 1968); a second feature is the increasing autonomy of Catholics' moral and doctrinal values from official church teaching; and the third is the emergence of pro-change groups in the church. This chapter focuses on the movement for change in official church teaching and practices. I examine the origins, purposes, and activities of the three groups of interest to this study – Dignity, the Women's Ordination Conference, and Catholics for a Free Choice. Before doing this, however, it is useful to consider the logic that drives their respective pro-change projects more broadly within the context of developments in post–Vatican II American Catholicism.

HUMANAE VITAE

In 1968, Pope Paul VI reaffirmed the Vatican's moral condemnation of artificial birth control. *Humanae Vitae* reasserted a universal sexual morality requiring that all sexual acts be within the context of monogamous marriage and should be open to life. In rejecting the moral legitimacy of contraception, Paul VI's decision negated several elements of the pluralist theology articulated at Vatican II. Most obviously, it reclaimed the supremacy of the church hierarchy's authority over personal conscience, the exercise of religious freedom, and lay interpretive autonomy. Second, its accent on sexual "acts" as opposed to Vatican II's terminology, "conjugal love" (Abbott 1966: 250–255), reclaimed an understanding of personal relationships defined by biology and physicality rather than by the couple's overall psychosocial development.

Humanae Vitae's pronouncement against birth control not only contravened the interpretive equality affirmed at Vatican II, but was itself a vehicle for reasserting the authority of church officials. In defending his stance, Paul VI stressed the "competence" of the magisterial authority as the "guardian" and "authentic interpreter" of the moral law. He also appealed to the continuity inherent in the "coherent teaching" of the church on the nature of marriage, articulated by the Council of Trent (1545–1563) and by his immediate papal prede-cessors (1968: 6–7).

Notwithstanding the Vatican's opposition to artificial contracep-tion, national survey data indicated that the majority of American Catholics did not regard contraception as sinful (Greeley 1977). Contraception was already commonly used by a substantial proportion of Catholics, and its use increased notwithstanding the Vatican's ban (ibid. 142–143). Indicative of Catholics' liberal stance on contracep-tion in the early 1970s, for example, a substantial 79 percent of American Catholics surveyed by the National Opinion Research Center (NORC) approved of providing birth control information to teenagers (Greeley 1989a: 91). Catholics' acceptance of contraception was supported by many priests who publicly affirmed recognition of a Catholic's conscientious decision to use contraception (Seidler and Meyer 1989: 94). Although there were other conflicts in the church, revolving primarily around Vatican II reforms, it was Catholics' con-tested response to *Humanae Vitae* that highlighted the "spiral of con-flict" publicly penetrating all levels in the church. Theologians, priests, and lay people variously challenged the Pope's and bishops' authority to demand adherence to a sexual morality that they in conscience believed to be impractical and unreasonable (ibid. 74–108). Although bishops in some European countries departed from the Vatican's stance, most American bishops upheld papal teaching and demon-strated their compliance with Rome by in some cases stripping dis-senting priests of permission to hear confessions (ibid. 94–104).

The impact of *Humanae Vitae* cannot be disconnected from its his-torical concurrence with the dialogical, pluralistic, and cultural emphases of Vatican II. It is likely, nonetheless, that independent of Vatican II, adherence to *Humanae Vitae* would have been personally difficult for many American Catholics given the historical context in which they received it. On the one hand, like other Americans in the late 1960s and 1970s, Catholics were exposed to the cultural and sex-ual turbulence of the sixties and the social and institutional changes that were set in motion. In particular, public debate about individual rights, equality, and personal privacy (ignited by the 1973 Supreme Court *Roe v. Wade* decision on the legal right to abortion) amplified new ideas which even the most conscientious of Catholics could draw on to derive a practical morality appropriate to their personal circum-stances. Equally important, the late 1960s and 1970s saw significant changes in the lifestyles of American Catholics. As extensively documented by Andrew Greeley's analyses of national statistical data (1977; 1985; 1989a), Catholics experienced substantial upward socioeconomic mobility indicated by increases in college graduation rates, greater participation in high-status professional and managerial occupations, and higher incomes. As Greeley (1989a: 79) emphasizes, "the proportion of young Catholics going to college has passed and exceeded the proportion of young white Protestants going to college."

It is probable therefore that the cultural milieu of American society coupled with the personal autonomy associated with professional socioeconomic status, would have made it difficult for many Catholics to obey the ban on artificial contraception even without the theology of conscience elaborated by Vatican II. Whether or not many Catholics were aware of Vatican II's affirmation of lay competence, the immediacy of the changes in Catholic sacramental life (such as in the Mass liturgy, and the fact that eating meat on Fridays was no longer forbidden) may have well suggested to some Catholics that the visible changes in a church that they had previously taken to be immutable might also extend to include a greater flexibility on sexual morality.

CATHOLICS' AUTONOMOUS DISCERNMENT OF DOCTRINE

Whatever the independent contributions of Vatican II, *Humanae Vitae*, and the social and cultural turbulence of the 1960s and 1970s on Catholics' worldviews, it is evident that the post–Vatican II period marked a significant shift in American Catholics' understanding of what constituted a sin (Greeley 1985: 216–217), and by extension in their attitude toward the church hierarchy. The public conflict in the church over birth control "symbolized a new era" for the American church, and the adoption of "a new mode of thinking for many Catholics" (Seidler and Meyer 1989: 104, 106).

Catholics' changed disposition toward Catholicism demonstrated a complex pattern. Andrew Greeley (1985: 53) points out that "the decline in church attendance began immediately after the birth control encyclical," with national surveys demonstrating a precipitous decline in the proportion of Catholics in all age groups attending Sunday Mass. In 1968, the year *Humanae Vitae* was issued, 65 percent of American Catholics reported weekly Mass attendance; in the ensuing years church attendance declined steadily so that by 1973 it was only 55 percent (ibid. 54–55). Church attendance rates stabilized, however, in the late 1970s and 1980s at around 52 percent (Hout and Greeley 1987: 332). The abrupt end of the trend toward decreasing church attendance highlights the theological revolution that occurred among American Catholics starting in the late 1970s: Catholics' disagreement with official church teaching on sexuality no longer prevented them from attending Mass and participating in the Eucharist (Greeley 1985: 50). Thus Hout and Greeley's statistical analyses lead them to conclude, "The active Catholics of the 1980s are less influenced (in their attendance habits) by disagreements with the hierarchy than were the formerly active Catholics who have curtailed their participation" (1987: 340).

Hout and Greeley argue that the decline and subsequent leveling in church attendance was the consequence of a one-time shock response to *Humanae Vitae* (ibid. 341), and their data contradict the notion that falling attendance was due to displeasure with Vatican II liberal reforms. In fact, Hout and Greeley (ibid. 332) suggest that Vatican II changes (such as greater lay involvement in the liturgy) helped to stave off further defections. In short, since the late 1970s it is not necessarily adherence to the official teaching and the rules of the church, but loyalty to the Catholic communal and sacramental tradition (Greeley 1977: 272–273; Hout and Greeley 1987: 340–341), that is the hallmark of a religiously involved Catholic. Catholics today, as one study of women and spirituality has documented, are "defecting in place." They remain within the church but "leave the old way of relating and stay on [their] own terms . . . present in a whole new way" (Winter, Lummis, and Stokes 1994: 114–115).

The findings of many national surveys confirm that Catholic attitudes and beliefs are increasingly autonomous of official church teaching (e.g., D'Antonio et al. 1989; 1996; Fabrizio et al. 1995; Gallup 1994: 142–148; Goodstein and Morin 1995; Greeley 1985). While the actual percentages reported vary from study to study, almost all Catholics (93%) think that a person who uses artificial contraception is still a "good" Catholic, and a substantial majority express a similar view of Catholics who are divorced (85%) (Goodstein and Morin 1995). Although still a majority, somewhat fewer Catholics (51%) think that Catholics who engage in homosexual relations can be "good" Catholics (ibid.). Since abortion was legalized in 1973, the vast majority of Catholics have steadfastly supported women's legal right to have an abortion (see Cook, Jelen, and Wilcox 1992), and 69 percent think that a Catholic who has had an abortion can still be a "good"

Catholic (Goodstein and Morin 1995; see also D'Antonio et al. 1996: 43–64).

Catholics' views of the priesthood also differ from official church teaching. Support for women's ordination among Catholics has steadily increased from an initial low of 29 percent in 1974 to 63 percent currently (Gallup 1994: 144; Greeley and Hout 1996). The idea of married male priests has always been comparatively more popular than the idea of women priests; in 1971, 49 percent of American Catholics favored married priests, and more recently the proportion who endorsed the idea was 75 percent (Gallup 1993: 144; Greeley and Hout 1996). Trend data since the 1970s show that a majority of Catholic priests themselves favor celibacy as an option. While the proportion in favor has remained fairly stable (around 53%), it is noteworthy that in the 1990s younger priests were significantly less likely than their age peers in the 1970s or 1980s to endorse celibacy (Hoge et al. 1995: 204–205).

Clearly, Catholics' disagreement with official church teaching on sexual morality and the priesthood does not lead Catholics to refrain from attending Mass, participating in the church's sacraments, or remaining involved in the church in other ways. As underscored by the findings of a national survey of Catholics commissioned by the doctrinally conservative Catholic League for Religious and Civil Rights, a majority of respondents (64%) expressed the opinion that even if the church hierarchy did not change its stance on doctrinal questions with which they disagreed, they would remain committed to the church (Fabrizio et al. 1995).

In sum, since Vatican II there is a significant pattern of Catholics splitting their religious commitments and doctrinal values from official church teaching. In particular, post–Vatican II Catholic generations, including those with high levels of religious commitment and those educated in Catholic schools and colleges, favor a democratic understanding of the church and an approach to morality that is sensitive to people's diverse circumstances (D'Antonio et al. 1996: 84, 88, 95–98). For these Catholics, the teaching authority they encounter must be "both rational and reasonable" (McNamara 1992: 159). Contemporary Catholics are thus redrawing the boundaries of Catholic identity and in the process, as I will document, are demonstrating that doctrinal knowledge and the authority to interpret doctrine are not the prerogatives of the church hierarchy alone. Today, the question of religious authority is "located within the self rather than externally" (Roof

1993: 119). Thus in many instances it makes sense to refer to believers' autonomy from official church authority as the "privatization of
religion" (Demerath and Williams 1992: 289). Yet, in my view, the
notion of privatization detracts from the fact that at least for the pro-
change Catholics in this study, the interpretive autonomy they demonstrate critically engages the Catholic tradition. Their identities and
institutional projects are very much collective, public, faith-driven,
and reasoned.

PRO-CHANGE GROUPS IN THE CHURCH

The shifting symbolic and institutional reality of post–Vatican II
Catholicism is sharply illuminated by the visibility of pro-change
groups in the church. Vatican II's review of the church emphasized the
importance of achieving greater consistency between doctrine and
church practices. Vatican II did not elaborate how the ideas it formalized should be given practical interpretation. In the context of a
post–Vatican II and American cultural spirit of individual and collective agency, the challenge was taken up by Catholics themselves. One
expression of this, as discussed above, was evident in Catholics' decou-
pling of attitudes and behavior from sacramental participation.
Another manifestation was the founding of several Catholic-based
activist organizations during the late 1960s and 1970s.

The proliferation of Catholic groups was clearly influenced by the
egalitarian ethos of American political culture, and by the emerging
visibility of diverse social movements and social movement organizations (see Minkoff 1995) in American civil society. The move toward
Catholic collective action was probably pushed by the consciousness
that church leaders, as evidenced especially by Paul VI's stance in
Humanae Vitae (1968), could not be relied upon to realize the new
doctrinal and institutional possibilities they had endorsed at Vatican
II. Similar to the trajectory of organizational change in the economic
arena (cf. Hannan and Freeman 1989), those who occupied a "peripheral" location in the church were at the forefront of efforts to initiate
institutional change. It was primarily marginalized Catholics who took
advantage of the church's shifting from a hierarchical to a communal
"People of God" model, and of the "murky" institutional environment
(cf. Fligstein 1991: 315) caused by public conflict at all levels of the
church over *Humanae Vitae*. Once again, this clearly was not solely a
church-driven process. The contestation of equality in American soci-

ety during this time by feminists, gays and lesbians, and pro-choice activists abetted Catholics' mobilization for equality in the church.

The social movements generated in the post-sixties era share a concern with noneconomic post-material issues that focus on collective identities and "the grammar of the forms of life" (Habermas 1987: 392; Offe 1984: 176). As movements of the educated middle classes they are preoccupied with the problems associated with "quality of life, equal rights, individual self-realization, participation, and human rights" (Habermas 1987: 392). Their emancipatory purpose as expressed by Anthony Giddens (1991: 210–212) is to "reduce or eliminate exploitation, inequality, and oppression" and to prioritize "the imperatives of justice, equality, and participation."

Among other newly formed pro-change groups, in 1969 gay Catholics founded Dignity, in 1973 Catholics for a Free Choice was founded, and in 1975 the Women's Ordination Conference was established. Subsequently, groups committed to more broadly based multi-issue changes in the church, such as the Association for the Rights of Catholics in the Church (1980) and Catholics Speak Out (1981), were founded. The mobilization of Catholic pro-change forces was accompanied by a countermovement mobilization of groups opposed to change in the church (Ebaugh 1991; Seidler and Meyer 1989: 57–60). Thus, for example, in 1968, Catholics United for the Faith was founded to defend "Catholic truth" in liturgy, theology, and sociomoral teaching (J. Sullivan 1995: 108). The Catholic League for Religious and Civil Rights, established in 1973, sees its organizational agenda in part as the defense of the official teaching of the Catholic Church (Donohue 1995). In 1984, Women for Faith and Family was founded to counteract Catholic feminists by providing a voice on behalf of (what its founders considered to be) Catholic women who are "faithful to the church" (Hitchcock 1995: 164). In the Catholic Church, therefore, it is not solely pro-change Catholics who contest the authority of the church hierarchy. Conservative Catholics variously challenge the church hierarchy's social justice teachings and its opposition to the death penalty (Gallup 1994: 147), and what some Catholics regard as the marginalization of certain devotional practices and faith beliefs (see Cuneo 1997).

While pro-change Catholic organizations engage in traditional forms of public protest, they have primarily taken their protest cues from the strategy institutionalized by Vatican II, namely, an emphasis on dialogue. The three activist groups included in this book –Dignity, the Women's Ordination Conference, and Catholics for a Free Choice – differ from one another in considerable ways. Yet the primacy of dialogue with the rest of the church, especially with church officials, and with the Catholic doctrinal tradition are features common to their respective projects.

In an influential essay on organizational dynamics, Albert Hirschman has argued that for dissatisfied members in organizations, there is "a bias in favor of exit" (1970: 43), and that "voice," while complementary to exit, may be strategically used to postpone exit (ibid. 37). Hirschman thus tended to see voice as the option for those with restricted possibilities rather than a powerful strategy for institutional change in its own right. Contrary to Hirschman (ibid. 76–85), the data presented in this and subsequent chapters will show that pro-change Catholics' articulation of the possibilities of Catholicism is not a strategy dictated by powerlessness or an uncritical organizational loyalty. It flows, rather, from their deliberate commitment to remain within the Catholic community. With the option of organizational exit available to them, but rejected by them, pro-change Catholics work to achieve institutional change from within the church, and in the process they change some of the meanings and practices of Catholicism.[1]

DIGNITY

ORIGINS AND PURPOSE

It is no coincidence that Dignity was founded in 1969, the same year that Stonewall marked a major explosion in gay political consciousness. Yet awareness of the need to transform gay Catholics' invisibility in the church preceded Stonewall. In 1968, an Augustinian priest in San Diego named Patrick Nidorf, "inspired by Pope John XXIII's renewal message" and concerned that gay and lesbian Catholics were still "biblical lepers," began meeting with a small group of gay and lesbian Catholics in Los Angeles on a monthly basis. Within a few months, however, Nidorf was asked by the bishop to stop his work with the group. In the heady post–Vatican II days, the absence of a priest did not present the obstacle to communal worship that it would have just a few years previously. Embracing the idea of

---

1. Writing in 1970, Albert Hirschman did not recognize exit as an option available to church members (1970: 33) despite the history of voluntarism in American religion.

the church as the People of God, the group continued under a male lay spiritual/educational minister, and subsequently expanded to New York and other cities.[2]

Today, Dignity/USA is the largest national organization of gay and lesbian Catholics, with seventy-five autonomous chapters or local faith communities across the United States.[3] In 1979, it established a permanent national office in Washington, D.C., where it has one full-time administrative staff person, and since late 1997 a full-time executive director. Dignity holds a national convention every two years at which, among other activities, delegates elect national board members and committees with special responsibilities. The delegates, who are elected representatives from their respective chapters, also review and make any amendments that they deem necessary to Dignity's constitution.

Dignity's Statement of Position and Purpose was drafted in 1970 and endorsed by members at Dignity's first national convention held in 1973. Most noteworthy about the original statement of purpose are its Catholic theological and social self-consciousness, its affirmation of gay sexuality, its commitment to integrating gay sexuality, faith, and social justice, and finally its nonconfrontational tone.[4] Dignity argues for the "right," "privilege," and "duty" of gay and lesbian Catholics "to live the sacramental life of the church." The opening sentences of Dignity's statement mix Vatican II concepts with more traditional faith beliefs reminiscent of the Catholic "creed" recited as part of the regular Catholic Mass liturgy. It states: "We believe that gay, lesbian and bisexual Catholics are members of Christ's mystical body, numbered among the People of God. We have an inherent dignity because God created us, Christ died for us, and the Holy Spirit sanctified us in Baptism making us Temples of the Spirit, and channels through which God's love might become visible."[5]

It is also noteworthy that Dignity confronts both official church teaching that homosexuality is unnatural and social stereotypes of gay

2. This account is taken from "Los Angeles – Cradle of Organization Marks 15 Years." Dignity's national newsletter, March/April 1984.
3. As noted in footnote 1, page 5, Dignity/USA's formal mission and membership also includes bisexual and transgendered Catholics. With no disrespect intended, I use the summarized "gay and lesbian" phrasing in this book for ease of presentation.
4. Statement of Position and Purpose published as part of Dignity's proposed national constitution in Dignity's national newsletter, June 1975.
5. Dignity's Statement of Position and Purpose, Fall 1993.

promiscuity. The statement declares: "We believe that gay men and women can express their sexuality in a manner that is consonant with Christ's teaching. We believe that all sexuality should be exercised in an ethically responsible and unselfish way." In the statement's initial formulation, Dignity articulated its organizational objectives to unite all gay Catholics, and to be an instrument through which gay Catholics might be heard by the church and society. Driven by these broad and ambitious aims, it identified four areas of activity, each with more detailed and specific objectives: spiritual development, education, involvement in social justice, and the organization of social and recreational events.

Dignity's statement today is basically similar to its original formulation. What is new is evidence of a greater feminist consciousness reflected in the demarcation of "feminist issues" as an additional area of concern, and a greater confidence in the morality of same-sex sexuality. Regarding the latter, the Statement's paragraph on sexuality contains an additional significant sentence: "We believe that we can express our sexuality physically in a unitive manner that is loving, life-giving and life-affirming."[6] The absence of a vilifying attitude toward the church hierarchy despite the hardened Vatican line since the mid 1980s toward what it labels "the pro-homosexual movement in the church" (CDF 1986) is still a feature of Dignity's Statement of Purpose and of its organizational literature as a whole. Dignity continues, in its words, to offer "a ministry of witness to the larger Church and society," with a "vision that one day neither society nor our church will discriminate against people on the basis of sexual discrimination."[7]

The revisions to Dignity's statement of purpose are reflective of developments in Catholic moral theology and in feminist consciousness that have occurred since Dignity's founding. But they also point to tensions within Dignity as it seeks to execute its identity project on behalf of gay and lesbian Catholics. In particular, the revisions crystallize Dignity's evolving attempts to deal with its own ideological diversity. Dignity has faced two interrelated challenges concerning (1) questions of strategy and identity in relation to the church hierarchy, and

6. Ibid.
7. Dignity/USA, organizational literature. Demonstrating their commitment to ending discrimination against gays and lesbians in society as a whole, many Dignity chapters are active in community outreach activities toward gays and lesbians. Members of Dignity/Boston, for example, frequently lobby the state legislature on issues of gay rights.

(2) tensions among the membership concerning Dignity's "ownership" of and experimentation with the liturgy, especially its practical attempts to create a liturgy that is gay- and gender-inclusive.

RELATIONS WITH CHURCH HIERARCHY

One of the prominent themes that emerges in tracing Dignity's historical development is an emphasis on the importance of maintaining dialogue with church officials. Newsletters from Dignity's early years, in particular, record progress made with the church hierarchy as a result of formal meetings held between either individual Catholic bishops or committees of the National Conference of Catholic Bishops (NCCB) and Dignity national board members or local chapters.

A major accomplishment in 1975 was a meeting with NCCB's liasion committee, where two Dignity board members presented Dignity's organizational objectives and specifically requested the bishops' pastoral sensitivity and support for civil rights legislation for gays.[8] A report subsequently compiled by the bishops' representative at this meeting was later presented as a major submission to all of the bishops. That same year (1975), Dignity gave face-to-face testimony at a meeting on "family themes" organized by the U.S. bishops, at which the Dignity representative stated his "undivided support" for all the church's sacraments including marriage, and argued for recognition of the fact "there are significant numbers of Gay love relationships that are long lasting."[9] Thus at the end of 1975 Dignity celebrated its success in being "singled out as a force to be reckoned with" by the American bishops.

The possibility of continuing dialogue with church officials was seriously threatened when the Vatican issued its Declaration on Sexual Ethics (1976) affirming its opposition to homosexual behavior. The Vatican's declaration gave rise to diverse responses among Dignity's membership. Whereas some resigned their memberships on account of the "clear contradiction" between Dignity and the Vatican, other members took a more radical view, arguing that Dignity should cut its ties "with the official church as it continues to persecute and misunderstand" gay people.

Dignity's official response to the declaration appeared to indicate the emergence of a more confrontational attitude toward the church hierarchy. It rejected the Vatican's stance as "disappointing and nar-

8. See Dignity's national newsletter, July 1975.
9. Dignity's national newsletter, September 1975.

row-minded," and criticized its neglect of revised biological, psychological, and theological thinking on homosexuality. Yet it was clear
that Dignity did not believe a change in organizational tactics was necessary. To the contrary, it remained focused on maintaining dialogue.
Dignity's president at the time framed the document as "a continuation of the Church's struggle with the issues." He argued against the
adoption of either retreatist or offensive tactics, contending instead
that Dignity's intrachurch presence was necessary "to challenge the
Church's leadership to a more sensitive and realistic approach to sexuality."[10]

In the ensuing years, Dignity's conversations with the American
bishops continued. For example, despite the Vatican's Declaration on
Sexual Ethics, Dignity was invited by the U.S. bishops to send a voting delegate to their 1976 Call to Action conference in Detroit, a conference organized by the bishops to discuss issues of social justice and
lay involvement in the church. In addition, Dignity board members
continued to have meetings with individual bishops. Dignity Masses
continued to be celebrated in Catholic churches with the approval of
the respective bishops; the Richmond chapter, for example, had its
bishop attend one chapter meeting. Among other initiatives, Dig-
nity/Atlanta was invited to submit an article to the diocesan newspaper, Dignity/Ann Arbor began a program of outreach to parishes need-
ing assistance in addressing gay and lesbian issues, and the priests of
the Baltimore diocese endorsed Dignity's role in providing a supportive Christian community.[11]

By the mid 1980s developments within church and society provided a new context for Dignity's organizational identity. On the one
hand, the emerging high incidence of AIDS among gay men gave a
practical urgency to theoretical discussions of the ethics of gay sexual
relations. As one Dignity member wrote in a prescient newsletter article in 1982:

> the question of how God will judge those of us who have led
> promiscuous sex lives while not unimportant, seems to be of less
> of a concern than our own judgment about what open sex lives
> are doing to our health . . . while questions of moral sexuality

10. For Dignity's response to the declaration, see its national newsletter, February
1976.
11. Reports of these events are carried in Dignity's national newsletters for May
1976 through September 1980.

may have been debatable in the past, the current physical consequences should make those moral conclusions a lot simpler to come to. [12]

At the same time, Dignity's status within the church was dealt a strong blow with the Vatican's adoption of a more authoritarian stance toward "the pro-homosexual movement in the church" in its 1986 letter (CDF 1986: 382). Following the letter's publication, and Dignity's refusal to depart from its organizational agenda of seeking recognition for the validity of gay and lesbian sexual relations, several bishops refused to allow Dignity chapters to use churches and other diocesan property for liturgies and meetings.

From its founding, Dignity's position on the morality of same-sex sexual behavior was an underlying source of tension in Dignity's relations with the bishops. As an ongoing debate on sexual ethics within Dignity itself illustrated, it was not really clear what exactly Dignity meant by its statement that "gay people can express their sexuality in a manner consonant with Christ's teachings."[13] On the assumption that there are many ways in which sexuality can be expressed, the vagueness in Dignity's stance in some sense enabled Dignity to initiate and maintain dialogue with the bishops. Following the Vatican's 1986 letter, however, delegates to Dignity's 1987 convention clarified their position. They voted "overwhelmingly" in support of a resolution that stated: "We believe that we can express our sexuality physically in a unitive manner that is loving, life-giving, and life-affirming."[14] Confronted with Dignity's explicit affirmation of the physical integration of faith and sexuality, individual bishops responded by asking chapters in their dioceses to "distance" themselves from the national statement.[15] With Dignity members unwilling to distance themselves from what had been a deliberative process of reaching a consensual representation of members' views on sexual ethics, Dignity was subsequently barred from using church property in many dioceses.

12. See Dignity's national newsletter, April 1982.
13. As articulated in Dignity's statement of purpose.
14. This resolution was incorporated into Dignity's statement of purpose at their 1989 Convention. It was further elaborated in Dignity's formal document on "Sexual Ethics" issued in 1989 by a Dignity special task force committee which, based on a mandate from the national convention delegates in 1983, had been gathering data and working on the report for six years.
15. This was the approach, for instance, of Archbishop John Quinn of San Francisco. See Dignity's national newsletter, December 1988.

Dignity's 1987 convention thus marked a watershed in Dignity's organizational history and identity. As one Dignity member wrote, it "galvanized and strengthened the Dignity community, renewing its sense of mission to both gay Catholics and the wider Church."[16] Denounced by the Vatican and expelled from diocesan church property, Dignity's experimentation with Catholicism became even more independent of the official church. The break was ceremoniously ritualized by respective Dignity chapters whose members walked in procession from their "last Mass" in a Catholic church to their new Mass premises which, in most instances, was a liberal Protestant church. Simultaneously stigmatized and empowered by the institutionalization of their "spoiled identity" (cf. Goffman 1963), members appeared more willing to think of their Catholicism as prophetic, and equally important, to enact this emancipatory ideal. This was particularly evident in the emergence of gay- and gender-inclusive liturgies at chapter and national convention meetings by the end of the 1980s.

TENSIONS WITHIN DIGNITY

Although an emphasis on dialogue in the relations between Dignity and the church hierarchy is a central component of Dignity's organizational mission, the strategic value of dialogue alone is also an occasional source of tension within Dignity. At times there are signs of dissent from what some members regard as Dignity's "docile" approach. This is highlighted especially by the activities of Dignity's New York chapter. Taking a more militant stance than that apparently favored by the national president following the Vatican's 1976 declaration, Dignity/New York held "quiet watch-ins" in front of Saint Patrick's Cathedral. Their purpose was to inform people about alternative understandings of sexuality than that articulated by the Vatican. Further, in 1979, coinciding with religious celebrations of the church's one-hundredth anniversary, members from the New York chapter held a banner outside Saint Patrick's Cathedral calling for "Dignity for gay and lesbian Catholics."[17]

Pope John Paul II's American visit in the fall of 1979 also highlighted disagreements within Dignity. While several chapters were reported to have taken a generally positive view of the Pope's visit, the New York chapter framed the visit as a protest opportunity. They organized a vigil outside Saint Patrick's Cathedral with signs bearing pink

16. Dignity's national newsletter, October 1987.
17. See Dignity's national newsletters, April 1976 and July 1979.

triangles and the message "Lesbian and Gay Catholics have Dignity /
Now give us Justice" written in both English and Polish. They also
publicly distributed an open letter to the Pope in which they focused
on the "repressive teachings of the hierarchy on sexuality" and their
harmful effects on gays and lesbians. Following the Pope's visit, Dignity
newsletter columns and letters written by members from different
chapters further underscored sharp disagreements among the national
membership over whether the Pope was a "reactionary conservative"
or a "stabilizing" influence in the post–Vatican II church.[18]

Dignity's national membership have also debated the meanings of
the Catholic sacramental tradition and in particular how it might be
reworked to integrate Catholic ethics of equality. In large part, this has
involved testing the boundaries of liturgical rites. The content of the
debate changes over time and from chapter to chapter. Overall, however, members' negotiation of Catholic liturgical boundaries highlights
opposing views concerning historical consciousness, the church hierarchy's authority, and the challenge of realizing Dignity's commitment
to inclusivity.

A major division among Dignity members, particularly in its early
years, centered over whose "property" the Mass was. Seeing the bishops as the "chief guardians of the faith and the liturgy," some members
warned that Dignity's experimentation with the liturgy in order to
make it more reflective of its worship needs would run the risk of turning Dignity into a "heretical" and "separatist mini-church." Others, by
contrast, argued for a more diffuse concept of Mass ownership. This
view contended, as one member stated, that "as the gay component of
the People of God, the Mass certainly does belong to us. . . . By establishing small worshipping communities, we have assumed the responsibility of preaching the Good News to a Church which has abandoned
Gays . . . " Members who supported this latter stance embraced a broad
vision of Dignity's purpose, one which might extend beyond the "ultimate goal" of acceptability within the church to "take on a more
mature purpose . . . of discovering what it means to be gay in Christ."[19]

Notwithstanding divergent views on the ownership and purity of
the liturgy, the necessity for restructuring some of the symbols within
the Catholic tradition has long been advocated by women members of

18. See especially the exchanges printed in Dignity's national newsletter, June
   1980 and September 1980.
19. See the exchange of views in Dignity's national newsletter, April, May, and
   July 1977.

Dignity. Women have been a numerical minority within Dignity since its origins, comprising about one-third of the membership. With a view to redressing women's minority status, several programs were initiated at the outset to make Dignity more attractive to women's participation. An emphasis on celebrating women members' contributions to Dignity, and on recruiting more women to Dignity, remains a constant feature of national conventions and of articles in national and chapter newsletters.

By 1976, when a national Women's Caucus was established, several chapters had already formed their own women's groups to "help them cultivate their identity and increase their membership."[20] The goals of the Women's Caucus (currently known as the Committee on Women's Concerns) were to "support an outreach to gay and concerned women; to witness to the church the gospel imperative of justice for all oppressed persons, particularly women; and to promote cooperative interaction between the women and men of Dignity."[21]

Since the mid 1970s lesbian members have been in the forefront of efforts to change the liturgy. In 1978, the Women's Caucus argued that "language must reflect our belief that all people are equal in the one Christ." Accordingly, they focused on developing liturgies that were free from sexist language, and lesbian members led initiatives to hire women co-chaplains and co-presiders in different chapters.[22] It was clear, however, that lesbian members' desires for a sexist-free liturgy and worship service were difficult to realize. Dignity's organizational commitment to gender inclusivity, while sincere in intent, was easier to theorize about than to implement in practice. For example, in 1978, Dignity supported a boycott of American states that had not yet supported the Equal Rights Amendment (ERA), declaring that although Dignity had a predominantly male membership, its members wanted to add their voice to the promotion of women's rights.

Yet it was apparent that Dignity men in particular and some of its women members were unprepared to extend this egalitarian sentiment to Dignity's own practices by making changes to rites that they perceived as "sacred" and immutable. It was not until 1981 that delegates to Dignity's convention passed motions requiring the use of inclusive language in all informational materials and correspondence. High-

20. Dignity's national newsletter, February 1975.
21. Dignity's national newsletter, February 1978.
22. See, for example, reports in Dignity's national newsletters, December 1975 and October 1978.

lighting both the autonomy of local chapters and the contentiousness surrounding what was perceived as "tampering with the purity of the liturgy," the delegates strongly encouraged, but did not require, all chapters to extend gender-inclusive language to liturgical celebrations. It would take a further twelve years, until 1993, before the national delegates passed a resolution advocating the use of inclusive language in liturgy and hymns.

Despite the relative sluggishness of Dignity's evolving feminism, many women members were committed to remaining active in the organization.[23] While welcoming its formal commitment to women, they were realistic about the pace of change. As one woman stated, "It would be naive to assume that it won't take a great deal of perseverance to plow through the entrenched attitudes of the Roman Catholic Church that may still be reflected in Dignity. . . . [but] I believe that those women who fail to participate in Dignity because they fear the tide of male oppression are "copping out."[24]

Women members thus continued to both defend and critique their involvement in Dignity and in the church. While women are still a numerical minority in Dignity today, their visibility and influence is certainly strong. One of Dignity's recent national presidents is a woman, Marianne Duddy, and women serve in several regional and chapter organizational positions. Women's success in moving Dignity toward realizing its commitments to gender inclusivity is seen especially in the organization and content of Dignity's liturgies. That the protracted debate on inclusive liturgies had shifted in favor of "new understandings" was evident in the fact that by the mid 1980s, feminist liturgies were regularly held in several Dignity chapters; and women co-presiders accompanying the male priest, while a source of contention for some members, became a customary feature of Dignity's regular Mass liturgies. Illustrating how much change had occurred during the 1980s, one male member, reporting on Dignity's 1989 national convention in San Francisco, wrote approvingly:

> For Dignity members, liturgy is a central aspect of our shared experience. This has traditionally meant a Roman Catholic Mass presided over by an ordained priest. Some members, particularly

23. In 1983 some of the lesbians, dissatisfied with the male predominance in Dignity, formed the Conference for Catholic Lesbians (Nugent and Gramick 1992: 69).
24. See Dignity's national newsletter, May 1980.

those with a feminist consciousness, have worked to develop models of inclusive language and ritual for use at our traditional mass in our attempts at communal prayer. This convention was marked by prayer services with a decidedly feminist flavor, several of which were led by women.[25]

Despite such achievements, the limits of feminist restructuring in Dignity as in the larger church are underscored by the "glass ceiling" effect of co-presiding. Catholic women's continuing exclusion from ordination precludes them from being "priest-presiders." While some members of Dignity believe that Dignity should ordain its own women and men clergy, the majority view, and one expressed by prominent women in the organization, is that Dignity should deal with this issue by supporting the efforts of the Women's Ordination Conference. Thus at its twenty-fifth anniversary convention in Los Angeles (in 1995), Dignity delegates passed a resolution reaffirming support for women's ordination and for a more egalitarian priestly ministry in the church. They refrained from endorsing intra-Dignity ordination, stating that Dignity "does not, at this time, sanction the ordination of its own clergy." Delegates did, however, recommend that Dignity chapters engage in a collective conversation investigating the expansion of women members' roles in the liturgy.[26]

In sum, since its founding in 1969 Dignity has become a significant voice for change in the Catholic Church. While focused primarily on establishing the legitimacy of gay and lesbian Catholics, Dignity's practical interpretation of its agenda makes it push for broader changes in the doctrine, rituals, and practices of the church. Most remarkable in this effort is Dignity's commitment to maintaining dialogue both among its own members and between Dignity and the wider church, including the church hierarchy. It is noteworthy in this regard that the American bishops' 1997 pastoral statement, Always Our Children, which urged parents not to reject their homosexual children, was positively received by Dignity's national leadership with the hope that it might allow dialogue to be reinstituted between the bishops and Dignity.[27]

25. See Dignity/East Bay's (Berkeley, Calif.) newsletter.
26. Dignity's national newsletter, Autumn 1995, pp. 13, 16.
27. See the comments of Dignity/USA's current president, Robert Miailovich, "What Is Our Vision?" Dignity/USA Journal, Summer 1998, pp. 4–6.

WOMEN'S ORDINATION CONFERENCE

ORIGINS AND PURPOSE

The impetus for the founding of a Women's Ordination Conference (WOC) came from Mary Lynch, a Chicago social worker. In 1974, inspired by the impending International Women's Year, she called thirty-one of her acquaintances to a meeting in Chicago to discuss the appropriateness of women's ordination in the Catholic Church (Foley 1976: 5). Indicating the support that existed for Lynch's vision, several hundred American and some foreign Catholics subsequently attended the first ordination conference, which was held in Detroit a year later (Gardiner 1976: 209–237).

WOC's history and the deliberations of its first and subsequent conferences are well documented (see Gardiner 1976; Weaver 1985: 109–118, 132–136), and therefore those details will not be reviewed here. Briefly stated, WOC defines itself as "an international grassroots movement of women and men committed to the ordination of Roman Catholic women to a renewed priestly ministry." WOC believes that "the church in fidelity to its Gospel mission, must be equally open to the full participation of women and men in its ministries; and that women have an equal right with men to have a call to renewed priestly ministry respected and tested" (WOC organizational literature). WOC's headquarters in Fairfax, Virginia, is presided over by a national coordinator. It has a current membership of about 4,000, and like Dignity and Catholics for a Free Choice, WOC is part of the Call to Action lay movement of pro-change Catholics.

WOC's understanding of an inclusive church that corresponds to what it regards as the egalitarian ethics of Christ is underscored in its choice of nominees for its Prophetic Figure awards. Among those who have received WOC awards are Sr. Luke Tobin, one of fifteen women invited by Rome to attend one of the sessions of Vatican II and subsequently in the forefront of the movement for equality within the church; feminist Catholic theologians Elisabeth Schüssler Fiorenza and Rosemary Radford Ruether; Charles Curran, most noted for his theological work on the personalism of sexual ethics, for which he was silenced by the Vatican; Theresa Kane, who publicly expressed concerns about women's inequality to the Pope during his 1984 American visit; an ex-Jesuit priest, Bill Callahan, founder of Priests for Equality and director of the Quixote Center for Peace in Washington, D.C.;

and others involved in peace and justice work in Latin America.

Over the course of its history, WOC has organized and participated in several media-oriented public demonstrations against women's exclusion from ordination. In 1987, for example, WOC held a liturgy outside the Vatican embassy in Washington, D.C., on the occasion of the Pope's American visit with banners calling for Equal Rites for Women. In the early 1980s, WOC organized Take Back the Church rallies, also in Washington, while WOC members in other regions, including Boston and Milwaukee, organized local protests such as praying and picketing at their diocese's annual ordination ceremony.

RELATIONS WITH CHURCH HIERARCHY

Since its foundation, WOC's continuing commitment to the transformation of the church has involved it in dialogue with the American bishops, both locally and at the national level. In the early years, dialogue with the bishops centered on specific WOC petition-signing projects. WOC lobbied the bishops to push for changes in the Vatican's presentation of its position against women's ordination, especially its argument that women physically cannot mimic Christ. They also exhorted the bishops to recommit themselves to expanding the roles of women in the church and to removing sexist language from the liturgy.

Apart from specific initiatives, WOC was also engaged in an ongoing dialogue with the U.S. bishops. In the spring 1976 they were present at the National Conference of Catholic Bishops' (NCCB) meeting, at which they raised the question of justice for women, an issue which later that year featured prominently in the Bishops' Call to Action conference. Marking an historical precedent in intrachurch communicative relations, WOC representatives had a series of meetings between 1979 and 1982 with the Bishops' Committee on Women in Society and Church, at which WOC and the bishops each prepared position papers and read specific articles for joint discussion with a view to understanding and promoting women's full participation in the church.

In all, six major dialogue sessions testified to the participants' comprehensive examination of the obstacles constraining women's equality. In particular, the discussions focused on personhood as reflected in official church documents on gender; the nature of patriarchy as a social system and its implications for the structure of the church; and the scriptural, theological, and institutional bases for change in official church teaching and practices.[28]

Midway through the process, the participants published an interim report on the dialogue. The idea was that the report in turn would encourage WOC's membership and individual bishops to discuss the issues raised. In a WOC editorial,[29] WOC explained that the rationale for its discussions with church officials was Catholics' shared common ownership of the church. It argued:

> we are Church. We are not the whole Church, but then, neither are the bishops. Hence, communication is essential to the discernment of the movement of the Spirit in our times. We believe that the Church must renew its structures in order to achieve in our day an even greater faithfulness to the risen Christ. We recognize that the power to legislate these structural changes is held by the hierarchy.

Reflecting the church hierarchy's recognition of WOC's important pro-change voice in the church, the Bishops' Committee on Women invited WOC to send five representatives to a conference organized by the bishops in 1983, entitled Women in the Church: A Dialogue for Bishops and Women. The conference also included representatives from other Catholic pro-change and conservative women's organizations. The big question that emerged informally at the meeting was whether the bishops should prepare a pastoral letter on women.[30] Attempts to formalize a vote among the conference participants as to whether they favored the idea of a pastoral letter written jointly by the bishops and women's organizations were, however, ruled out of order by the bishops.[31]

Underscoring the church hierarchy's autonomy to unilaterally set the church's formal agenda, several days after the meeting the NCCB announced its intention to write a pastoral letter on women. From the

28. See the detailed accounts of these dialogue sessions as reported in the May 1981 and July 1982 WOC newsletters.
29. WOC's newsletter, May 1981.
30. In the Catholic Church, a pastoral letter has less official "teaching authority" than a papal encyclical but is still considered a significant statement of official church teaching.
31. For an account of this meeting, see WOC's December 1983 newsletter.

outset it was WOC's position that this was a misplaced focus. In its view, the bishops should not write a letter on women but on the problem of patriarchy in the church. WOC also contended that the letter should be written *with* women instead of *about* women; and that diocesan hearings should be set up in order to incorporate the experience of all Catholics into the letter.[32] Subsequently, two WOC members were appointed by the bishops as consultants to their letter-writing team, and WOC and several other women's organizations were formally invited to testify at closed hearings organized by the bishops. WOC members also participated in the various open hearings on women's issues held throughout the country by the bishops in 1985 as part of its letter-writing process.

After the bishops issued the first draft of their letter (U.S. bishops 1988), WOC actively engaged its membership in discussions about its contents. It organized a Take a Bishop to Breakfast program encouraging women at the grass roots to talk with their bishops, and submitted several detailed amendments to the writing committee based on discussions of the first and second drafts. Following publication of the letter's more conservative and what WOC considered to be an inferior second draft, which aimed to meet Vatican concerns that the letter was not sufficiently direct in clarifying official church teaching on women, WOC wrote an open letter to the bishops arguing against its publication.[33]

WOC instead asked the bishops to be "prophetic" at their upcoming November meeting. Specifically, they called for a program that would include dialogue with WOC on the values of ministry, celibacy, and the establishment of an international and interfaith study on women's ordination.[34] Arguing that "women should be included in the conversations about us," WOC's national coordinator stated that: "It is time the pope met with us and other feminist women from around the world for a real dialogue. . . . What is needed now is women's ordination and a restructuring of the hierarchical patriarchal church."[35]

The ensuing history of the bishops' "failed" pastoral letter on women is well documented. Following the intervention of the Vatican, the letter underwent two more increasingly conservative drafts. The

32. See WOC's September 1984 newsletter.
33. See WOC's newsletter, May–October 1990.
34. Ibid.
35. Text in WOC's newsletter, November 1990–June 1991

Vatican questioned the bishops' methodology, namely its discussions with diverse women's organizations and the inclusion of Catholic women's experiences based on its nationwide hearings. The Vatican also argued that insufficient stress was given to what official church teaching regards as women's unique identity differences from men.[36] The fourth draft of the letter failed to receive the necessary support of two-thirds of the bishops at their November 1992 meeting. The final text was thus issued as a lower status committee report rather than as a more authoritative pastoral letter.

The defeat of the pastoral letter may in one sense be seen as vindicating WOC's position that the bishops should not have embarked on writing about women, but should have focused on patriarchy. The defeat also highlighted that unlike sociopolitical questions of economic justice and nuclear policy, two issues on which the American bishops issued influential pastoral letters in the 1980s, the direct challenge to the church hierarchy's authority posed by women's equality in the church could publicly fracture the collective consensual voice of the bishops.

Although the bishops' conservatively leaning women's letter was not endorsed as an official teaching document, the fact remained that women's intrachurch equality had not advanced in any significant way since the WOC-bishops dialogues initiated in the mid 1970s. Moreover, as was highlighted by the Vatican's negative response to drafts of the pastoral letter, it was clear that the Vatican remained unequivocally opposed to the idea of women's ordination.

Reflecting WOC's frustration with its inability to shift official church thinking on women's ordination, WOC issued an open letter to Pope John Paul in 1993 on the occasion of his visit to Denver. The WOC letter argued that "the sin of sexism" – as it was called by the U.S. bishops (1988: 762–763) – was "strangling the life and credibility of our church." Discussing examples of women's ministry in scripture and in the early church, the letter contended that the injustice stemming from denial of women's intrachurch equality was especially serious in the United States in light of a shortage of priests. Noting the public support among American Catholics for women priests, WOC concluded that: "The hour has come to resurrect our gospel roots, our authentic tradition of gender equality in ministry, our openness to the

36. See the details about the Vatican consultation as reported in "Concerns Expressed about U.S. Bishops' Draft Pastoral on Women," *Origins* 21 (June 13, 1991): 73, 75–76.

Spirit." WOC asked the Pope to join them in their push to realize a transformed, "renewed priestly ministry based not on power or privilege, but on a ministry of mutuality." Using the language of Vatican II, they also urged the Pope to participate in WOC's effort by beginning "an open and honest dialogue" with them.[37]

Less than a year later, WOC received a "reply" to its letter with the publication of Pope John Paul's "Ordinatio Sacerdotalis," in which, as discussed in Chapter 3, he ruled against women's ordination and the legitimacy of debate about it. Demarcating John Paul's stance as a "new chapter" in the contestation of the issue, WOC insisted that their advocacy of women's ordination would not be silenced. The Vatican's subsequent clarification that the Pope's statement was to be treated as part of the "deposit of faith" coincided with WOC's 1995 twentieth anniversary conference. WOC characterized the Vatican's statement as "a new effort to stifle all discussion of women's ordination" and alerted the membership to the "creeping infallibility" represented by the Pope's stance. WOC rejected the legitimacy of the statement's claims to infallibility on the grounds that it lacked theological consensus among Catholics. It also framed the Vatican's response as an attempt "to sanctify the sin of male domination and sexism at a new level of solemnity in an outmoded papal power pyramid."[38]

TENSIONS IN WOC BETWEEN ALTERNATIVE MODELS OF PRIESTHOOD

The theme of WOC's twentieth anniversary celebration in 1995, Discipleship of Equals: Breaking Bread, Doing Justice, was a fitting statement of WOC's emancipatory agenda. "Working for the rights of women within our church" – WOC's subtitle since 1983 – does not call merely for women to be ordained as priests in the current hierarchical structure; it also involves a commitment to transforming the church into a "discipleship of equals." This model of the church follows Elisabeth Schüssler Fiorenza's (1983/1994: 286, 324) understanding of the early Christian communities as nonhierarchical communities grounded in equality and reciprocal service among all of the members as they seek to live out the ethics of justice and equality exemplified by Christ's life.[39]

37. The text of the open letter was published in WOC's newsletter, May–October, 1993.
38. WOC letter to its members dated December 8, 1995.
39. It is not just feminist theologians or post–Vatican II writers who emphasize an egalitarian and communal understanding of the Catholic tradition. Writing

Although the 1995 conference title was intended to signal "a paradigm shift in the women's ordination movement" (Redmont 1995: 16), the discipleship model has been at least implicitly present since WOC's early foundations. The very idea of women's ordination to a "renewed" priestly ministry, articulated from the outset as WOC's primary goal, paralleled Vatican II's project of church renewal by indicating a commitment to the re-examination of the meanings of priesthood. Moreover, several of the members who participated in the first ordination conference viewed that conference as initiating the process of church transformation. Calling for a "renewal in basic structures," they argued for a "listening church" that would be "more aware of the real needs of the Christian Community." Participants also saw their project as providing "an impetus within the Church to move from unjust structures to practicing the Christian message the Church verbally preaches." In sum, participants saw the first conference as "an exciting step in projecting alternative futures for the Church."[40] Synthesizing the first conference's deliberations, one participant summarized the conference as emphasizing the need for a reinterpretation of priesthood, bonding among women, and maintaining fidelity to the church's tradition (Turner 1976: 136).

Restructuring the church was also a major theme at WOC's second conference, held in 1979. Participants discussed a new concept of priesthood wherein the hierarchical model would be displaced by an inclusive priesthood based on baptismal equality. The ambiguities and tensions contained in this emergent vision, particularly those associated with the structural limits of "reinterpretation," posed a strategic challenge to participants. The dilemma focused on whether to accept ordination in the current hierarchical structure and subsequently work to effect further changes from within, or whether to deprioritize women's ordination unless it was part of a comprehensive package of institutional change.

In the mid 1980s, feminist theologian and WOC board member Mary Hunt argued that the idea of women's ordination needed to be reexamined in light of changes in women's religious participation, specifically what she saw as their move away from the institutional

before Vatican II, Yves Congar stated that "it is the visible, organized body of Christians that is the Body of Christ. There is nothing in [Scripture] to suggest a dissociation between a community of faithful . . . and the system . . . of dogmas, sacraments, powers and ministries exercised under apostolical authority" (1957/1965: 33).

40. Task force members quoted in Gardiner 1976: 182–186.

church and toward small faith communities. From her perspective, Hunt found it "difficult to imagine . . . how the whole apparatus of the institutional church will be dismantled and reconstructed." Rather than restructure the existing church, Hunt argued that the formation of new groups and the development of "basic covenant communities" was easier to envision.[41]

Thus in 1985 WOC organized an Ordination Reconsidered conference to discuss the different visions related to the question of women's ordination.[42] Following the conference, Hunt revised her earlier assessment of WOC goals. While restating her preference for the "woman-church" strategy (of local groups gathered as church for liturgy, sharing, and support), Hunt suggested that this should not be seen as competing with the intrachurch reform strategy. It was thus Hunt's assessment that WOC needed to contain a "both/and approach," without prioritizing either strategy, in continuing its advocacy for women's ordination.[43] Another contributor argued for the necessity of a "multi-form strategy" that would variously draw on diverse types of feminism. This participant's evaluation of women's ordination was that WOC should either "go for it – or forget it."[44]

Over twenty-five years after its founding, therefore, WOC is still struggling with the strategic dilemma of how to effect changes in the structure of the Catholic Church. It is evident, however, that irrespective of whether an intrachurch or parallel woman-church strategy is preferred, WOC members remain committed to the idea of ordained Catholic women, a view which is dominant among American and European Catholics as a whole.[45]

CATHOLICS FOR A FREE CHOICE

ORIGINS AND PURPOSE

Catholics for a Free Choice was established in 1973, the year that the U.S. Supreme Court legalized abortion. CFFC's emergence was

---

41. Mary Hunt, "Ordination Reconsidered," WOC's newsletter, February 1984.
42. See WOC's newsletters, January 1985 and May/June 1986.
43. Mary Hunt, "Reflecting on WOC's Past, Present, Future," WOC's newsletter, March/April 1986.
44. Mary Frohlich, "Women's Ordination: Go For It – Or Forget It," WOC's newsletter, January 1985.
45. See Greeley and Hout's (1996) discussion of American and European survey data on this and other church reform questions.

thus part of the new public context set by the court's action for the subsequent contestation of abortion in America. Unlike Dignity and WOC, CFFC is not a membership-based organization. It relies instead on a small group of volunteer activists dispersed around the country in addition to the paid staff at its Washington, D.C., headquarters. Local chapters called Catholics for Choice affiliate with CFFC. Compared to WOC and Dignity, CFFC appears more secure financially, with some of its operating costs underwritten by foundation money.

Up until the early 1990s, CFFC defined itself as "an international organization that supports the right to legal reproductive health care, especially family planning and abortion," and which works to "reduce the incidence of abortion and to increase women's choices in childbearing and child rearing through advocacy of social and economic programs for women, families, and children."[46] Paralleling concerns among CFFC board members that the concept of "free choice" did not give sufficient recognition to the moral complexities of abortion, it is noteworthy that since 1994, CFFC has presented a more substantive explication of its mission. Its current organizational self-definition states:

> CFFC shapes and advances sexual and reproductive ethics that are based on justice, reflect a commitment to women's well-being, and respect and affirm the moral capacity of women to make sound and responsible decisions about their lives. Through discourse, education, and advocacy, CFFC works . . . to infuse these values into public policy, community life, feminist analyses, and Catholic social thinking and teaching.[47]

Paralleling the respective ways in which Dignity's public presence highlights a Catholic voice alternative to the church hierarchy on homosexuality, and WOC's on women's ordination, CFFC's activities show that there is not a monolithic Catholic position on abortion. The contents of CFFC's quarterly publication, aptly named *Conscience* to reflect its theological emphasis, demonstrate CFFC's commitment to explicating the morality of a woman's decision to have an abortion. Similar arguments are elaborated in several booklets and theological

46. For a statement of CFFC's aims, see *Conscience*, Spring/Summer 1993.
47. For this redefinition of CFFC aims, see *Conscience*, Autumn 1994. See also Rosemary Radford Ruether, "Reflections on the Word 'Free' in Free Choice," *Conscience*, Summer 1994.

commentaries published by CFFC. CFFC uses its resources primarily to call attention to what it regards as the church hierarchy's disrespect for moral pluralism. It also highlights historical changes in church think-ing about the ensoulment of the fetus, and the fact that the church hierarchy has never invoked papal infallibility regarding abortion.

CFFC's focus on the more publicly visible and politically charged issue of abortion makes it a more "political" group than either WOC or Dignity.[48] But quite apart from the politicization of abortion in America, CFFC's public stance on abortion provides an important counterpoint to official church arguments defining abortion as the crys-tallization of the "culture of death" (John Paul 1995a). CFFC's organi-zational presence is significant on account of the stimulus it provides in reorienting Catholics (and others) to the fact that the morality of abortion is a more contested and complicated question for Catholics than is suggested by the absolute nature of official church teaching.

RELATIONS WITH CHURCH HIERARCHY

The Catholic bishops' active involvement in the American abor-tion debate, unlike their more institutionally confined opposition to homosexuality and women's ordination, clearly marks CFFC as both a moral and a political opponent of the church hierarchy. For church officials, the insidiousness of CFFC's moral-political stance on abor-tion is intensified because it is taken in the name of Catholics, thus publicly undermining the authoritativeness of the church hierarchy's public policy position on abortion.

The decision whether or not to talk with CFFC presents a much greater dilemma for the bishops than that occasioned by dialogue with other pro-change Catholic groups. Since bishops frequently decline to share public platforms with pro-choice politicians and have reserva-tions about invitations extended by Catholic colleges and universities to pro-choice spokespersons, they are clearly hesitant in lending cred-ibility to CFFC by talking with its representatives.

---

48. Some of the central figures in the Catholic pro-change or Call to Action movement are actively involved across the issues of concern to Dignity, WOC, and CFFC. In particular, the theologians Mary Hunt, Rosemary Radford Ruether, and Daniel Maguire are involved in WOC and CFFC and in several other related organizations. Although Mary Hunt is not involved in Dignity, but in the "alternative" Conference for Catholic Lesbians, and New Ways Ministry, her lesbian theology makes her a favorite among some women mem-bers of Dignity/Boston.

CFFC's comparatively more antagonistic relations with the church hierarchy can be traced to a pre-*Roe* conflict over state abortion legislation that pitted the New York diocese against a group of Catholic women who were subsequently instrumental in founding CFFC. The high point in tension between the church hierarchy and CFFC occurred, however, in the early 1980s. Ten years after the legalization of abortion, CFFC focused on Catholic women's absence from pro-choice activism. CFFC identified what it considered to be Catholic women's acquiescence to the subordinate gender role assigned to them in official Catholic teaching as the primary reason for this political inaction.[49] CFFC thus embarked on a public strategy designed to demonstrate that the church hierarchy was not the only "authority" on abortion and that the church's official teaching was not universally shared by Catholics.

In the political context of the 1984 presidential campaign, during which Catholic bishops denounced the pro-choice position of the Democratic vice-presidential candidate, Geraldine Ferraro, CFFC placed a full-page advertisement in the *New York Times*. CFFC's Catholic Statement on Pluralism and Abortion highlighted the diversity of views on abortion among committed Catholics and argued that "even direct abortion, though tragic, can sometimes be a moral choice." The names of almost one hundred prominent Catholics, several of whom were nuns, were printed at the bottom of the advertisement indicating concurrence with CFFC's stance. CFFC stressed the importance of intra-Catholic dialogue on abortion. While acknowledging its support for the role of the church hierarchy in "providing Catholics with moral guidance on political and social issues," CFFC argued that "responsible moral decisions can only be made in an atmosphere of freedom from fear of coercion."[50]

The impact of CFFC's advertisement on Catholics' attitudes toward pro-choice activism obviously cannot be measured. The church hierarchy's punitive response to the statement,[51] however, managed to keep intrachurch conflict on abortion, and equally important the church's hierarchical structure, as public news for at least two years following the statement's 1984 publication. Responding to an editorial in the *National Catholic Reporter* that was critical of CFFC's "stand

49. CFFC editorial, *Conscience*, May 1983.
50. *New York Times*, October 7, 1984.
51. Most notably, the Vatican began disciplinary procedures against several of the nuns who signed the statement, which, in turn, ignited public controversy among American Catholics.

against institutional structures," CFFC's president, Frances Kissling, defended CFFC's stance as "a position of conscience" that fights against both hierarchically coercive silence and "self-censorship."[52] Overall, in CFFC's perspective, the Vatican's response and actions by local American bishops against pro-choice Catholics had demonstrated the church hierarchy's vigilance in trying to silence Catholics' public rejection of its abortion position.[53]

The heightened intrachurch tensions surrounding abortion in the 1980s may have undermined the church hierarchy's credibility on abortion among Catholics and non-Catholics alike. But at the end of the decade, the Supreme Court's 1989 *Webster* decision acknowledging states' rights in protecting fetal life, gave the bishops, who had submitted a friend-of-the-court brief favoring restrictions (see Dillon 1995), both a moral and a political victory.

The pro-life tilt in the abortion policy arena, and what CFFC regarded as the bishops' commitment to greater political activism as evidenced by their declaring abortion their number one concern, pushed CFFC toward a reorientation of its intrachurch political strategy.[54] Coinciding with the bishops' annual pro-life Respect Life Sunday, CFFC called for "reflection on the true meaning of respect" and argued that "the essence of respect is mutual understanding through sincere and open dialogue." CFFC thus proposed that 1991 become a Year of Dialogue. Condemning what they considered to be the church hierarchy's role in polarizing both Catholics and non-Catholics over abortion, CFFC suggested the establishment of reciprocal "listening sessions."[55] While noting that dialogue was "integral to CFFC's mission at all times," CFFC argued that the "degeneration of the discussion" caused by the bishops' harassment of pro-choice Catholic politicians and health care professionals pointed to the "need for an extraordinary effort toward dialogue."[56]

CFFC's call for dialogue was partly "successful." Although several bishops declined requests from local CFFC activists to engage in conversation, some bishops met with individuals or small groups to discuss

---

52. *Conscience*, September/October, 1985.
53. *Conscience*, January/February, 1986.
54. See *Conscience*, May/June, 1990.
55. A "listening session" model had already been implemented by Archbishop Rembert Weakland of Milwaukee in order to hear the concerns of people, especially women, in his diocese.
56. *Conscience* editorial, vol. 12, no. 3

differences on abortion, and the information director of the NCCB's pro-life committee debated CFFC's president at a Boston College forum. The possibility of any rapprochement between CFFC and the church hierarchy was dampened when in late 1990 the bishops hired a Washington, D.C., public relations firm to conduct their pro-life public advocacy, a move that was sharply condemned by CFFC. A CFFC editorial in early 1991 by Frances Kissling argued that if the church hierarchy wanted to reduce the incidence of abortion, it should instead "come into the mainstream" and "give up its unrelenting opposition to birth control."

It was evident nonetheless that CFFC remained committed to taking a more complex approach to debate over abortion. In the same editorial in which she criticized the bishops, Kissling acknowledged that a change in the articulation of pro-choice values was necessary. Echoing the CFFC slogan that "no woman wants to have an abortion," Kissling elaborated that "abortion is not in itself a positive good." She thus argued that the pro-choice movement needed to "acknowledge that fetal life has value." Echoing the emphasis in both official Catholic teaching and CFFC literature on the social dimensions of justice, Kissling stressed that abortion, while "a profoundly personal matter," was also "a fundamental social phenomenon."[57] CFFC's more emphatic articulation of the need for dialogue and a "permit but discourage" approach to abortion was reiterated in subsequent *Conscience* editorials.

CFFC's credibility in arguing for moral pluralism on abortion was denigrated in the wake of the publication of Pope John Paul's encyclicals, "Veritatis Splendor" (1993) and *The Gospel of Life* (1995a). In late 1993, for example, referring to the increased media visibility of CFFC spokespersons during the Pope's visit to Denver, the U.S. bishops clarified that Catholics should not think of CFFC as an "authentic" Catholic organization. Stating that CFFC has no formal or informal affiliation with the church, the bishops charged that "CFFC has rejected unity with the church on important issues of long-standing and unchanging church teaching." The bishops stressed moreover that "there is no room for dissent by a Catholic from the Church's moral teaching that direct abortion is a grave wrong." CFFC subsequently rejected the bishops' accusation that they had rejected unity with the church, and argued that their continuing affiliation as Catholics was

57. *Conscience*, January/February, 1991.

indicative of their commitment to the church. They also stated that while they made "no claim to speak for the institutional church," they often expressed positions that reflected the views of the majority of Catholics.[58]

Relations between CFFC and the church hierarchy were further strained by their divergent interests at both the U.N. International Conference on Population and Development (Cairo, 1994) and the Beijing World Conference on Women (1995). The Cairo conference in particular caused a rift between the Vatican and the American delegation over the prominence of abortion as a policy option in world population control. Reminiscent of CFFC's *New York Times* statement in 1984, CFFC once again took a proactive stance in articulating the diversity of views among Catholics. Specifically, they published an open letter to President Clinton in which they highlighted the church hierarchy's restricted view of women's role in church and society, and urged him to consider the global implications for women of the Vatican's population policy.[59]

CFFC also offered a "Catholic feminist" perspective on a Vatican report published before the Beijing conference. It cautioned government and nongovernmental organizations accredited to the Beijing conference to "read with suspicion" the positions taken by the Vatican. In particular, the commentary warned delegates about what it framed as the fundamentalism of the Vatican's anthropology of women.[60] Further, *Conscience* published a "Memorandum" written by Elisabeth Schüssler Fiorenza and addressed to the Vatican delegation to Beijing. Schüssler Fiorenza reminded the delegation that Catholic women can speak for themselves, and she argued that Vatican teaching on gender, women, and family values "does not serve the welfare of women and their children." Schüssler Fiorenza then elaborated what she defined as women's demands for a just and radically democratic global society.[61]

Following these international events, CFFC's attention became refocused on its American constituencies. In March 1996, the automatic excommunication of Catholic members of pro-choice and other

58. *Conscience*, Winter 1993/1994.
59. *Conscience*, Winter 1994/95.
60. This was part of an initiative of member groups of the Women-Church Convergence, a coalition of women's groups and organizations grounded in the Catholic tradition. *Conscience*, Spring/Summer 1995.
61. *Conscience*, Spring/Summer 1995.

organizations including CFFC and Call to Action by Fabian Bruskewitz, the bishop of Lincoln, Nebraska, found CFFC once again defending the Catholic authenticity of its agenda.[62] Responding to the threat of excommunication, CFFC rejected both the canon law validity of the bishop's action and its applicability to abortion. CFFC also noted, as supported by the public statements of individual bishops, that Bruskewitz's strategy did not have the support of his confreres. CFFC pointed out moreover that if all the Catholics who disagreed with official church teaching were excommunicated, there would be "a very small church indeed."[63] CFFC elaborated its response in a press release wherein it challenged Bishop Bruskewitz to document how membership in CFFC was incompatible with Catholicism. It concluded its statement by addressing the bishop: "Persuade us to follow your teachings through reason and compassion, not through the ecclesial equivalent of brute force."[64]

As seems to be a pattern since CFFC's founding, the Bruskewitz affair provided CFFC with another opportunity whereby public controversy caused by the actions of a member of the church hierarchy enabled it to draw attention to its own organizational agenda. CFFC used the event to stress the church hierarchy's rejection of moral pluralism and to emphasize the values underpinning its commitment to change in the church.

---

62. Bishop Bruskewitz issued a formal canonical warning of excommunication "to all Catholics in and of the diocese of Lincoln" forbidding them to be members of organizations which he deemed to be "perilous to . . . and . . . totally incompatible with the Catholic faith." In addition to CFFC and Call to Action, the forbidden organizations included Planned Parenthood, the Hemlock Society, the Freemasons, and the Society of Saint Pius X (the Lefebre Group). See the *National Catholic Reporter* (April 5, 1996): 3–5. In canon law the penalty of excommunication excludes a Catholic from the sacramental and communal life of the church. Richard McBrien (1995: 500–501) explains that excommunication is "considered a very serious penalty . . . used for very serious offenses." The offense in question must be "strongly repudiated by the Christian community" and the "unrepentant perpetrator is to be to a certain degree, repudiated by the Christian community and disbarred from full communion therein." McBrien (ibid.) notes that excommunication in itself "says nothing about the moral standing of a given person before God; rather it addresses a person's relationship with the Christian community."

63. Denise Shannon, CFFC executive vice-president, quoted in *Conscience* (Spring 1996): 32.

64. CFFC news release, March 25, 1996.

EMERGING TENSIONS FOR CFFC

Compared to WOC and Dignity, no visible tensions emerge in the public organizational history of CFFC. The absence of tension would seem to be largely reflective of the fact that CFFC is not a membership but an advocacy organization which, in addition to its paid employees, selectively recruits highly committed volunteer regional activists. The apparently tension-free nature of CFFC is also reflective of the ideological breadth of its organizational agenda. Since CFFC's commitment to maintaining legal abortion is informed in part by recognition of the "right to privacy," it integrates its stance on abortion with the right to reproductive decisions in general and with issues of sexuality. Thus it is "logical" that CFFC also endorses the rights of gays and lesbians in church and society.[65] By the same token, CFFC's focus on women's equality and its advocacy of social and economic programs that enhance women's life choices means that it opposes any institutional barriers against women's equality. Accordingly, it is a strong advocate of women's ordination in the Catholic Church. There thus appears to be a "CFFC worldview" that by virtue of its pro-choice stance on abortion tends to embrace a relatively predictable ideological position on several other issues.

Although CFFC's agenda is not constrained by intramembership disagreements, there are some external credibility tensions associated with its organizational public self-presentation. One of these relates to the moral and ideological weight associated with the advocacy of "free choice." Dissociated from the historical and public policy context in which CFFC was established, the concept of "free choice" in the late twentieth century may suggest a certain hedonism or moral vacuum. More specifically, the use of "free choice" in CFFC's organizational label detracts from CFFC's own emphasis on the moral complexity of the abortion decision and on the social and economic context in which it occurs.

CFFC board members are evidently conscious of the legitimation problems associated with their organizational identity. Reflecting concern that the moral complexity of abortion be appreciated, they have pondered the question of a name change for CFFC. In a 1994 *Con-*

---

65. The "common theology" that CFFC sees connecting abortion and gay and lesbian rights is elaborated in an article by CFFC representatives Mary Jean Collins and Margaret Conway in Dignity/USA's newsletter, April 1990, pp. 11, 14. The title of the article is "Common Theology, Common Cause: Abortion and Gay and Lesbian Rights."

science editorial, feminist theologian and CFFC board-member Rosemary Radford Ruether discussed the ideological drawbacks associated with the use of the word "free," but also stressed the rationale for its use. Ruether explained that CFFC believed that abortion was not a discretionary, morally neutral decision, but that it was one which women should nonetheless be "morally free" to make.[66] Whether or not CFFC can construct a new name for itself that will reflect the complexity of its political and church agendas remains to be seen. In any event, CFFC is unlikely to yield its claim to Catholic identity.

A second source of tension in CFFC's public self-presentation derives from the partiality of its embrace of official church teaching. Whereas CFFC rejects the church hierarchy's stance on abortion, it affirms official church teaching on social justice. CFFC's emphasis on the importance of appreciating the communal socioeconomic context of individual lives is located squarely in Catholic social teaching. While the majority of American Catholics are, as noted at the outset of this chapter, also variously selective in their acceptance of official church teaching, the public nature of CFFC's doctrinal selectivity can be jarring and can undermine its legitimation strategies.

The irony attendant on CFFC's recourse to official church teaching in defense of its social justice commitments was apparent in CFFC's critique of the establishment of the Catholic Alliance, a subsidiary organization of the politically conservative, and predominantly non-Catholic, Christian Coalition. The Catholic bishops sharply denounced the Catholic Alliance. The bishops rejected its legitimacy to present a public Catholic voice, especially on political questions on which its policies deviate from the church's commitment to advocating greater socioeconomic equality.[67]

---

66. *Conscience* editorial, Summer 1994.
67. Specifically, the bishops condemned the Catholic Alliance for the "clearly partisan tone of their documents . . . and the inference that they speak for the Holy Father." While "not denying the right of Catholics to join whatever organization they choose or to support whatever public policy issues they espouse in conscience," the bishops emphasized that "[t]he Christian Coalition and the Catholic Alliance . . . is much more a political and partisan organization than the expression of a particular religious perspective. It seeks the formation of a Catholic-Christian voting bloc, which puts it on a collision course with our political responsibility statement." These are the remarks of Bishop Howard Hubbard concerning the Catholic Alliance, presented to a closed executive session during the U.S. bishops' fall meeting, November 14, 1995. See *Origins* 25 (December 7, 1995): 417, 419.

Much like the bishops, CFFC denounced the alliance's self-promotion as a Catholic organization (notwithstanding the church hierarchy's rejection of CFFC's Catholicism). Joined by other pro-change Catholic organizations, CFFC issued a public statement and mobilized Catholic individuals and organizations against the Catholic Alliance. Explicitly associating itself with Pope John Paul II, CFFC invoked the Catholic social justice tradition and argued against the legitimacy of the Catholic Alliance's Catholicism. CFFC stated: "The agenda embraced by this group represents the antithesis of our core beliefs and those espoused by the leadership of the Catholic church, including Pope John Paul II in his recent visit to the United States." Furthermore, echoing the church hierarchy's denunciation of the misuse of the Catholic label by different groups (including CFFC), CFFC pledged "to resist the political strategy of using Catholics as a front for a right wing agenda . . ."[68]

Although the CFFC is indeed committed to a Catholic social justice agenda, its strategic appeal to the church hierarchy's legitimacy on social justice draws attention to its own rejection of official church teaching on abortion. On the other hand, unlike the Catholic Alliance, the Catholic roots and theological engagement of CFFC render it organically closer to the Catholic doctrinal tradition.

CATHOLICS' RECLAIMING OF INTERPRETIVE AUTHORITY

In sum, the post–Vatican II period bears witness to American Catholics' engagement in redefining the church's doctrinal and institutional boundaries. Vatican II's emphasis on balancing the church hierarchy's authority with interpretive equality appears to have stabilized from below in favor of equality, as indicated by the autonomy of Catholic attitudes from official church teaching on a range of doctrinal issues. It is also reflected in Catholics' engagement in specific issue-oriented activist organizations seeking transformation of church doctrine and practices. These Catholics seek recognition for the multiple bases of Catholic identity. This study uses data from pro-change Catholic activists and professional Catholic theologians in order to illuminate how it is possible for Catholics to remain Catholic and maintain their commitment to building an inclusive church. The in-

---

68. Statement published in *Conscience* (Spring 1996): 15. For more details concerning CFFC's response to the alliance, see *Conscience* (Winter 1995/96): 34.

vestigation of these processes comprises the remainder of this book. I begin in the next chapter by illustrating how participants in Dignity/Boston negotiate their multiple identity affiliations as gay or lesbian and Catholic.

CHAPTER FIVE

Gay and Lesbian Catholics: "Owning the Identity Differently"

"I think when Catholic lesbians come out, it's like a double oppression. Like Black women have a totally different view of what oppression is about. And I think that's true for lesbians too because when you don't get privilege you feel it, you really can see it and you're hurt by it. And I think that's why a lot of lesbians just can't stay connected with the church. I think I wanted to stay connected because my spirituality has always kept me sane. It's always really made me feel better about myself. It's who I was and helped me make sense of the world when nothing else did. Catholic spirituality worked for me. I've always been really lucky to have been exposed to the progressive stuff. I was exposed to Vatican II. There was a priest in my parish who did folk masses. They wouldn't let him do it at the church but he did it at the VA. And so it's like that little stuff, the fringe stuff that keeps me alive. . . . I just don't know why. I have this thing about "No, I'm still Catholic." It's like a gene thing. Nobody can take that away and tell me that I'm not. I want to stay connected to that spirituality and also this social justice stuff, you know. That's real. And there's a way in which ritual – there's lots of rituals in the world – but there's a way in the ritual, although I struggle with it at times, a way that I can't even name. But I think in some ways it's familiar. And it touches different parts of me. There are pieces that touch my childhood like saying the Our Father. And it isn't always at a conscious level. It feels like an important piece of history for me that right now I still want to carry with me and sort of build. I'm pretty clear that it may change – who knows what next year or tomorrow or ten years from now will bring for me? – but I'm also really clear that my spirituality is not the Church and

115

that the Church is not my spirituality. It's a place to go to celebrate that spirituality. I feel incredibly disconnected, and rightly
so, from the hierarchy of our church and the governing body.
When I call myself Catholic I really feel like I'm naming a spirituality or a historical spirituality that has evolved and not a
structure because I feel so disconnected from the official church."
(Julia, Dignity/Boston)[1]

The eloquence with which Julia, a college-educated woman in her
mid-thirties, talks about Catholicism speaks to the riches and the tensions encountered in holding a lesbian and Catholic identity, and to
some extent made different by the "maleness" of the official church, a
gay and Catholic identity. Several of the themes that Julia identifies
will resurface throughout this chapter. The Dignity/Boston interview,
questionnaire, and observation data will document the strong pull of
Catholicism experienced by participants, and the strategies by which
they disconnect their Catholicism from the authority of the church
hierarchy. It will also show how they use their interpretive autonomy
to reappropriate the symbolic resources of Catholicism and rework its
sacramental rituals in ways that affirm the validity of a gay or lesbian
Catholicism. It is these strategies that keep Dignity participants
vibrantly connected both as a local worship community and with the
broader Catholic tradition. At the same time, underscoring the difficulties involved in realizing an emancipatory vision, Dignity's community practices will also illuminate how the inequality institutionalized
by the church hierarchy is easily transposed and not so easily transformed at the local level.

REPOSITIONING MARGINALITY

Dignity/Boston was founded in 1972 as a local chapter of Dignity/
USA, the national association of gay and lesbian Catholics. It aims to
"serve as a model community which recognizes the inherent dignity of
all people" (Dignity/Boston, organizational literature). In sociological
terms Dignity/Boston can be characterized as a responsive community,
that is, one that aims to be responsive to the "true needs" of all

---

1. All personal names used throughout this chapter are fictitious in order to pro-
    tect the anonymity of interviewees.

its members in terms of the values it fosters and puts into practice (Etzioni 1996: 1–2). Members' committed openness to one another despite issues of major disagreement suggests, as my findings will illustrate, that Dignity/Boston comprises a strong "trusting" community integrated by "ties of mutual obligation, vulnerability, understanding and sympathy" (cf. Mansbridge 1993: 340). The chapter has approximately seventy gay and thirty lesbian members who live and work in the Boston metropolitan area. Almost all of the members are white, and the vast majority are college-educated and employed in professional or managerial occupations. Although Dignity welcomes family members and friends who are not gay or lesbian, almost all of the regular participants in Dignity/Boston are gay or lesbian. The community's main activities include a weekly Sunday Mass liturgy and various social activities and local community outreach events. The chapter opened a new suite of offices in downtown Boston in the summer of 1995, where it holds committee meetings and some social events and keeps a library of materials primarily relating to Catholicism and sexual issues. Since Dignity is prohibited by the church hierarchy from using Catholic church facilities, it holds its weekly Mass in a Protestant church located in Boston's Beacon Hill district.

As a community whose lifestyle is in open contradiction to official church teaching on sexuality, Dignity's "outsider" status in the church provides a particularly valuable case study for exploring how pro-change Catholics negotiate their conflicting identities. More than that of any other marginalized group in the church, the identity of gay and lesbian Catholics is pathologized because, as discussed in Chapter 3, official church statements construe homosexuality as an objectively disordered condition.

THE PULL OF CATHOLICISM

It is not possible to quantify how many gay and lesbian Catholics leave the church on account of the church hierarchy's teachings on sexuality. Clearly some join other denominations or refrain from participating in institutionalized religious activity at all. On the other hand, as is highlighted by the religious involvement of Dignity participants, many gay and lesbian Catholics choose to continue to be actively committed to Catholicism notwithstanding the Vatican's condemnation of their sexuality. Interview data from Dignity participants invariably focused on the pull of belonging to what respondents saw as the larger culture, history, and tradition of Catholicism. The "gene thing" referred to by Julia serves as an appropriate metaphor to synthesize most respondents' understanding of both the given nature of their religious identity and the fact that it is experienced as something that respondents cannot easily discard. Regardless of whether respondents had positive or negative experiences growing up as gay or lesbian Catholics, the Catholic doctrinal and communal tradition provides them with the framework infusing their sense of what comprises a "legitimate" identity. In other words, although Dignity participants actively challenge the official boundaries of Catholicism, their sense of identity is both nurtured and constrained by a strong consciousness that they are Catholic and thus part of a larger tradition. The interpretive autonomy of Dignity, and of individual members to construct an identity that is both gay and Catholic, is thus informed by what "feels right" in terms of Catholicism.

Almost all (88%) of the Dignity survey respondents stressed the personal importance they attach to inclusion in the broader church community and their quest, as one member stated, for full acceptance as "part of the Body of Christ." Yet this acceptance, clearly, has to integrate members' identity as gay and lesbian Catholics. Thus, for example, several respondents stated that the original reason they were attracted to Dignity was to reconcile their faith and their sexuality, and they attributed their continuing regular participation in Dignity to the way in which the Dignity community nurtures their dual identities as gay or lesbian Catholics. A professional man in his mid-thirties reflected the views of many when he said: "My faith is very important to me. But I didn't want to give up my sexuality." Other respondents stated that they wanted to be "in the company of other men and women who are celebrating their religion and sexuality." Another professional man said that he "was looking for a supportive setting. . . . a community which integrates spirituality and sexuality in a healthy, life-giving way."

For the vast majority of Dignity participants it was evident that personal narratives were deeply embedded in specific communal attachments. For them, community was not something that could simply be picked up or created out of whole cloth. The attraction of the Dignity community appeared rather to be grounded in the commitments and ties by which it linked members to Catholicism. Many of the respondents expressed the emotive pull they felt toward retaining their links with the broader Catholic tradition and remaining an accepted part of what Bellah and colleagues (1985: 153) would call their "community of memory."

Bellah and his coauthors lament the weakness of communal bonds that are grounded in egocentric individualism and the shifting superficiality of self-oriented relationships. They argue that in the absence of collectively shared "communities of memory" inscribed with links and obligations to larger civic or religious traditions, community "for the therapeutically inclined . . . is something hoped for, something yearned for, something sadly missing most of the time . . ." (1985: 134–138). In contrast to the therapeutic culture central to Bellah and associates' characterization of American middle-class life, Dignity participants were searching, as different respondents indicated, for "a worship community," "a faith community that shared [their] beliefs, social justice views and gayness," a faith community that would, in short, challenge them to "keep priorities right." For almost all of the respondents, then, it seemed "natural" that this community be Catholic because even for two Dignity respondents in the sample who converted to Catholicism, Catholicism was a formative source in grounding their values and identity.

The context in which Dignity respondents affirm their faith, therefore, must not only be open to their sexuality but in continuity with what they hold to be their Catholic heritage. One woman phrased the sentiment of many respondents when she said: "I wanted a place where I could feel connected with my spirituality in a community related to my Catholic heritage. I wanted a community not only based in faith but also based in the celebration and validation of my life." One middle-aged man said: "The Catholic religion is my heritage. . . . Dignity is my spiritual home." Another man said: "I wanted to maintain my Catholic tradition but never felt as though I really belonged at any mainstream parish." Participation for others was explained simply as "Catholicism is inescapably part of my life," or "Catholicism is an encompassing identity for me." Being Catholic thus assumes a certain overarching character for the Dignity respondents. They experience it as an inherent part of their self-understanding and consequently find that its rumbling presence in their lives cannot easily be silenced. Catholicism's institutionalized collective memory (cf. Schudson 1992: 2–3) connects Dignity respondents to the past as well as shaping their present and future practices in ways that demand continuity with a communal tradition that transcends the diverse experiences of participants' lives.

The pull toward Catholicism is clearly not experienced as a process of unruptured involvement in the church. One man whom I interviewed, Cole, presented a somewhat typical profile of the cyclical fall away from and return to the church and to Dignity that characterized many of the Dignity respondents. Cole's narrative captures how various doctrinal and social pressures can lessen involvement in religious activities. It also illuminates how life cycle fluctuations in participation in institutionalized religion in general are reflected in Dignity as the church writ small. Cole is currently active in Dignity, and his story is one of the recovery of religious self-fulfillment; importantly, this is not solely a privatized fulfillment but one achieved through communal participation.

"When I was just out of college in the mid-80s I had already known about Dignity so I went a few times and I didn't really feel comfortable with the surroundings I guess at the church. At the time they were meeting in the basement of a church. Somehow I just didn't really feel like it was for me. I felt it might have been too progressive. Not quite what I wanted, not traditional enough. So I stopped going. Maybe I'd gone about three or four times. And I stopped going for about six years. And then I stopped going to church altogether and I was involved in other things. I was studying for exams and I needed to concentrate a lot of time on that and so I was ignoring my spirituality. And in a way I kind of felt lost. I was really kind of sad in a way. I was really missing out on something. And I couldn't figure out what it was. I didn't know how to get that back or even really what it was I was really missing. And then I was talking to a friend . . . and he was involved in Dignity. And I said maybe I should go back and try it again. And this was spring of '92. And it kind of clicked that time. . . . The homilies were very special, very personal. It's the first time I could really relate to homilies and to what the priest was saying to me. And it was really an incredible feeling. I have a lot of other activities. I do volunteer work. I play sports. . . . So I was heavily involved in all of these other activities and they are all still important to me but over the years Dignity has become more important and the other activities have become a little less important. . . . When I was growing up my family was always involved with the church. I liked the church. We never heard any horror stories at church [that sex was sinful]. My parents were pretty conservative. . . . but they were never bigots. They were really open minded and fair and I think by example they passed that on to all their kids without knowing it. So I always had a good church experience and I think that continued and I really missed that when I was not going to church. I always felt a strong spirituality and a strong connection with God. So I felt good that I went back. It has changed my life a lot. It has actually helped me through a lot of hard times, being back in church and being more focused."

Although Dignity participants' desire to worship communally as gay and lesbian Catholics is not driven by a therapeutic ethos, their community practices are not devoid of expressive and therapeutic elements. Dignity values expressivity, indicated in particular by a strong emphasis on communal singing during Mass. The therapeutic needs of the individual are also integrated as part of communal worship. This is perhaps best illustrated by the inclusion of a "healing ceremony" midway through the Mass, generally on a monthly basis. During one such occasion it was striking how the presiding priest linked the more therapeutic elements of personal healing with the doctrinal emphasis in Catholicism on social relationships. The priest focused his homily on compassion. Speaking about God as a God whose "first outburst is always compassion," the priest's message stressed that "God wishes to care for us, to heal us, to bind up our wounds," and importantly, that God gives people the energy to be compassionate toward others. The priest's perspective on compassion was noteworthy in that it challenged the values of self-fulfillment and individual autonomy that dominate American culture (e.g., Bellah et al. 1985; Etzioni 1996). He stressed that compassion was not so much a feeling, but an energy and a deeply experienced awareness of our connectedness to one another and to nature. Being connected, the priest acknowledged, is a cliché, but to really be connected, he argued, we must act out of our interdependence in a time when people are "compassion fatigued." At the end of his homily, the priest invited three "healing teams" or what Dignity calls "anointing groups," each comprised of three Dignity members, to take their respective places in the church, one on either side of the altar and one at the right side of the church. Then the whole congregation stood up and recited a special healing prayer distributed at the beginning of Mass, after which those who wished to be prayed over and anointed were invited to approach any of the three groups. With piano and guitar music as background, several people, mostly men, went up individually to the respective groups where they quietly talked and prayed together. Once the healing encounters were over, the Mass liturgy continued.

An emphasis on healing is not a Dignity innovation per se, since the sacrament of reconciliation or "confession" is central to the Catholic doctrinal tradition. Yet since most Catholics today tend to go to confession infrequently,[2] it is striking that Dignity participants have established a refashioned healing ritual as a regular feature of their Mass. The inclusion of healing ceremonies may reflect Dignity members' quest for some kind of therapeutic outlet, but it may also be seen as indicative of members' commitment to communally enacting various elements of Catholicism.

Clearly, gay and lesbian Catholics, as I will further demonstrate in this chapter, own the Catholic identity in ways that are different from those of other Catholics. The preceding discussion highlights the fact that one facet of their identity negotiation is the self-conscious aspiration that their identity be Catholic and that it be celebrated in a communal setting with other gay and lesbian Catholics. For Dignity participants, the voluntarism of American religion (cf. Warner 1993: 1074–1080) is manifested by their choice to stay Catholic and to live a Catholicism that openly affirms their identity as gays or lesbians notwithstanding the church hierarchy's declaration of the contradictory nature of these dual identities. Despite the declining significance of denominational identity for the post–World War II generations of religiously involved Americans (Wuthnow 1988), Dignity respondents demonstrate that denominational attachments still matter in particular contexts. Unlike their gay and lesbian peers who join explicitly nondenominational Christian churches such as the "gay" Metropolitan Community Church,[3] Dignity participants want a gay and lesbian worship community that specifically invokes Catholic identity

2. For example, in a 1993 Gallup poll conducted among American Catholics, 54 percent of whom described themselves as either "very strong" or "strong" Catholics, only 14 percent of the total sample reported having gone to confession within the previous thirty days (Gallup 1994: 144).

3. Although as Stephen Warner (1995: 86) notes, the MCC "resists being called 'the gay church'" since it wants to be "universal enough to reach out to all

and tradition. Although religious identity may be less "primordially rooted" (Warner 1993: 1077) than it was in past times, Dignity participants experience Catholicism as a tradition that they do not want to forget, even while that same tradition is used by the church hierarchy to denounce their sexuality.

The specifically Catholic identity of Dignity thus contrasts with the communal basis of some contemporary religious congregations where the importance of a shared doctrinal identity is underemphasized. Stephen Warner's study (1988) of evangelical Protestants in Mendocino, California, found that a common migratory history rather than denomination was a central dimension of the congregation's collective memory. Similarly, although the Metropolitan Community Church has communal worship and uses an eclectic mix of Christian liturgical forms (Warner 1995: 88), the primary bond that unites MCC participants is to a large extent their gayness and not the sharing of a specific denominational tradition, even though, as Stephen Warner (ibid.) observes, the church does have an evangelical Pentecostal culture. Dignity participants, by contrast, do not uncouple their religious-communal worship from its specific doctrinal roots. For them it is important that their community be a community of religious memory rather than one based on other commonalities of sociobiographical history. In short, for gay and lesbian Catholics in Dignity/Boston, the salience of their Catholic heritage cannot be split from other aspects of their personal biographies. For them, Catholicism is important precisely because it integrates them with a larger communal tradition, one whose collective historical memory is inscribed in their personal memories.

SEXUAL IDENTITY

Just as the choice of Dignity participants to stay Catholic is driven by what they experience as the communal pull of Catholicism, it is also enabled by how they construe their sexual identity. The emergence of new domains of knowledge (e.g., gender, sexuality, ethnicity) and new subjects of knowledge (e.g., women, gays and lesbians) legitimated by the protest movements of the 1960s and 1970s (Seidman 1994: 235), was accompanied by changes in the conceptualization of identity. It is

God's children," the vast majority of participants in MCC churches across the United States are gay men, along with a smaller number of lesbians.

thus common today for some social theorists (e.g., Hall 1992) to emphasize the fluidity of what were traditionally regarded as ascribed and immutable cultural identities. Rather than seeing gender or sexuality, for example, as essentially fixed and constraining, theorists stress the socially constructed, historically changing, and malleable nature of the role expectations and behaviors associated with different identities (see S. Epstein 1987 for a critical review).

An emphasis on the social construction of identity is framed especially by academics as emancipatory since it opens up the possibility of institutional transformation. This view highlights the arbitrariness of categorical distinctions (such as male versus female) and the ways in which these distinctions are used to exclude groups of people from participation in social and political life. Constructionist approaches point to the systematic way in which inequality is socially reproduced on the basis of purportedly innate differences, and reject the predetermined consequences of ascribed identities. In this view, for instance, it is inherently unjust that being born female as opposed to male means that one is automatically denied access to opportunities and life chances solely on the random biological basis of genitalia. A constructivist view of sexuality – and one frequently at odds with how people actually experience sexual identity – similarly maintains that since a person's sexual preferences are fluid and may shift back and forth over the life span, discrimination on the basis of sexual orientation is equally arbitrary and unjust.

By contrast to a constructionist vision of equality which rejects group discrimination, a constructionist framing of identity can be used to argue against the equal rights claimed by, for example, gays and lesbians. An emphasis on the social as opposed to the natural basis of identity may lead to the politically conservative view that since identities are not pre-given but chosen, then people cannot legitimately expect special protection under the law or demand public policies designed to mitigate conditions associated with their (chosen) identity. A shadow is thus cast on the notion that the granting of group-specific rights is necessary to override the legacy of past injustices.

Clearly, theorists who take a radical constructivist view arguing that nothing about identity is given fail to appreciate the important ways in which, as Cathy Cohen notes (1996: 367), people's everyday reality and life chances revolve around the salience of particular group memberships and participation in group-specific experiences. By the same token, an emphasis on the innate and predetermined "culture" of specific categories of people (e.g., Pope John Paul's [1995b] view of women) contributes to the perpetuation of inequality and the invidiousness of ranked comparisons (cf. C. F. Epstein 1988).

To avoid the intellectual and practical pitfalls associated with the extremes of either perspective, it is necessary for sociologists to pay more attention to how people who occupy different identity categories themselves perceive identity. My interviews with Dignity participants contribute to an expanding empirical literature documenting the subjectively experienced complexity of sexual identity (see, for example, Stein 1997). Highlighting the abstract nature of views that emphasize sexuality as socially constructed, all of the gay and lesbian respondents in the Dignity study expressed an essentialist understanding of their sexuality. Similar to the findings of other studies of gay Christians (e.g., Thumma 1991; Warner 1995), the view reiterated by Dignity survey respondents was that sexuality was natural, innate, and divinely prescribed, and that differences in sexuality did not detract from individual integrity or relational wholeness. Importantly, Dignity participants' essentialist interpretation of their sexuality was not located simply in a biological identity but in what they see as a God-given sexuality. Respondents emphasized, as one stated, that "sexuality in general is a gift from God to be embraced and celebrated." Others similarly argued:

"Gay people are born gay."

"God created everyone in his image without looking over what makes us different. God equals love; love of human life, no matter how that genuine love is expressed."

"Being homosexual does not mean that God does not love me. It just means that I am different."

"The spirituality of a relationship is more important than the mechanics of it; all loving relationships are valid before God."

"It is a cherished gift from God. We are all different and bring different gifts and talents to the community."

"Homosexuality is part of God's creation."

In short, in the experience of the gay and lesbian participants in

Dignity, "if you're gay," as one respondent phrased it, "you're gay as a creation of God. There is no choice involved."

Dignity respondents' interpretation of their sexuality reflects their acceptance of personal experience as a source of objective authority. Similar to the primacy of self-validation discussed in other studies (e.g., Bellah et al. 1985; Roof 1993: 119), Dignity participants maintain that if one experiences something as natural or if something "feels right," then it must be good. There is a sense of personal entitlement; since they "are this way," and made by God to be this way, it is their right to be gay and to be accepted for being gay irrespective of alternative views on homosexuality. At the same time, of course, in view of the Vatican's teaching on the disordered nature of homosexuality, gay and lesbian Catholics have a strategic interest in articulating an essentialist view of the self and of sexuality. Like other gays and lesbians who are advised to change their sexual orientation, they may, as Steven Epstein observes, "have more than a passing investment in the claim that they've 'always been that way' – that their gayness is a fundamental part of who they really are" (1987: 12).

By presenting their sexuality as natural, Dignity respondents eliminate the possibility derived from a social constructionist framing that their sexuality is pliable and accordingly could, or should, be changed to fit with the church's official teaching. For them to adopt a constructionist understanding of sexuality would be personally threatening, as it would compel them to defend their "choice" of a sexuality that official church doctrine defines as disordered. Dignity respondents' anticonstructionist view of sexuality could thus be seen as a strategic rejection of the church hierarchy's constructionist view that engagement in same-sex relations is a willful decision to choose homosexuality over heterosexuality or to act on a natural but disordered sexual inclination. Depending on the institutional and sociocultural context of their use, therefore, both essentialist and constructionist framings of identity can serve diverse strategic purposes (see also Bernstein 1997).

INTERPRETING THE CHURCH HIERARCHY'S POWER

Although Dignity participants reject a constructionist understanding of sexuality, they take a constructionist stance, in part, toward the institutional church. Similar to the church hierarchy, they are selective both in what they present as immutable and in rendering as immutable those aspects of life which protect their own identity interests. The church hierarchy, as discussed in Chapters 2 and 3, presents Catholic moral doctrine and institutional practices as divinely prescribed and immutable, whereas it applies a constructivist interpretation of gay and lesbian sexual relations. Gay and lesbian Catholics, by contrast, regard sexuality as divinely ordained and see the institutional church, in part, as socially constructed. Thus, while the church hierarchy sees gay and lesbian sexuality as disordered, gay and lesbian members of Dignity view aspects of the church hierarchy's teaching as a deviation from the justice ethics they identify with Christ's life.

The vast majority (91%) of Dignity survey respondents saw the church hierarchy's teaching on homosexuality not as an isolated issue but as part of a larger problem related to its stance on sexuality in general and its use of power. One man in his early fifties stated: "The church is still focusing too much on sexuality and too little on commitment to Christ, peace, and social justice. The vision of Vatican II has yet to be realized because church leaders are too fearful of the unknown and of letting go of the past." It was the view of a man in his early thirties that: "The Church's actions on gay issues are part and parcel of its current and historical roles in issues of race, gender, religion and international power. The hierarchy has become an organism more concerned with self-presentation and self-perpetuation than with the growth and healthy development of the people it serves."

Another man argued:

"The institutional Church is based on an ancient sexist hierarchy. And the people in charge will do anything to preserve their power. Eventually, however, the real church will win. The real church is the people. And the people of the church will no longer tolerate having a small group of men validate and invalidate their lives. The issue of GLBTs [gay/lesbian/bisexual/transgendered people], women in the priesthood, and birth control are all linked. They all are examples of the power these elitist men have over millions of people. As each of these issues is attacked it puts chinks in the armor for all of them."

One woman said:

"Homophobia is, I believe, always linked to underlying sexism, and the 'woman issue' is a fundamental problem in the institutional church. But even beyond that, the Church's stance on homosexuality seems to reflect their unwillingness to let people think/discern for themselves in good conscience, their obsession with maintaining power and control, their infantilization of people and demonization of sexuality. It also epitomizes the 'we get to say who is good and who gets to belong and you can't get to heaven without us' mentality that I so often experience from the institutional church."

Such quotations illustrate that while Dignity participants reject the constructionism underpinning official church teaching on homosexuality, they turn this constructionism back on the church hierarchy to map out what they perceive as its failure to focus on the "essentials" of Catholic doctrine. For them, what is "essential" is the message of equality and justice, and as the earlier quotes concerning participants' understanding of sexuality have underscored, the sanctity and goodness of the human person.

Given the mix in respondents' views between an emphasis on sexuality as divinely prescribed and church doctrine as constructed, it is interesting to note how they talked about the impact of Catholicism upon their coming out as gays or lesbians. Two-thirds (66%) of the Dignity survey sample saw Catholicism as accentuating the difficulties they encountered in acknowledging their sexuality and coming out. Despite their belief in the naturalness of their sexuality, negative societal and religious constructions of homosexuality were powerful voices in defining their self-identity. Their recollections of growing up as gay or lesbian Catholics evoked a sense of disempowerment, or as one man in his late twenties described it, a "disenfranchisement" by the church. Irrespective of age or gender, themes of sin and guilt dominated these retrospective negative accounts of coming out. Typical of the respondents' remarks were those of one professional man in his early thirties who said: "Being brought up Catholic predisposed me to a huge amount of guilt in dealing with being gay. How could I be as good a person as so many family and friends knew me to be and yet be gay?"

One man in his late forties who has been a member of Dignity since the 1970s elaborated, stating: "We are talking about the 1960s when Vatican II was just underway. There 'were no gay people' as 'role models.' Those 'identified' as gay were objects of ridicule . . . and they were going to hell, to eternal damnation. No wonder it was so easy to contemplate suicide as an adolescent especially if you were a product of a parochial school."

Another man said: "I am 53 years of age. I was raised in a strong Catholic neighborhood and attended the Catholic parish school K–12, a Catholic college, and graduate school. Every sexual thought, feeling, word, and especially act, was looked on as sinful. It was very hard to wrestle with sexual maturity and even more difficult once I realized (at age 21) that I am gay."

For a woman in her mid-forties who had recently come out, "Homosexuality was such an abomination it was not even discussed when I was growing up in my family. . . . My parents never knew I was gay. However had they known, they would have been devastated, not just because of the shame or embarrassment to our family, but because they would have been genuinely concerned about my salvation (as I used to be)."

The expanded public discussion of sexuality which began in the 1960s, and post–Vatican II changes in the theological understanding of sexuality and relationships, appeared to have had little impact in easing the personal identity burdens confronted by young Catholics growing up in the 1970s and 1980s. For these Catholics, as for their older counterparts who grew up in a more sexually repressed church and society, the dominant message appeared to be one that echoed the Vatican's condemnation of homosexuality. One woman in her early thirties said: "I was a practicing Catholic still following the strict rules of the church and it was difficult to come out when the Catholic church said homosexuality was wrong and evil."

Another woman in her late twenties stated: "I was raised to believe that my sexuality was a deliberate choice against God – that I was willingly committing a sin and that my unwillingness to 'repent' was a mark of arrogance and betrayal."

A professional man in his late twenties said: "Growing up in the Catholic Church we were taught that gay people were intrinsically evil. Throughout childhood and adolescence I struggled constantly with what the church said about gays versus what I knew of myself. I knew that I was not evil inside, but it took me many years before I was able to accept this and live freely – without guilt – as a gay man."

In addition to the negative accounts reported above, some of the Dignity survey respondents (24%) saw their Catholicism as a mixed blessing or irrelevant to the process of coming-out, and a small minority (10%) stated that growing up Catholic provided images and stories that made it somewhat easier for them to come out as gays or lesbians. Notwithstanding the church hierarchy's negative view of homosexuality, other aspects of Catholicism provided these members with a framework for confronting and understanding their "difference." The multiplicity of meanings contained in the Catholic tradition was well captured by one respondent, a woman in her late forties, who said: "The church hierarchy makes it harder [to come out]; my belief in God and in the church's positive teachings – about honesty, witnessing, social activism – made it not only easier but absolutely necessary."

A man in his early thirties said: "I truly believe despite what others may say or may write, God created each of us to be unique individuals, encompassing all aspects of our lives/personalities. The belief that God loves us for ourselves was a large part of the manner in which I was raised as a person and as a Catholic."

A professional man in his early thirties said: "I wasn't raised to feel ashamed of my sexuality. Homosexuality was never put down by my family or at the church or school I went to as a child. I was always taught that God loves me for who I am. God created me because he/she loves me."

Similarly for a man in his mid-forties: "My experience of God happened at a very early age. My Catholicism as it was lived in my Spanish/Italian family was always about love, not laws."

These quotations point to the tension in individual lives between conflicting essentialist and constructionist understandings of sexual identity (see also S. Epstein 1987; Stein 1997). On the one hand, from their current relatively emancipated standpoint as gays and lesbians who are out, Dignity respondents are unequivocal in maintaining that sexuality is innate, fixed, and divinely sanctioned. At the same time, it is clear that for the majority of respondents the emotional recognition and acceptance of their sexuality was an extremely painful process. The apparent naturalness of their gayness was not a sufficient buffer against the external voices stigmatizing homosexuality.

PRACTICING GAY AND LESBIAN CATHOLICISM

Gay and lesbian participants in Dignity choose to stay Catholic because they want to maintain their connection to the larger Catholic community with which they identify and which they experience as a deeply felt, faith-based community of memory. They legitimate the authenticity of being gay or lesbian and Catholic by, on the one hand, defending their sexuality as fixed and divinely prescribed and, on the other, by uncoupling commitment to Catholicism from acceptance of the church hierarchy's authority and doctrinal views that they regard as socially constructed.

What are the consequences of this identity construction for Dignity respondents' practice of Catholicism? How do participants maintain solidarity with the larger Catholic community while simultaneously rejecting doctrinal teaching that denigrates being openly gay or lesbian and Catholic? This section will address these questions by probing the routine community practices of Dignity/Boston.

Dignity participants strive to give recognition to their gayness and their Catholicism. Although they understand both their sexuality and their Catholicism as "natural," the choice and their sense of entitlement to being gay or lesbian and Catholic demand that they work at constructing an identity which integrates both, and which in the process aims to be emancipatory.

The identity negotiation efforts of Dignity/Boston need to be understood as part of the chapter's continuing attempts to put in practice the inclusive values of the "model community" that it aspires to be. The task of being culturally inclusive obviously poses a wide range of practical and political challenges. Although a model inclusive community needs to pay attention to prejudices associated with an array of differences (including gender, sexuality, ethnicity, race, social class, and physical disability), in practice the composition of specific local communities results in the prioritization of particular sources of inequality. For Dignity/Boston, whose members are predominantly white and middle-class, the challenge of being an inclusive community revolves primarily around the tasks associated with creating gay- and gender-inclusive practices. It is to these practices that I now turn.

IDENTITY WORK: DIGNITY/BOSTON'S MASS

Communal worship, as Nancy Ammerman (1997: 55) observes, is a ritual event that expresses both "the unifying vision of the congregation" and the "internal differences that belie the picture of ritual unity." As it is for many other Catholics and Christians, the weekly Sunday Mass liturgy is Dignity's core communal worship event. Since Dignity is prohibited by the church hierarchy from using church facilities it celebrates its weekly Mass, as already noted, at a Protestant church, inconspicuously situated among office buildings and residential apartments. At around 5:20 P.M. any Sunday, the casual passerby taking a late afternoon stroll down the street where the church is located would probably be curious as to the nature of the event taking place at the address of Saint John the Evangelist. As one approaches within twenty feet of the church the harmonious sounds of an earnest choir rehearsing hymns can be heard, while outside a few men and two or three women are customarily hanging out on the steps leading up to the church's door.

By 5:30 P.M., however, the appointed time for Mass to begin, the interior of St. John's looks like many a traditional Catholic Mass setting. Most participants are in their seats having warmly greeted many of the others present. The women tend to sit together in the front rows on the left facing the altar, and the men scatter behind them and in seats on the right aisle. The dark formality of the church with its simply adorned altar at the top of the central aisle indicating the sacramental presence of Christ, and awaiting the physical presence of the priest, signals to anyone familiar with a Mass liturgy that a Mass is what is about to begin. Perhaps the main overt difference between the Dignity/Boston Mass gathering and many "regular" Catholic Masses is the remarkable warmth and intensity of the community atmosphere that permeates the gathering.

Dignity's Mass is customarily celebrated by one of several Roman Catholic priests who are associated with Dignity. Most but not all of the priests are gay members of Dignity, and some of the priests have been denied permission by their respective bishops to celebrate Mass on account of their openly gay lifestyle. The Dignity roster also includes an Eastern Orthodox priest. Occasionally a woman or a nonordained male member of Dignity/Boston join the presiding priest on the altar as an active co-presider of the Mass, including the sacramental consecration of the Eucharist (also known as Holy Communion). Thus, unlike some other Dignity chapters such as Dignity/Chicago, where nonordained members of the chapter lead the liturgy at all times, Dignity/Boston maintains the core ritualistic Catholic tradition of having an ordained male priest as either the principal or sole celebrant of its Masses. The roster of priests and all other organizational details pertaining to the liturgy and the chapter's other activities are controlled by chapter members. The principle of communal control is so well established and so at odds with what happens in traditional congregations, that it is easy to be taken aback by the custom of one of the regularly presiding priests, who just before beginning the Mass liturgy, thanks his fellow community members for inviting him back to preside.

Dignity/Boston's weekly Mass illustrates both the interpretive possibilities of Catholicism, and the tensions inherent in trying to enact an emancipatory Catholicism. Lay responsibility for the liturgy and chapter members' consciousness of the deliberativeness of their participation in Dignity means that members take seriously the doctrinal meanings and implications of what they are doing. In collectively creating "the body of Christ" from which they are officially excluded, participants work at demonstrating the legitimacy of both their Catholicism and their gay or lesbian identity. They accomplish this by innovatively working with and around the traditional Mass liturgy.

Presiding priests make subtle references throughout the Mass to "Christ's gay and lesbian brothers and sisters," and the generative values embodied in committed gay relationships are affirmed during sermons. One priest in particular makes a point of stressing the "worthiness" of participants to receive communion. This emphasis contrasts with the regular Mass liturgy (and the broader Catholic penitential tradition) wherein people acknowledge the unworthiness conferred by original sin by communally stating aloud: "Lord I am not worthy to receive you, but only say the word and I shall be healed." When, instead, Dignity participants state "Lord I am worthy to receive you," it is clear that they are not claiming a superiority over their coreligionists. Rather, they are using the liturgy to affirm the Catholic theological emphasis on the redemptive presence of a loving God in the world and in their lives.[4]

Underscoring lay involvement in the liturgy, Dignity's Masses frequently involve the innovative use of someone other than the presiding priest as the homilist during Mass who talks about the meanings of the day's scriptural readings. Invited homilists are usually chapter members, or less frequently visiting Dignity leaders from other chapters. Another notable way in which Dignity Masses differ from regular Masses is the reflective but not heavy-handed effort made by homilists to connect scriptural readings to the daily routines and challenges of

---

4. The *Catechism of the Catholic Church* (1994: 87) states, "The doctrine of original sin is, so to speak, the 'reverse side' of the Good News that Jesus is the Savior of all. . . ." Accordingly, Dignity's "I am worthy" may be seen as an affirmation of the reverse side of the doctrine of original sin (salvation) and not as the negation of original sin.

being gay or lesbian. These homilies, as many members emphasized, are experienced by the congregation as powerfully inspirational.

Pentecost Sunday occurs seven weeks after Easter Sunday and commemorates the descent of the Holy Spirit to the Apostles fearfully locked in a room as they await Christ's return to earth. In the course of my research, Dignity/Boston marked Pentecost as a special occasion deserving of six co-presiders: three women and two men in addition to one of the regular priest presiders. The Mass also included other special features, including an evocative spiritual dance by one of the women members designed "to welcome the Spirit." The celebration of pluralism signaled by the presence of six presiders on the altar and by the theological symbolism inherent in the scriptural account of a Holy Spirit speaking in many tongues was qualified somewhat by the homily given that day by another member, a woman in her early thirties. Her homily, while replete with hope, was also a gentle and sober reminder that people who are "different" must deal with the limits imposed on the enactment of pluralism. She said:

> "As I reflected on Pentecost and who the Holy Spirit is in my life, I thought of my own struggle to come out. I reflected on the relationship between my personal closet and the room where the Apostles hid. For me as for the Apostles, there were different levels of trust and coming out. As I look at my life, I can see where the Spirit worked to give me hope. As a young child and teenager I always felt different and as if I didn't fit in anywhere. I would read as much as I could about Jesus. I loved to hear of Jesus's compassion and love. During Jesus's life, the Apostles spent time with him. They learned of his love. As in my own life this was a safe place to be. Then Jesus asks for more. Always more. After Jesus's death the Apostles lived in fear. They hid in the room so as not to be found and hurt or killed. They lived in fear not knowing why they trusted. Not understanding fully Jesus's message. As I began to struggle with my own sexuality, I felt trapped in the darkness of my closet. I trusted Jesus and yet I felt alone. The message of Jesus was acceptance and love, yet I was taught growing up that what I felt was bad, not normal. . . . Yet something deep inside me kept me going. At the beginning of my coming out to myself, I lived in fear. . . . My coming out came when I truly trusted the Spirit within me. Only then could I speak the

words and come out of my own personal closet. This was only the beginning. It wasn't until the Holy Spirit entered the Apostles that they had the words to speak and the courage to come out. . . . The Spirit has given me the courage to come out and to risk being ridiculed and possibly abandoned. . . . When the Apostles received the Spirit they could come out of their room without fear. . . . Our stories are all quite different. But we wouldn't be here if the Spirit wasn't working within us. . . ."

As this homily suggests, the creation of a gay and lesbian Catholicism engages Dignity in systematically linking faith and sexuality and publicly affirming the boundlessness between them. Another way in which this task is accomplished is through Dignity's practice of celebrating same-sex couple relationships through commitment or what Dignity calls Holy Union ceremonies. These are ritually celebrated during the part of the Mass at which the sacrament of marriage occurs during regular Catholic Church weddings. Although commitment ceremonies are relatively infrequent at Dignity/Boston, one occurred during my study. With the theme of "walking in faith," Dignity celebrated the Holy Union of two men, both of whom are active members of the chapter.

When I arrived for the regularly scheduled 5:30 P.M. Mass at about 5:20, the chapel was already filled with people and the atmosphere had all the excitement and sense of anticipation that one associates with regular weddings. Ushers accompanied guests of the couple up to their seats in the front pews, while Dignity members who were not part of the immediate wedding party occupied the middle and back rows. After the opening song, the wedding party of four male witnesses walking in pairs followed by the male couple proceeded up the center aisle from the main door at the back of the church to the altar. The Mass was led by one of Dignity's regular priest members and it basically followed the standard wedding Mass liturgy. In his homily, the priest emphasized that God looks for ways to penetrate the cracks in people's lives and that relationships are one expression of God's love for people. While noting that some relationships are bad, the priest stressed that God blesses lasting committed same-gender relationships as holy unions just as he blesses male-female relationships. The priest concluded his homily by emphasizing that God is a God of love and of inclusiveness and diversity. Following the homily, prepared prayers were offered for other couples to have the courage to publicly affirm their commitment, for divorced couples, and for people who are vulnerable or economically disadvantaged. It was noteworthy that among the spontaneous prayers spoken by Dignity members, one offered thanksgiving for the public witness of love shown by the couple, and another echoed the prayer that other couples similarly make such a commitment. After these prayers, the couple exchanged vows to respect, love, care and to "be always there" for each other. The liturgy then continued through communion and at the end of Mass the congregation was invited downstairs for a light reception.

I did not see this commitment ceremony as an "exotic" practice; what was striking, rather, was the "normalcy" of the event, and the important symbolic role it played in affirming both the sacredness of same-sex couples and the sacramental power of communal life. In interviews and informal conversations with Dignity participants in the weeks after the ceremony, many people spoke about how much they personally valued witnessing the holy union and the hopefulness that it inspired in them that gay and lesbian couples were in fact as blessed as heterosexual couples. The positive excitement caused by the ceremony was in some respects surprising. Since many of the participants in Dignity are engaged in long-term relationships of several years duration (some of them have had or are planning to have commitment ceremonies of their own), "couples" are very much part of the Dignity community scene. On reflection, it seemed that what I had witnessed at the ceremony was the crystallization of the sacramental power of community. On the one hand, notwithstanding the division of the congregation during the ceremony between wedding guests and Dignity members, there was a very strong sense throughout the liturgy that the gathered community was united in blessing this couple and in commiting themselves to nurture them through their relationship in the times ahead. This precisely is what the sacrament of marriage is, in part, supposed to be about (even though many of the invitees at any given wedding ceremony may more likely comprise a group of relationally uninvolved individuals than an emotionally connected community). At the same time, demonstrating the reciprocity of communal life, the couple was not just receiving the blessings and support of the community. The two men's courage in publicly declaring their commitment to one another was in fact contributing to making the community stronger by formally demonstrating both the existence of committed relationships and, by extension, the necessity of nurturing community in order to facilitate individuals' quest for enriching social relationships.[5]

PRIDE SUNDAY

The mutuality between faith and sexuality and between individual and communal identity is also demonstrated at Dignity through the integration of gay and lesbian festival days into the liturgical calendar. Such events are celebrated as (what some members call them) "high-holy days." Coming-out Sunday, for example, is demarcated as a special Sunday in October to encourage gay and lesbian Catholics to come out and to affirm the coming-out decisions of others. A major event for the community is Pride Sunday, which marks the culmination of the annual national Gay Pride Week. In 1995, Pride Sunday coincided with Trinity Sunday, which celebrates Catholics' belief in the three persons of God (Father, Son, and Holy Spirit), one of the core elements of the Catholic faith. Several features of Dignity's Pride Sunday Mass highlighted how members routinely claim their dual identities as gay or lesbian Catholics. I will use this occasion to illustrate how Dignity participants redefine their marginal status in the church to one of entitled and committed ownership.

Participants' ownership of the Mass was signaled from the outset by the choice of the prelude hymn, "Open our hearts to know your wonder, open our eyes to see your truth," which was composed by one of Dignity/Boston's longtime members.[6] A colorful procession up the central aisle of the dark church marked the start of Mass. Members carried Dignity/Boston's rainbow banner embroidered with the slogan Praise God with Pride. They were accompanied by other members carrying a crucifix, pole streamers, and flags, who were followed by the two copresiders: a priest robed in regular Mass vestments, and a woman wearing a simple alb (a long white tunic). Before the formal prayers began one of the founding members of the chapter walked up to the altar and presented the priest presider, Frank, with a stole (a long, nar-

5. Since 1997, Dignity/USA has had a national Registry for Holy Unions formally documenting same-sex unions that meet its guidelines; and individual chapters, including Dignity/Boston, have set up a Couples' Ministry designed to support couples in committed relationships through various spiritual, educational, social, and ministerial/mentoring activities.

6. "Open Our Hearts" (Chris Connors). Copyright 1997, Perfect Blue Publishing. Reprinted with permission. Prophetsongs, P. O. Box, 1535, East Arlington, Mass. 02174.

row, scarf-like garment). What was symbolically significant about this stole was that it was not inscribed with the customary Catholic symbols of the cross or fish, for example, but embroidered with the rainbow colors of gay liberation, thus injecting new inclusionary meanings to the donning of a garment that customarily signifies the exclusive hierarchical status in the church of the male priest as the icon of Christ.[7]

The ways in which insignia can be appropriated from their customary setting and given a new meaning was further explicated in the priest's opening remarks. Frank began the Mass by commenting on the coincidence of Pride and Trinity, and noted that the Trinity was not very popular among some Christians on account of its male-centered symbolism. He then pointed to changes in the use of the triangle as an early symbol of the Trinity; he also observed how it had become transformed from a means of identifiying gays in Nazi Germany to its current use as a symbol of hope and pride for gays and lesbians.

As is the custom at Dignity/Boston, the two official, church-prescribed scriptural passages for the day were read respectively by a man and a woman and were followed by the responsorial psalm. The readings were accompanied by a spiritual dance performed by one of the women members, a relatively recent innovative practice found in some other Catholic churches on special-occasion Masses. The gospel book was then carried in dance fashion up and down the central aisle and brought back to the two co-presiders, Frank and Miriam, who stood in the middle of the aisle as they jointly read aloud the Gospel. Following this reading, and underscoring the attempt to make co-presiding a shared activity notwithstanding the different "sacred" statuses of the two co-presiders, it was Miriam who gave a very brief homily.

Miriam remarked that the feast of Trinity brought together for her the mixture of Easter and Pentecost that she saw converging – using the feminine pronoun for God – in "a celebration by God of Her gift to us." Emphasizing that God's gift was a "celebration of truth, sexuality, the body, and community," Miriam stressed how important it was for Dignity to be a supportive community. In the spirit of building community and to celebrate Pride, three members of Dignity (as had been previously arranged) then shared with the rest of the gathering what Pride means to them personally.

7. Extending the inclusivity of this gesture, members attending the Dignity/USA 1997 national convention in Boston, received similar rainbow-colored stoles.

The first person to tell a "Pride story" was Joe, a man in his early twenties who had been out for about two and a half years. Joe said that he found it difficult to find a story to explain Pride and could only think of "snippets" such as his nervousness riding the subway going to Boston's South End for fear of violence against gays, or moments of difficulty in acknowledging his homosexuality to others. These snippets, Joe said, reminded him of how important it is to stand up for his sexuality and to reach out to others who may be scared and who need to know that there is a supportive community for them.

The next person who spoke was Susan, a middle-aged woman who highlighted two occasions of Pride that stood out in her life. What was so moving about Susan's story was that the personal events selected simultaneously highlighted the transformation in her personal journey and the changed but enduring depth of her Catholic commitment. Susan's first experience had been sixteen years ago when she had celebrated her profession as a nun, and the second had been two and a half years ago, when she had come out as a Catholic lesbian.

The third storyteller was a middle-aged ex-priest named Peter. He related going to his rector before he was to be ordained and telling him that he was gay and "not worthy" of ordination. The rector, nevertheless, told him he was worthy, and so Peter was ordained. Having "laid low" for several years fearing he would be "found out," Peter eventually came out in the early 1970s but found that he still had fears as a gay man. Even today, he said, there are times when he is nervous about wearing gay insignia; but he related an anecdote of a chance encounter with a lesbian woman on public transport which reminded him of the importance of visible gay symbols in creating bonds among gay and lesbian strangers.

All the storytellers received very warm spontaneous applause from the congregation when they told their Pride stories. At the conclusion of the three stories, there was a standing ovation, and Miriam went to each of the three storytellers at their seats and hugged them. Although the stories shared by members were a departure in content from the parables related in scripture or frequently told in homilies as a way of illustrating Christian virtues, the morals of the Pride stories bore a striking resemblance to the morals of scriptural stories, with their emphasis on the importance of honesty, courage, truth, and community. What was different about the stories told at Dignity was not just their "gay" content or the fact that they were told by community participants rather than by the priest. Their powerful charge was enhanced by their grounding in the raw reality of participants' experiences and the immediate concrete salience of the individual stories to almost all of the people listening.

As in regular Masses, this portion of the Pride Sunday Mass was followed by the "prayers of the faithful." Rather than using the recommended official church prayers, Dignity used prayers that, as is the chapter's custom, were prepared by one of the members of its liturgy committee. Continuing to distinguish the different identity of the gathered community, Dignity's formal prayers were offered for the homophobic, for lonely men in bars, and for people to have courage to come out. Spontaneous prayers spoken from the congregation further underscored the shared identity of the community participants: one comparatively older man prayed for the memory of his parents, whom he said couldn't help being homophobic. Prayers were also offered for those who marched in the Pride parade on the preceding Saturday, and for the delegates to Dignity's upcoming convention. At the same time, other prayers pointed to the "normalcy" of the people present in the sense that they were similar to what might be heard during the spontaneous prayer portion at any Catholic Mass. One person prayed for a sick mother, another for someone who had died of AIDS; a man who said that his son and daughter-in-law were expecting their second baby, prayed that he would be a good grandfather.

Following the prayers of the faithful, the congregation joined the choir in singing another hymn composed by the same member whose song had been featured at the outset of the Mass. Titled "Prophets to the World," it spoke about themes that gave resounding expression to the sense and aspirations of the people gathered: "Trusting a God of Justice . . . Trusting a God of Freedom . . . Speaking from our pain. Living a life with justice will finally break our chains. Trusting a God who loves us, we speak our truth to all. Transcending fear and hatred to answer the Gospel call. Celebrate our promise! Celebrate with Pride! Together we share a power that cannot be denied."[8]

Appropriately, the high point of communality was during the "offertory prayer," the time of Mass which affirms the shared "communality" of all Catholics and commemorates Christ's Last Supper with the consecration of the Eucharist. All the people present assembled around

8. "Prophets to the World" (Chris Connors). Copyright 1997, Perfect Blue Publishing. Reprinted with permission. Prophetsongs, P.O. Box 1535, East Arlington, Mass. 02174.

the altar rather than staying in the pews and joined hands for "Table-prayer," a collectively sung version of an offertory prayer.[9] At the con-secration, Frank held up the bread, and just as a "normal" concelebrant male priest at a regular Catholic Mass would have done, Miriam then held up the chalice as they both spoke aloud the words of consecration.

A gender-inclusive language version of the "Our father" beginning "Our father/mother who art in heaven" preceded the distribution of communion, which was given out by eucharistic ministers from the chapter. Another touch demonstrating the inclusivity of Dignity's practices was the provision of "consecrated" grape juice instead of wine for any communicants who had an alcohol problem. With grape juice instead of wine, they could still mimic receiving the "body and blood of Christ" as intended by the transubstantiation of the bread and wine effected during the consecration. As is the practice at most American Catholic Masses today and at Dignity's Masses, almost all of the approximately eighty people present on Pride Sunday received com-munion.

Before the blessing at the end of Mass, as is customary at Dig-nity/Boston and at many other Catholic Masses, a member of the board welcomed visitors and newcomers and announced upcoming events. The Mass then concluded with the singing of "City of God" with its joyously commanding tones exhorting people to seize a new en-lightened reality.[10] At the conclusion of Mass, as is the practice at Dignity/Boston and at some regular Catholic Masses, about one-third of the people went downstairs to the church basement for refreshments and informal conversation.

THE CHARISMA OF CATHOLIC COMMUNALITY

Dignity's use of a Protestant rather than a Catholic church underscores the fact that gay and lesbian Catholics are objectively excluded from the official church. Yet as I hope my account of Dignity's Pride Sunday Mass illustrates, it is evident that Dignity participants continue to experience the charisma of belonging to the broader Catholic doctri-nal tradition. They demonstrate their ownership of Catholic iden-

9. "Tableprayer: God of Life and of the Living" (Michael Joncas). Copyright 1988, G.I.A. Publications Inc., 7404 South Mason Avenue, Chicago, Ill. 60638.
10. "City of God" (Dan Schutte, S. J.). Copyright 1981, North American Liturgy Resources, 10802 North Twenty-third Avenue, Phoenix, Ariz. 85029.

tity by reworking the ritualistic and sacramental elements of Catholicism. By experimenting with the symbolic resources of Catholicism, Dignity members forge a meaningful representation of their gay and lesbian Catholic identity. For Dignity participants, worshipping together is experienced as something "extraordinary" and "transcendent"; it is not, as Peter Berger (1992: 96) might argue, a politicized redefining of worship as simply "a gathering of ordinary people enjoying the experience of community."

As is indicated by their holding of a weekly Sunday Mass that is customarily celebrated by a priest, Dignity members want to preserve the Catholic sacramental tradition. Further highlighting its maintenance of traditional church practices, during most of its Masses Dignity/Boston upholds the physical intrachurch segregation between the priest in the altar area and the people in the pews. Moreover, notwithstanding the democratic intent of having nonordained members preside during some Masses, they too wear an alb or some other insignia to indicate their different status during the liturgy. Unlike many of the women associate pastors interviewed by Ruth Wallace (1992: 130–132) in her study of priestless parishes, Dignity members value the visibility of "priestly" distinctions, even though those distinctions are being attached in some cases to nonordained presiders, and more frequently to priests who no longer have official approval to celebrate Mass.

Paralleling the strategic value of presenting an essentialist understanding of sexuality, Dignity participants would also seem to have a strategic interest in publicly embracing the institutionalized symbols of the Mass. Not to maintain the Mass's distinctive characteristics could be taken as indicating tacit acknowledgment that what they are doing is "not really" Catholic and never could be authentically Catholic, since in official church teaching their status as active gays or lesbians contradicts their Catholicism.

While maintaining several of the traditional symbols of Catholicism, Dignity participants reconstruct such symbols and practices to give public recognition to their shared identity as gay and lesbian Catholics. The use of openly gay priests and women co-presiders, invited homilists from within the community, gay- and gender-inclusive images, language, and themes throughout the traditional Mass liturgy, the sacramental celebration of same-sex "holy unions," and the recentering of personal "healing" as integral to Catholic communal life, serve as examples of how Dignity recombines into a new synthesis the traditional practices of Catholicism with ones that make room for and affirm the multiple identities of its participants. Dignity Masses thus enact a communality where the overwhelming message conveyed is that their sacramental celebrations are very much in the Durkheimian (1912/1976: 206–214) understanding of an organically connected com munity worshipping, in part, the sanctity of its communal solidarity. Dignity preserves what it considers to be the fixed symbols and mean- ings of Catholic faith and communal memory, but simultaneously injects them with new understandings that are in tune with the reali- ty of being gay or lesbian and Catholic. In its practical ability to rec- ognize emergent possibilities from within the Catholic tradition, Dignity constantly testifies to the fact that the "communities of mem- ory that tie us to the past also turn us toward the future as communi- ties of hope" (Bellah et al. 1985: 153).

Experimenting with being an inclusive "community of hope" is, as I will discuss, not without its conflicts and tensions. It is evident, nonetheless, that members experience participation in Dignity as emancipatory insofar as it collapses the boundaries between their mul- tiple identities and destigmatizes their "difference." Dignity partici- pants are empowered to worship as a "lifestyle community" while simultaneously remaining connected to a broader doctrinal tradition of which they are critically self-conscious and appreciative. Many of the Dignity survey respondents emphasized that participation in Dignity provides them with the communal context in which they can cele- brate their sexuality and their Catholicism. One professional woman in her late thirties said that Dignity is "a community that feeds my faith and sense of self." Another respondent stated that Dignity "offered an affirming space where my faith and sexuality are affirmed – a community that validates my same-sex relationship." A woman who converted to Catholicism from a fundamentalist church before she joined Dignity stated: "For me Dignity is a place of healing, a place of refreshment. . . . it is a place to celebrate being Catholic, being spiri- tual and lesbian. . . . it is with gratitude to Dignity that I have been empowered to live my life as a Catholic woman and lesbian."

Other respondents spoke more generally about the impact of the "power of community" in Dignity on their self-acceptance and person- al growth. One man stated, "I was affirmed, embraced and accepted for who I was, all of me, and it was a community." Another younger man who is involved in a relationship and has been an active member of Dignity for over six years said: "It is a community that for me is an invaluable source of strength, comfort and joy in my life." Several other interviewees variously said they valued Dignity's "sense of community," its "open affirming community," and the fact that it provides "a safe space." Some respondents who had stopped attending Dignity liturgy for a while but then returned, said that they "really missed the sense of community." As one older college-educated man emphasized, he returned because Dignity provides "the sense of community that I don't seem to be able to find in other areas of my life."

Other participants discussed Dignity as the context in which they could be "home" in communion with other Catholics. As one woman in her early thirties expressed this: "I needed to find 'home' again where my lifestyle was accepted by a Catholic community." Another professional woman in her early forties, who said that she did not necessarily agree or feel comfortable with every aspect of Dignity, was nonetheless adamant that "this is truly my first church 'home' and I am very grateful for its existence." While the metaphor of "returning home" suggests warm images of connectedness and security, some participants also commented on the pain and vulnerability associated with Catholicism as "home," and how Dignity helps them to reclaim a trusting security. One woman whom I interviewed discussed the positive and negative experiences of growing up Catholic, and reflected on the new pluralistic sense of identity that she was forging:

"And so, you know, church has both meant something that has been safe and something that has been incredibly rejecting and abusive. . . . I went to a Catholic high school and I had a very difficult time negotiating the fact that I knew my sexuality was different, and I think at that time I experienced a deep fracture. In that sense, I live with the belief that the opportunity to go home again is there in the church but at the same time I live with this very haunting voice that always says, 'Be very careful because the people in whom you trust in the church are the ones who can hurt you the most with their policies.' . . . So the church is a place that I'm incredibly committed to and incredibly frightened of. And that's a hard tension to hold. . . . And I think, you know, it's taken me a while to sort of get rid of my mother's voice or my father's voice in the background saying, 'You know, if you're a Catholic and you don't play by all the rules, then you're not really a Catholic.' I've had to undo a lot of that stuff and say, 'That's not true.' But it's only in the last few years that I've gotten that enthusiasm, that sense of security and confidence back. And it's creeping back. It's a lot better than it was. And so I can own the identity differently."

As the above comments suggest, Dignity/Boston models the owning of multiple identities that reconcile particularistic claims with claims to participation in a larger communal tradition without negating the validity of either. Rather than presenting as contradictory identities, being gay or lesbian and Catholic becomes unproblematic, especially during the seventy minutes or so of Dignity's Mass when the boundaries between both identities are dismantled and "forgotten." The emancipatory charge that can accompany this sense of the seamlessness or "naturalness" of multiple identities was expressed by several Dignity participants. One woman, for example, although she has been out for many years at work and to her family, said that Dignity's Mass "is the place where I really forget that I'm out – I feel so comfortable." A man who grew up in a very accepting Catholic family, has been out for fourteen years, and is involved in many social activities expressed a similar sentiment. He commented: "I've always felt like an outsider in many organizations and in many situations even growing up and I think it might be typical of growing up gay that you always feel like an outsider. And Dignity's the first time where I don't feel like an outsider."

Another member, an ex-priest, explained how the process of involvement in Dignity was transformative for him:

"It was hard for me to get to know people in the community because coming through those doors for the first time was a big step for me, and going downstairs afterward for coffee was a bigger step. . . . And there were times when I kind of just stood there and felt very isolated. It was somewhat awkward and painful. You know I wasn't sure how to talk and act as a gay person who had come out and was in a community with other gay people. So it took me a while to find my way, find my own particular style of doing that. What was most comforting to me I think was the sacramental part. The preaching particularly was very clear in terms of encouraging me and allowing me to integrate my spirituality and my sexuality. And I think that that was the biggest contribution made to my life in terms of change, was hearing that message from the puplit in a community of gay and lesbian persons. . . . It was a message that I didn't preach a lot myself [when I was a priest]. I mean when I was beginning to come out before I left the priesthood from time to time I would mention the word gay or lesbian in my homily, usually in the context of being inclusive and respecting the dignity of other people. But never forcefully. And I found that one of the big obstacles for me in my priesthood was there was this big gap in my spirituality because I was good at preaching and I could make others feel comfortable with their spirituality but there was this big gap in mine where I could only take myself so far. And then I'd bump into this thing called being gay and I cringed. I couldn't figure out how all that fit together. . . . Dignity helped me to rework my own spirituality and my own images of God. I was able to pull a lot of things together in my life and work toward a sense of integrity and wholeness in my spirituality."

A woman who at college had been very involved in Catholic activities, described the emancipatory impact of her initial experience of Dignity:

"The second week that I went there, XX was presiding and after the Eucharistic prayer he said to people, 'I want you to really watch your negatives, because, you know, the church really teaches us that we're not worthy and tonight when you say this I want you to say "I am worthy." ' And I just started to cry because it was the first time that anybody had ever said that. And that to me was my most profound invitation to be at Dignity and it didn't have to do directly with my being lesbian. It had to do with me being called as a sort of an equal member that was okay. And I felt like aside from being gay, it was just like maybe I can be a spiritual person and have a spiritual community. And that has always been a cornerstone of what Dignity is to me. . . . My family infused me with this kind of Irish-Catholic stuff that *you're not worthy and you're not worthy* [emphasis hers]. You have to really work hard to earn somebody's love or respect or tolerance or whatever. And the fact that you don't have to earn it, that it's there, and it was done for you by Jesus, that's very powerful and I can't understand why we don't, why the church doesn't espouse that because that to me is one of the most incredible gifts of Christianity. It doesn't mean that you're not humble, that you're not in awe because I think you can be very reverential and very in awe without saying you're bad and not worthy."

Other respondents elaborated on their participation in Dignity by emphasizing what they considered to be Dignity's prophetic role in bridging the diversity within the larger Catholic community in an inclusive and people-centered way. One woman, a committed feminist who is very active in Dignity, explained her continuing participation in the church:

" . . . the image I think I hold onto the most, and I don't mean this in a self-aggrandizing way but I mean it because it gives me great hope, is to think about the image of a prophet and I think about that because it comforts me to know that the people who have had wisdom and who have been gifted to speak have often been those who have not been accepted in their communities or their homes, at least not well until after they died. There's so much we need to hear from people like that. I believe in prophets these days. I believe that they're there and if I'm really honest with myself I believe in some ways that perhaps I might be one of those prophets in the sense of trying to stay faithful to witnessing when its very difficult to do that and finding ways to work in the system and around it. . . . the church is about relationships, communal relationships. Not independent relationships, but communal relationships that involve reverencing whatever is sacred. And cultivating that and sharing that and rejoicing in that. And that's where my heart is. That's how we, thank God, have managed to create the environment at Dignity. . . . And as a religious community, Dignity/Boston I think is interested in belonging to ourselves and also to the larger church. And in order to do both I think that there are ways in which we have to pay attention to our own spiritual needs and take risks and break free from the institution, but we need to do it also with an appreciation for our need to be connected and to belong to a larger community, to people who share our faith. And so I think we need to do that carefully. And I think we see that reflected in the liturgy because there's a way in which we tend to our own spiritual needs really well and other ways in which I think we sometimes need to sacrifice those needs to feel a sense of belonging to the larger church. But I see those as important, both of those. And they may at times be competing needs. But I think that we have a need like so many of us do to be connected and to be independent at the same time."

Another woman said:

"I am sometimes really taken aback by how many people really struggle to be part of the church. I mean I consider us [Dignity] Catholics but I consider us Catholics in the more universal sense. . . . If the Pope wrote an encyclical tomorrow and said it was okay to be sexually active with a gay person, I think that a lot of people would go back to the parish and leave Dignity. And for me it's really different. It's taken on a life of its own for me. It isn't just that it's okay for me to be with my partner there. It's really about a way to look at my spirituality and my faith in a way that is more, it seems to be, more true and more searching and more prophetic and more the kind of thing I think that we're called to be as Catholics in the most ideal sense. And I don't mean to sound disrespectful of the institution or the Vatican but I think that I don't like it when we place dogma and institution and the hierarchy above the principles of the faith and social justice. . . ."

The foregoing comments suggest that the Dignity/Boston community succeeds in integrating participants' identities as gay or lesbian Catholics so that they can feel not only "at home" and in a "safe space," but personally and communally empowered to see their identities as having emancipatory possibilities for personal and institutional transformation. The process of negotiating ownership of a gay or lesbian Catholic identity confronts members with the challenge of interrogating and reinterpreting Catholicism's symbolic resources while retaining its "sacred meanings." In creating and maintaining an egalitarian and inclusive "community of hope" that affirms their sexuality and their Catholicism, participants are challenged to build a transformative community that still remains faithful to what they understand to be the communal memory of Catholicism. This task engages Dignity participants in an ongoing and often contested conversation about the boundaries of an authentic Catholicism. Members' deliberations become most sharply focused when they seek to craft practices that express the communal identity that participants perceive to be collec-

tively theirs. It is to the challenges of trying to institutionalize emancipatory practices that I now turn.

TENSIONS IN THE INSTITUTIONALIZATION OF EMANCIPATORY PRACTICES

As its principal community activity, Dignity's Mass can easily be
come a site of contested meanings. The organization of the structure
and content of Dignity's Mass is the responsibility primarily of the
chapter's elected ten-member liturgy committee. At the time of my
research, the committee's monthly meetings were held in different
members' homes over pot-luck dinners; since late August 1995 they
have been held in Dignity's new office suite. One of the committee's
main items of discussion is the selection of presiders, and whether to
have co-presiders and invited homilists for a set number of forthcom-
ing liturgies. The choice of readers and Eucharistic ministers is more
routine given their less controversial role in the traditional Mass structure.

The liturgy committee is faced with the difficult task of constructing a Mass that dismantles the exclusionary boundaries of the official
church in order to mirror more closely what Dignity participants
regard as the inclusivity of Christ. Most notably, then, in addition to
official church teaching on homosexuality, the church's gender-based
inequality cannot be reproduced in Dignity's justice-oriented "model
community." As articulated in Dignity's statement of purpose, members "dedicate" themselves to "work toward the eradication of all constraints on our personhood based on the ascribed roles of women and
men." For almost all of the women in Dignity/Boston, and for the
majority of its men, Dignity's theoretical commitment to gender equality has to be in evidence throughout its community practices.[11]
Particularly for many women members, ownership of Catholic identity demands a radical integration of faith, sexuality, *and* gender. The
feminist slogan that "the personal is political" means that the sacraments, as one woman stated, should not be "used as weapons" but as
"important symbols of life and growth and how we think." How
Dignity deals with women's representation in its sacramental life is

11. As an indicator of this sentiment, in personal interviews with Dignity participants, all but one of the thirteen women and all but four of the thirteen men
emphasized the personal importance to them of the fact that Dignity strives to
affirm an egalitarian ethic in its practices.

thus an ongoing source of underlying tension in the community, and it also means that women and men in Dignity are, to some extent, negotiating two different sorts of "gay" Catholic identity.

Establishing gender-inclusive practices is difficult. Underscoring the challenges involved in realizing emancipatory ideals, at Dignity/Boston the possibility of "normalizing" women's equality with men is shadowed both by its members' perceptions of the limits of Catholicism and by the chapter's own historical memory of earlier attempts to be more gender-inclusive. Dignity/Boston experienced a major conflict among members in the mid to late 1980s over gender inclusivity that has continued to inhibit the experimental tendencies of the chapter. As members retrospectively describe the conflict, it was basically a power struggle between "feminists," who were pushing for gender-inclusive language, women presiders, and specially focused women's liturgies, and "traditionalists," who resisted such initiatives as threatening to the authenticity of a Catholic Mass. The conflict was not resolved amicably. To the contrary, many traditionalists left Dignity, choosing instead to worship at one of the downtown Boston parishes that are relatively welcoming of gays and lesbians. Some of those who left did so apparently with bitterness, as they had been instrumental in establishing the chapter and had a strong sense of ownership over its identity.

The experience of community conflict and the fragmentation occasioned by the defections during the late 1980s is a critical story in Dignity/Boston's history. It functions as a cautionary reminder to the current membership, many of whom joined after the early 1990s and consequently did not witness the conflict first hand, that the strength of their created community is quite fragile. A genuine sadness and regret is notably evident when members who were active in pushing for change, and who sincerely believe in the rightness of their feminist case, reflect upon the experience. The enduring "chilling effect" of the past communal fracture on innovation in current liturgical practices is evident in the deliberations of the elected liturgy committee. At the two liturgy committee meetings that I attended, the committee's overarching concern was to avoid giving cause for divisiveness among the membership as a result of the Mass liturgies they planned.

Dignity's priests, as noted earlier, preside at the invitation of the liturgy committee, and most of them are also regular gay members of the chapter. Consequently, while they are well respected by the membership on account of their pastoral and spiritual "gifts" (as Dignity participants frequently refer to members' talents), they do not have the comparatively privileged status and leadership role that priests in parishes traditionally enjoy. Nonetheless, the chapter has a fairly stable roster of presiding priests, and the committee and the membership as a whole seem appreciative of the different "gifts" each priest brings to his role. Rather than displacing priests as the principal celebrants of the Mass in favor of a lay-led liturgy, the ethos among the membership appears to favor ordained priests. In this regard, Dignity/Boston is more conservative than some chapters such as Dignity/Chicago, where lay-led liturgies are customary.

The preoccupation of Dignity participants with both the boundaries of "the traditional Mass" and sustaining connection with the larger church means that members' reservations about moving toward a lay-led liturgy help to constrain the liberal tendencies of those on the liturgy committee. At one committee meeting, for example, in discussing the roster of priests for the fall, it emerged that there was no priest available to preside on two Sundays. One committee member suggested having a lay-led liturgy on the two Sundays in question. She defended her idea by appealing to the communal emphasis of Dignity, stating that she didn't "feel comfortable when we have presiders who just pop in on an ad hoc basis." Although others present seemed to share her sentiment, the response adopted was amazingly attentive to the "juridical" constraints on the committee. One person, for example, was quite adamant that the decision would have to "go through the [member elected Dignity/Boston] board," and another emphasized that "all the potential priests would definitely have to be unable to preside." The committee then discussed how great it would be to have occasional lay-led liturgies, but agreed that the time may not yet be ripe to "open the community to it." As one member noted, "We have promised them [the members] that we would talk about it with the community first. . . . We have given our word to the community that we are listening to them." The committee thus agreed on the need to plan a survey of how members felt about the possibility of some lay-led liturgies and to organize educational and "listening" evenings to discuss the issue.

"Listening nights" are used by Dignity on a fairly regular basis to provide members with an opportunity to express their views and to hear other people's concerns about potentially divisive issues. Dignity's listening nights demonstrate, as Wood and Bloch (1995) have also shown, that issues that are controversial for religious organizations can

be discussed with civility and in a manner that further binds participants as a "community of discourse." Two listening nights were organized early in the summer of 1995 to discuss proposed motions for
Dignity's upcoming national convention. Their purpose was to provide
the four elected women delegates from Boston with a "sense" of how
the membership felt about motions proposed by other chapters that
would be discussed and voted upon at the convention. During these
democratically structured "listening" sessions, which took place after
evening Mass in the church basement, chapter members were encouraged by the moderator to "talk about what they feel about the issue"
rather than focus on the specific wording of the proposed motions.

During the first listening night, discussion centered around a
motion proposing that all ceremonial roles in Dignity liturgies should
be reserved for ordained priests. After preliminary comments about the
upcoming convention and the various motions, the members in attendance broke into six small discussion groups with about eight members
at each table and discussed this and two related motions for about
twenty-five minutes. For some groups, including the group of six
women I sat with, the issue seemed straight-forward, as there was a
strong consensus that lay-led liturgies should be the practice at
Dignity. For other groups it was evident that the question was somewhat more controversial. Participants at one table, for instance, had an
engaged discussion about the role of ministry in general at Dig-
nity/Boston. At the end of the group conversations, one participant
from each table shared the table's consensus with the rest of the gathering, and this was followed by an open and courteous exchange of
views. There was clearly a diversity of opinion among the participants
in the discussion, with many strongly disagreeing with restrictions on
ceremonial roles and others endorsing the view that Dignity practices
should maintain parity with official church practices. One man, in particular, took a negative view of the changes that might be wrought by
women presiders, but overall there was not a clear gender division in
the views presented. Although it was evident that the diverse opinions
expressed were strongly felt, the participants spoke in a nonaggressive
tone and behaved courteously toward one another. Nonetheless, the
moderator, indicating the importance members attach to civil discussion, reminded members that they "should speak in turn and be
respectful of other people's opinions."

The consensus that emerged favored greater communal equality in
ceremonial roles. The dominant view was that if the motion in ques-

tion were endorsed, it would eliminate Dignity/Boston's occasional practice of using co-presiders (as seen at the Pentecost and Pride liturgies). Additionally, several women pointed out that if the motion were endorsed it would also eliminate the women's liturgy. Women's liturgies involve about twelve women members who meet together on a monthly basis at different participants' homes to share a liturgy based on a selection of scriptural and/or nonscriptural readings, prayers and poetry, and an (objectively nonconsecrated) bread-breaking ceremony celebrating their communal friendship. Participants, as several whom I interviewed stressed, find the women's liturgies "really nourishing" spiritually.

Two other related motions discussed were whether Dignity should ordain its own members as priests, and whether a task force should be set up to study the question of a priestly ministry which would be less hierarchical than the current official church system. Most participants agreed with the idea of a task force, but several expressed reservations about its mandate and structure. Highlighting the democratic culture of the chapter, some members pointed out that ministry was a broad issue and encompassed tasks other than those associated with priests. These speakers stressed that it was important to maintain the diverse ministries in the chapter that drew on the talents of several members. In a similarly democratic vein, other participants raised questions about the composition of the task force and suggested that it should not be weighted toward "expert" members who had previously, for example, been nuns or priests.

The issue of Dignity ordaining its own priests was the most controversial motion. In the discussion that occurred, several women and men disagreed with ruling out Dignity's possible future ordination of clergy. They argued that this was too definite a step that if endorsed would preclude Dignity from action on the question in the future. One woman suggested that since Dignity was "already in violation of the Roman Catholic tradition . . . with its women's house Masses and special liturgies, that maybe we should ordain our own people." Another woman took a different view, suggesting that if Dignity took this step it might alienate current and potential members from Dignity. She said that in view of the fact that previous members had resigned because they already found Dignity "too radical," for Dignity to ordain its own priests would "really shut the door." Although this member said that she personally favored the ordination of women in the Catholic Church, she argued that for Dignity to do this "would be making a stand to seize power and keep people out," an option with which she thus currently disagreed. At the same time, she stressed her hope that "Dignity would continue to be prophetic" without necessarily taking this radical step.

In a subsequent interview, a woman member who was opposed to Dignity ordinations elaborated on some of the practical implications if Dignity were in fact to ordain "its own people." She argued:

> "We have to have a definition of ordination. It's a contract – if you look at all my friends who are priests, they basically promise to give their life to the church, and the church promises to take care of them. Can Dignity do this? We need to be really clear about what we mean when we say that we will ordain our own people. It makes a very powerful statement. . . . Ordination is not our only beef with the church. Roman clergy cannot marry, some dioceses will accept gay priests and others won't. In general, they ignore who has the call and who has the gift."

It was this interviewee's assessment that most members were not ready to accept the legitimacy of a Mass celebrated by a nonordained priest. She elaborated: "the community is not at the point where we are ready to have a Sunday Eucharist without a priest, except maybe for the annual liturgy in celebration of women and then some members [a few men and one or two women], because they know in advance, will also go to a regular Mass." She welcomed nonetheless the fact that members in Boston and nationally were talking about the issue. She stated:

> "We avoided talking about presiders for a long time. . . . We have a lot of talking and education to do, not brainwashing. So we know where we all are and what we are talking about. Many members are not ready to lose having the priest. At the convention [Los Angeles 1995] people who were ex-religious [ex-priests or ex-nuns] were more liberal on the presider issue than the rest of us. Even at Dignity, the 'laity' I think are still not used to feeling empowered after their years in the pews."

Dignity's negotiation of its commitment to be an inclusive community while maintaining its Catholic identity finds an uneasy balance in its occasional practice of using nonordained members as co-presiders accompanying the ordained priest. The use of co-presiders is controversial, and some of the questions that it raises transcend the issue of gender. Since many members have strong reservations about the use of co-presiders, the liturgy committee, in its restrained push toward change, schedules co-presiders on an intermittent rather than a weekly basis. Currently, the overall commitment of Dignity/Boston to gender inclusivity means that when there is a co-presider it is most usually a woman who is chosen to "balance" the male priest. Independent of who the co-presider is, some members believe that a co-presider should not be on the altar at the same time as the priest during the portion of the Mass when the Eucharist is consecrated. One woman reported that a couple of years before when she was co-presiding, the priest asked her to join with him in speaking aloud the actual words of consecration, which she did. This took the Mass participants by complete surprise and offended some in attendance who believed it violated the validity of the sacrament. According to the co-presider, she got "raked over the coals" by the liturgy committee for doing something they had not approved.

Although many Catholics have a somewhat vague understanding of what they believe actually happens at the consecration, they nonetheless understand it is a "sacred" rite. The sacred meanings that people inject into it vary. For some, as for this woman who co-presided, the sacredness comes from the fact that the whole liturgy and the communal presence of the people gathered "transforms the Eucharist." For others, the sanctity of the Eucharist is derived from the specific words of consecration stated by the ordained priest. Notwithstanding the different meanings Catholics attach to the Eucharist, for many participants at Dignity/Boston the use of gender-inclusive liturgical language and co-presiders are important minimal expressions both of the communal values of the Mass and the chapter's commitment to gender inclusivity.

But even with the use of gender-inclusive language, which is customary at Dignity/Boston, people occasionally slip back into the male version of the liturgical prayers. At one of the Masses I attended, for example, the priest made a faux pas, stating "Through him, with him, and in him," instead of "Through Christ, with Christ and in Christ." He immediately apologized for his "mistake," stating that old habits die hard. While such a slip-up is quite understandable, it also underlines the symbolic hurdles involved in dismantling gender boundaries and what some women see as the deep-rooted "naturalness" of the gender exclusivity in some Dignity practices.

One woman, Anna, talked about the theological resistance among some members over gender-inclusive liturgy and music. She said that what she finds offensive is "the implication that the power of God, that being saved, only comes through being male. And I just don't believe that. To say that, 'well Jesus was a male, so it's okay' is really being offensive. It's still connecting in a real serious way the saving power of Jesus to being male. And that wasn't his saving power. His saving power was his relationship to God." Many women, in particular, believe that unless the church hierarchy changes its opposition to women priests, some Dignity members will continue to resist changes at Dignity that give women a more central role in liturgical celebrations. Some of the women interviewed expressed their frustration and personal pain over what they see as their fellow members' reproduction of the church hierarchy's view of women's sacramental unworthiness. As Anna argued:

> "Many of the men sort of just don't get it. They say that it's not about feminism. They say we love you but don't mess with the Eucharist. . . I think there's a fair amount of men at Dignity who if the church changes its stance on homosexuality, they're back in. That's all they need. That's their only issue with the church. Whereas for most of the women, because we're women and because we're lesbian, this is not just about being gay. It's a whole avenue of justice issues and that's where we are hit because for them it's not about claiming Eucharist, it's about being accepted as gay. If we get that everything else is hunky dory. You know that's it. . . . I just think that the question of sexuality is so linked with the sexism in the church that you cannot separate them and I just don't think the guys get that at all."

For Anna, participation in the monthly women's liturgy provides a "women-owned space" wherein the participants are able to "let go of the power of the connection to Christ the man." Yet she also values and wants to be part of the regular Dignity community Mass because she sees it as an important public context wherein gay and lesbian Catholics can worship together and affirm their connection to the larger Catholic tradition. Thus she attends Dignity on a fairly regular basis, even though on some days there, she said, "I feel like I'm a betrayer or something," because the Mass reminds her that she is participating in the sexism of a "male church."

Quite apart from gender issues, the difficulties of trying to be an inclusive community are also illustrated by the selection of co-presiders and invited homilists from within the community. This practice raises questions concerning the "credentials" of the people chosen. If the priesthood is a vocation given by Christ, who really is "called"? And why should model "egalitarian" communities such as Dignity reproduce the meritocratic structure of the larger church and society? Such questions go to the heart of challenging official church practices while simultaneously trying to maintain the validity of a Catholic Mass that is recognizable both to members and to outsiders. Although members want to be inclusive, this does not necessarily mean that "anything goes" and that everybody is equally qualified or suited to being a co-presider or a homilist.

Although most of the priests associated with Dignity do not object to co-presiders, some do not like yielding their homily time to an invited homilist on the grounds that they value the homily as a pastoral opportunity to share their understanding of the scriptural readings. In addition, many members are critical when invited homilists give a homily unrelated to scripture or use the opportunity to make what some participants regard as a "political speech." How to include more voices from the community in the Mass liturgy while ensuring that a certain standard of "professionalism" is maintained is thus a dilemma both for the liturgy committee and for some members, who themselves would like to be more actively involved in leading the liturgy. The fact that some members believe that they have a vocation to preside can lead to feelings of exclusion and cause misunderstandings between members if such people are not asked or are asked only sporadically to co-preside. The infrequency with which co-presiders are featured and the relatively large pool of talented members available means that choosing co-presiders from within the community is fraught with tension.

Unlike priests who come to Dignity already ordained, co-presiders have to be chosen in the absence of explicit guidelines as to the qualities and qualifications of the person sought. The relative arbitrariness of who is chosen and how frequently they are asked to preside means that the co-presider has an ambiguous status that, while in keeping with the democratic nature of the chapter, can become politicized or personalized for a variety of reasons. Since the larger context involves the question of the co-presider's legitimacy in an "authentic" Catholic liturgy, co-presiding can become a lightning rod for intrachapter tensions. These may be further exacerbated if the co-presiders are identified as "feminist" and thus seen by some members as undermining Dignity's integration with the official church.

One co-presider is Miriam, a professional woman in her early thirties. Miriam is a warm, reflective, and charismatic woman with a gift for pastoral/therapeutic spirituality. She consistently struck me while I observed and interacted with her on several occasions as a "natural" priest. Miriam first co-presided in the late 1980s and was at the forefront of efforts within Dignity/Boston at that time to have co-presiders and special women's liturgies. Miriam explained the mix of feelings she has experienced about co-presiding:

> "I think for me the special part of it is feeling that a community that I care very much about has recognized that there may be something about the gifts that I may have to offer that are important. And I appreciate that because that has not been my experience in lots of different ways as a lesbian, as a woman, as a Christian. It's very hard to have one's voice heard and appreciated and respected and to me I just sometimes can't get over my own level of appreciation, the feeling that there is something worthwhile that I have to offer that they call forth in me. And I want to do my very best every time. And I worry about it for days before it's time to speak about anything wondering if it's something worth saying. And I have gotten such wonderful feedback that it makes me remember that maybe in fact I have something to offer. And I think that's quite telling because one of the things that I know about myself is that the mask I portray or the confidence I may portray and in part believe in, isn't the whole story. And a lot of the battering that I've taken around my identities, all of the identities have left me feeling profoundly empty in ways. . . . But for me, the healing is now . . . in feeling that I can bring the best of who I am and know that it connects truly and genuinely to the people around me."

When I later asked Miriam whether it was a source of tension in general for the community that some people are chosen to co-preside and others are not, she responded:

"Well, it's a source of tension for me, to tell you the truth. And I think it is for more and more people. In fact, on the women's retreat this last month, we began a very difficult conversation about inclusivity and who gets included and whose voices are heard and whose aren't. And people fall on lots of different points on that continuum, but I tend to think we need to do a better job. Always reminding ourselves that the gifts are dispersed. And I think it's really easy for me to forget that. . . . For a few years after I first presided a few times, then I wasn't asked. And I felt like I was sort of waiting to be called forth. And I saw other women friends of mine being asked, and I wondered was it something that I may have done in the past that folks didn't like. . . . I wonder sometimes if it was because I was part of a lot of that controversy in the late 80s. So I wondered in part if it was political or wondered if maybe folks got the impression that I wasn't ready or willing to do that. You know, I wonder. I don't know. There could be lots of reasons. . . . I feel in the last year or so that I've been called a really good amount . . . and I feel like it's time to give someone else a chance . . . but I hope it doesn't mean that in giving other people a chance in the next year there wouldn't be a place for me because it's something that I would like to continue."

Miriam's views crystallize the practical hurdles that confront a community that tries to be democratic in its own practices. No matter how fair the selection procedures may be, selection inevitably means exclusion. Miriam's comments demonstrate the internal personal conflict between an earnest desire to be a regular co-presider and sincerity in believing that other people should also be recognized. It is also quite striking that even for those people who are chosen as co-presiders, there is a sense of "unworthiness" associated with the perception that they are not asked frequently enough. The reality is that despite the community's attempt to be pluralistic, the opportunities to co-preside are limited. As in the official church, presiding in Dignity reproduces a sense of inequality, but for different reasons. At Dignity, inequality stems from the limited number of co-presiding opportunities available; the inclusion of other people as co-presiders means that there is less opportunity for Miriam to "give back" to the community. In the church as a whole, by contrast, inequality is inscribed in the Vatican's interpretation of doctrine which prohibits women priests notwithstanding the shortage of priests to celebrate the church's sacraments.

Dignity members' understanding of the church as, in part, a social-ly constructed institution facilitates their experimentation as an inclu-sive and egalitarian worship community. Their experiences enable them to shift the boundaries in official church teaching. Thus partici-pants are not bothered by the fact that they celebrate their weekly Mass, the primary context of their identity work as gay and lesbian Catholics, in a Protestant church, using gay priests and innovative liturgical strategies that affirm the values of a gay sexuality. Partici-pants' constructionist understanding of Catholicism is only partial, however. It is constrained by inscribed memories of Catholicism and the known demands of its doctrinal tradition. Thus, although going against official church teaching by actively creating a gay-inclusive Catholic worship community, some members resist liturgical changes that would extend Dignity's gender-inclusive practices. As highlighted by the tensions over co-presiding, maintaining the charisma of what some Dignity participants consider to be a "normal" Mass tends to get prioritized over the chapter's commitment to enacting broad-based egalitarian practices.

Dignity's relative success in creating a worship community that is gay-inclusive but only partially gender-inclusive underscores the fact that the enactment of emancipatory identities is invariably a piece-meal and fragmented process. As underlined by the identity con-sciousness of many of the Dignity women, multiple identities do not just cause tension at the communal and societal level; they are also the source of internal personal conflict and feelings of self-betrayal. The inextricable link between sexuality and gender means that until Dignity is able to forge communal liturgies in which sexual and gender distinctions are invisible, not because they are suppressed but because they have become irrelevant, these women can only partially experi-ence the emancipatory charge that they so appreciatively recognize as emergent in their participation in Dignity.

SUMMARY

Owning an identity, no matter how creatively forged, is not a purely personal psychological state or strategy. Identity emerges rather from the context of intergroup relations (Tajfel 1978) and depends on the availability of plausibility structures (Berger and Luckmann 1966) that contextualize and legitimate identities as reasonable and real. For respondents in this study whose marginality in church and society renders them "different," participation in Dignity empowers a gay or lesbian Catholic identity. Dignity provides its members with a "subuniverse of meaning" (Berger and Luckmann 1966: 79) that confirms the validity of their reclaimed identity as gay or lesbian and Catholic, and enables them to creatively maintain that identity against its stigmatized counterdefinition. In a sense, involvement in Dignity enables its participants to comprise what Nancy Fraser would call a "subaltern counterpublic" (1992: 123), providing members with a relatively safe "enclave of protected discourse" (Collins 1990: 95; Mansbridge 1996: 58) where they can experiment with forging new identities. The experimentation is held in check, however, and avoids the dangers of ideological insularity and values distortion that can characterize protected enclaves (cf. Mansbridge 1996: 58–59) by participants' shared commitment to the larger Catholic tradition and to the integrity of a Catholic identity, notwithstanding their contestation of what that entails. Thus, as documented, Dignity participants assume the authority to interpret doctrine in ways that, autonomous of official church teaching, fit with their identity goals, but in this process they also set (contested) limits as to what they may legitimately change.

Since the Catholic tradition, as discussed in Chapter 2, is not monolithic, it is not surprising that in Dignity as in any community or organization where the weight of tradition is heavy, questions of whose memory is to be consulted and what elements of the tradition are to be remembered are both contested and constraining of future options (Powell 1987: 35–36). Dignity participants are engaged in an ongoing experiment with how to live out an identity that is in continuity with Catholicism yet affirming of their gay or lesbian sexuality. For Dignity participants as a whole it is evident that commitment to shifting official church teaching on sexuality does not extend indiscriminately to a rejection of other aspects of Catholic doctrine. It would seem rather that for gay and lesbian Catholics who choose to stay Catholic, empowerment to shift the boundaries of Catholicism is itself dependent on their holding constant to varying degrees some of the "traditional" aspects of Catholicism. The holding of a weekly Sunday Mass liturgy in itself highlights the anchoring role of Catholicism in Dignity members' lives. Dignity participants are so accustomed, moreover, to the "normalcy" of a Catholic Mass, and so committed to retaining their links with the larger church tradition that they continue to endorse the liturgical leadership role of priests and, less so, of nonordained co-presiders.

The malleability of symbols is what makes identity projects potentially transformative. As the co-presiding priest on Pride Sunday observed, and as several sociologists discuss (e.g., Hall 1973; Zald 1996), symbols are not static in their meanings. They are transformed in response to particular historical and cultural contexts. The process of ideological contestation is thus simultaneously a process of creating new meanings.[12] Otherwise, if the content and practical meanings of symbols were immutable, it would be difficult to unmask established "truths" to see that institutional routines are culturally rather than divinely prescribed.

How Dignity deals with the process of symbolic contestation is itself notable. Retaining the solidarity of Catholic communality confronts Dignity members with the mutual tasks of maintaining both their Dignity/Boston community and their participation in the larger Catholic community. Whether or not any specific innovation is institutionalized by the chapter is, as documented, arbitrated through engagement in a democratic consensus-building process. For some members, the preservation of certain Catholic symbols and liturgical forms is motivated by their sincere belief that the symbols in question are essential to maintaining an authentic attachment to the Catholic doctrinal tradition. Other members take a contrary view, sincerely believing that embracing change is realizing justice ethics that are equally central to the Catholic tradition but selectively enforced in official church practices.

Underscoring the value that members place on the importance of sustaining their own local Dignity community, it is striking that participants who favor change tend to proceed slowly, hoping that by their continued although personally conflicted participation in Dignity, change can be forged. As illuminated by the deliberations of the liturgical committee, members temper their articulation of pro-change demands out of concern that pushing for change may fracture the communal solidarity of the chapter as a whole. Yet members' commitment to being an inclusive community means that gender equality,

---

12. As Mayer Zald (1996: 262) notes, "symbols, frames and ideologies are created and changed in the process of contestation."

for instance, cannot be sacrificed in order to maintain the solidarity derived from members' shared sexual identity. Consequently, motifs of gender equality are always "naggingly" present in members' communal routines. In this regard, Dignity/Boston gives concrete expression to Jane Mansbridge's important point that "when we compromise with justice, we must design our lives and our institutions so that the justice that is compromised remains nagging, in the margin somewhere, in a bracket that does not go away, to pique our souls and goad us into future action" (1996: 59). Until that future action is realized, communal cohesiveness may be understood at some level as a partial betrayal of personal values and of the community's own ideals.

Some scholars (e.g., Bellah et al. 1985: 71–75; Etzioni 1997: 64; Habermas 1987: 393–395) suggest that the celebration of particular identities leads to subcultural segmentation and severs ties with the broader communal tradition that has historically perpetuated the inequalities at issue. This is clearly not the case with Dignity/Boston. Like all communities, Dignity/Boston is not monolithic. Members have different views of what it means to be a moral community in practice. Nonetheless, its participants strive as a community to recognize the identities and the tensions with which they are confronted. Maintaining a gay and lesbian Catholic community is thus an ongoing experimental and dynamic process. In seeking the restoration of their dignity in a church in which they are officially marginalized, gay and lesbian Catholics show that achieving an identity that maintains links with a larger community of memory is a constant process of communally self-conscious negotiation over what meanings should be prioritized. Dignity's community practices demonstrate that interpretive diversity does not inevitably undermine communal solidarity. Rather, they indicate that it is possible to engage the symbols of the Catholic tradition and inject them with new meanings that allow participants to retain links with the past while anticipating new and more emancipatory future possibilities.

CHAPTER SIX

Using Doctrine to Critique Doctrine

The preceding chapter illustrated how participants in Dignity affirm the compatibility of their sexuality and their Catholicism. As documented, Dignity respondents transform the disordered identity given to them in official church teaching by interpreting Catholicism, sexuality, and the church hierarchy in ways that enable them to embrace the Catholic tradition and rework its exclusionary symbols. This chapter focuses more formally on how pro-change Catholics legitimate an emancipatory agenda. Specifically, I examine how members of the Women's Ordination Conference (WOC) and volunteer activists for Catholics for a Free Choice (CFFC) argue for a more participative and pluralistic church, and how in the process they validate the authenticity of their Catholicism.

Institutional and Doctrinal Transformation

This chapter will engage important theoretical questions in sociology concerning the prospects and resources for achieving institutional change. As discussed in Chapter 1, Jürgen Habermas views communicative reason as the primary means by which people can reach a negotiated agreement about a course of action that benefits the common good rather than the instrumental interests of particular actors. In Habermas's "ideal speech situation," participants engage in reasoned communication which is unconstrained by differences between the participants in status, power, and language capabilities, and where the weight of tradition, dogma, and emotional attachments is bracketed. In this model of a deliberative community "no participant has a monopoly on correct interpretation" (Habermas 1984: 100). The understanding negotiated is achieved through the soundness and persuasiveness of the reasons that participants offer and reciprocally critique in support of a particular course of action.

As will be recalled, Foucault, by contrast, takes a skeptical view of the ability of reason or knowledge to transform the world (1982/1997: 130–131). Foucault's suspicion of the self-reproducing power of existing institutional procedures leads him to celebrate noninstitutionalized, playful experimentation as the way to create new schemas of social relations (1984b/1997: 165). Foucault's stress on the inventiveness necessary to achieve social transformation gives little recognition to the creative potential of communicative reason. For Foucault, the search for "truth" via reason is sabotaged, since the categories people use to argue against power are themselves the products of a particular institutional power context. Accordingly, rather than valuing talk and the practical ethics that might emerge from reasoned communication, Foucault instead emphasizes the liberating potential of experimental behavior that is outside the bounds of established rules (ibid. 172–173). In this understanding, identity transformations are creatively lived rather than intellectually construed.

This chapter takes account of the different theoretical assumptions of Habermas and Foucault. But rather than engaging in abstract theorizing, it provides empirical data illustrating how in actuality prochange Catholics' legitimate their transformative agendas. Since the institutional context for this discussion is the Catholic Church, the findings also illuminate the place of reason in doctrinal debate. As discussed in Chapter 1, for Habermas, the sphere of reasoned communication excludes religion, which he sees wholly in terms of tradition and unquestioned dogma rather than as a differentiated body of beliefs, social ethics, and institutional practices. Habermas (1992) argues that if there were to be a self-critical reasoned discussion about religion, it would have to be uncoupled from the "event of revelation," and consequently it would lose its distinctive theological character. Habermas's premium on reason thus elevates the emancipatory potential of reasoned communication while simultaneously silencing the critical use of symbolic resources, such as doctrine, that in his view subvert reason.[1]

1. Explaining the reasons for his tendency not to engage with theologians' critique of his theory, Habermas states that "silence on the grounds of embarrassment" would be justified since theology remains for him personally "an insufficiently reconnoitered terrain." He maintains nonetheless that since American and

Contrary to Habermas's narrow understanding of religion, the doc-trines and practices that comprise the Catholic Church are, as dis-cussed in Chapter 2, contingent on historical, cultural, and social fac-tors. In particular, the church has, among other strands, a tradition of doctrinal and institutional reflexivity. Doctrine is thus used to critique church doctrine and practices. Catholic doctrine develops, in part, in response to shifts in the practical understanding of social ethics (e.g., equality) and the church's attempt to ensure that faith and reason underlie its institutional practices. In this sense, the church is, as Francis Schüssler Fiorenza argues, a "community of interpretation" whose role is "to engage in a critical reconstructive interpretation of [its] normative religious and moral traditions in relation to social and political praxis" (1992: 67). The identity negotiation of WOC and CFFC respondents will show that faith and reason are compatible in practice for contemporary Catholics, and enable them to critique and transform aspects of Catholicism while simultaneously preserving its doctrinal and communal tradition.

CONTESTED DOCTRINE

Before discussing the themes used by WOC and CFFC respondents to legitimate change in church teaching and practices, it may be helpful to recall official church teaching on the issues respectively contested by them. As discussed in Chapter 3, the church hierarchy bases its opposition to the ordination of women upon three main arguments. One, the Vatican maintains that since Christ did not call women to be apostles, the church hierarchy is prevented from ordaining women because it cannot act counter to the will and example of Jesus. A sec-ond argument is that because Christ was male, priests as icons or rep-resentatives of Christ must maintain the natural physical resemblance to Christ, thus precluding women from symbolizing Christ as priests.

The third reason highlights the fact that Catholic doctrine is not derived from scripture alone but is complemented by the church's institutional tradition. The Vatican defends its continued opposition

German theologians have for decades reacted to his writings, "In this situation, silence would be a false response: the person who is addressed and remains silent, clothes himself or herself in an aura of indeterminate significance and imposes silence." Thus for Habermas (unlike Foucault), silence is reactionary (Habermas 1992: 226).

to women priests on the ground that an exclusively male priesthood is part of the church's constant tradition. In the Vatican's view, this male hierarchical tradition is structurally core to the church's identity. Nonetheless, as noted in Chapter 3, the church hierarchy stresses women's equality to men and insists that women's exclusion from the priesthood should not be interpreted as evidence of their inferiority. Rather, official church teaching sees gender role differentiation as reflecting complementary differences in the nature of women and men.

Unlike opposition to women's ordination, which is seen by the Vatican as part of the deposit of Catholic faith (CDF 1995), the church hierarchy regards abortion as a trans-Catholic issue of universal morality. Official church opposition to abortion is grounded in the understanding that human life begins at conception and thus that abortion kills innocent human life. Accordingly, the church hierarchy is absolute in its opposition to abortion irrespective of the stage of embryonic development or the contextual circumstances surrounding a woman's decision to have an abortion. As noted in Chapter 3, the Vatican sees the prevalence of abortion as crystallizing a contemporary "culture of death" (John Paul 1995a) which it associates more generally with moral relativism and individualism.

Although official church teaching on women's ordination and abortion have practical relevance for women, the issues clearly are substantively distinct from one another. The two issues are grouped together in this chapter in order to give a broad sense of the interpretive resources pro-change Catholics use to contest doctrine. Given this purpose, therefore, it is how respondents link the question at issue to their understanding of Catholicism, rather than the substance of each issue, that is important here.

DATA SOURCES: WOC AND CFFC RESPONDENTS

Although WOC and CFFC respondents are members of discrete organizations focusing on separate issues, they share a common commitment to institutional change in the Catholic Church. This chapter uses WOC respondents' understanding of women's ordination and CFFC respondents' views on abortion to illustrate how pro-change Catholics legitimate doctrinal and institutional transformation. The WOC data is based on written answers from a survey of 210 randomly selected ordinary members of WOC, and the CFFC data are based on written answers from a survey of thirty-two CFFC volunteer regional activists.[2]

In the WOC and CFFC questionnaires, respondents were asked several open-ended questions tailored to the issues raised by their respective projects. This chapter presents data based on responses to three questions asking how respondents' pro-change agendas fit with Catholicism, and what theological and sociocultural reasons favor women's ordination or a pro-choice stance on abortion. Each of the questions received thoughtful and detailed written answers from the WOC and CFFC respondents.[3] I pooled the replies to the three questions into one extensive answer because the responses offered to each question overlapped somewhat. Although it is possible to code respondents' answers along a number of different dimensions, I coded them for themes of doctrine and power in accord with underlying theoretical interests, and for gender in view both of the gender specificity of the two issues and official church teaching on gender differences.[4] Given the disproportionality in the WOC and CFFC sample sizes, this chapter uses more illustrative data from WOC than from CFFC respondents in discussing the pro-change arguments used.

RESPONDENTS' PRO-CHANGE ARGUMENTS

DOCTRINE

The analysis of respondents' answers revealed a remarkably strong emphasis on doctrinal reasoning. It was strikingly evident that it was their experiences and knowledge of the Catholic doctrinal and institutional tradition itself, rather than their cultural status as Americans, that primarily drove respondents' doctrinal contestation.[5] The respondents appeared to share the strategic view expressed by one WOC

2. Four of the 214 respondents in the WOC sample did not provide written responses to the relevant questions.

3. On average, WOC respondents wrote 39 words in response to question one, 23 words in response to question two, and 24 words in response to question three. CFFC respondents wrote 54 words in response to question one, 42 words in response to question two, and 57 words in response to question three.

4. Using doctrine, power, and gender as thematic categories, each narrative was coded exhaustively for multiple themes by two coders working with the questionnaires independently. Both coders were unaware of the sources of the materials and of the study's theoretical interests.

5. The thematic analysis of WOC respondents' questionnaires showed that in the

respondent, a woman nurse practitioner in her early forties, who said:

"If we make a case for women's ordination using only social mores and not grounding this in God's word, we will be easily (and rightfully) dismissed by the church. Only Christ's teaching and New Testament Guidelines should be referred to in making a case for ordination."

It was thus noteworthy that the vast majority of both WOC (88%) and CFFC (84%) respondents located the validity of their respective agendas within Catholicism.

As Catholics who choose to stay within the church, respondents assume the authority to reinterpret Catholic theology rather than abandoning it as hopelessly patriarchal. Pro-change Catholics take core symbols in Catholicism and use them to argue for interpretations alternative to those presented in official church teaching. Variously drawing on scripture, Vatican II, early church history, Catholic sacramental practices, and the church's social justice tradition, WOC respondents provide a compelling doctrinal case for women's ordination.

Underscoring the hold of a Christocentric paradigm in nurturing a changed understanding of priesthood, 65 percent of WOC respondents explicitly invoked Christ-related themes in discussing their views on women's ordination.[6] Whereas official church arguments defend the exclusivity of a male-only priesthood by pointing to the single act of Jesus in choosing only men as apostles, WOC respondents focus on the social dimensions and relational meanings of Christ's life as a whole. For them, narrative accounts of Christ's life lead to an alternative the-

responses to the open-ended questions, only 4 percent of respondents used "rights language," typically stating, as one respondent phrased it, that "[w]omen have a right to have their call to ordination tested."

6. This finding is significant in view of purported tensions among some advocates of women's ordination as to whether they want ordination in "Jesus's church" or in some alternative theological "woman-church" (see Redmont 1995). In their use of doctrine, WOC respondents invoked multiple subthemes. For example, in addition to the Christological emphasis, 36 percent drew on Vatican II concepts such as universality or baptismal equality, 18 percent emphasized issues of institutional credibility for a church grounded in Christ but which discriminates, 18 percent referred to the examples offered by women in scripture and in the early church, and 23 percent emphasized the sacramental implications of a shortage of priests.

ological interpretation that illuminates an inclusive rather than a discriminatory Jesus. Several respondents thus linked their pro-change aims to the activism personified by Christ on behalf of equality and justice. As expressed by these WOC respondents:

"Basically I experience Jesus in the New Testament as being with the causes – standing with all who are on the journey for truth. I believe in equality and justice and I hope for the dawning of the day when both women and married priests experience fullness within Catholicism."

"To me, being a Catholic means to participate in the Church established by Jesus. Jesus always seemed to espouse the dignity of humankind. To realize that dignity, all people need to be afforded the opportunity to follow their calling, to utilize their individual gifts and talents given to them by their creator. To deny that dignity to half of humankind does not fulfill the example set by Jesus to be Catholic."

"If we take to heart Jesus' words about equality, we must be willing to look at institutions and our individual lives and be willing to *live* accordingly [emphasis in original]."

Stressing a different dimension of the Christological narrative, some WOC respondents emphasized the humanity of Christ. Highlighting the universalism of Christ's humanity, they challenged the distinctiveness of his maleness and the iconic significance attached to this in official church statements. These respondents pointed to the symbolic-theological implications that flow from the church hierarchy's exclusion of women from the sacramental imaging of Christ. One young woman who is a pastoral counselor stated: "If the most important thing about Christ is maleness, are women saved? The Vatican's Christology is warmed-over misogynistic-androcentric daydreaming."

Other WOC respondents argued:

"If Christianity teaches that all are redeemed in Jesus Christ then it is a contradiction to exclude women in the full ministry. It is a denial of redemption. Either Jesus is savior of all or what we believe is false."

"The universality of Catholicism must reflect the universality of gifts, given by God to be used for the good of all. The ordination of women will demonstrate the universality of God's call, without distinction or human-ordered restrictions. The more complete image of Jesus, the Incarnate One, will be made manifest when women assume the overt and visible role of priest/shepherd."

Many other respondents similarly invoked scriptural references to equality, and/or to Vatican II's emphases on baptismal equality and the church as the People of God, to argue for women's ordination. As interpreted by these respondents, a church that claims to be universal and inclusive of all humanity undermines its foundational ethics by institutionalizing what respondents regard as arbitrary, gender-based boundaries of exclusion.

Some WOC respondents (18%) explicitly framed women's ordination as an issue of institutional credibility for a church grounded in a Christ-embodied ethics of justice and equality. These respondents emphasized how church practices deviate from the redemptive narrative of Christ's life and the doctrinal values central to the church's identity. One middle-aged man summarized the views of many of his WOC peers:

"Equality, fairness, even-handedness – all are values that the Catholic Church has and does espouse. These are good mature values – human, humane, and person-enhancing. Preaching equality and practicing it in actuality *must* go together, or else it's just words [emphasis in original]."

Other WOC respondents variously echoed this stance, stating:

"Catholicism is important to me because it has provided the framework in which I could exercise my belief in God and in the life and work of Jesus. I need the Church to show the way to live justly. I wish it would begin with following more closely the message of Jesus."

"I believe women reflect something of God as do men. The Church should be in the forefront of creating an equal place for women. I think oppression of any type (bigotry against women, non-Caucasians, the poor, gays and lesbians) has to be eradicated. That's part of the Gospel message and has to be the mission of the Church."

"I feel that the Catholic Church should be a leader in justice issues. I feel that the ordination of women is a justice issue and therefore the Catholic Church should act justly and ordain women. I think women are discriminated against in this issue despite the fact that the Church says that this is not discrimination. I can't believe that Jesus would discriminate in this way. If Jesus did select only men for ordination, it was because it was the norm for the times, it isn't now."

"We have to accord human rights and equality to all if we are truly Christian. Patriarchy, domination of any one, discrimination of all kinds are all irreconcilable with Christianity. If Catholics are truly followers of Christ, we can't do it."

"I don't believe we can say one thing or have a vision of reaching out to embrace all, yet put up boundaries or limitations on people and how they minister within the community. I believe that goes against the innate nature of the church and the reality of the Gospel."

Another way that WOC respondents engage the church's tradition is in their reconstruction of scripture and of early church history to critique the church hierarchy's opposition to women priests. Contesting the church hierarchy's emphasis on the constant tradition of an exclusively male priesthood, many WOC respondents (18%) highlighted the role of women in the bible and the examples of women's leadership and ministry in the early church. These respondents stated, for example:

"God did not create male and female for procreation only. In the early days of the church women played an extremely active role. They were strong when many of the men were weak. Jesus *always* had women with him. He *needed* them! Why does the church continue to deny what it does?" [emphasis in original].

"There were deacons in the early church – Junia for example. Women are valuable in the church and to God. It does not matter that the Apostles were male; they were also Jewish fishermen. How many Jewish fishermen are currently in Catholic seminaries?"

Some WOC respondents' arguments (23%) also included references to the practical consideration posed by the current shortage of priests in America. In this line of reasoning, the Vatican's continuing opposition to women priests even in the face of the shortage of male priests and its practical implications for the church's sacramental continuity is seen as undermining the church's tradition. As argued by one WOC respondent:

"The Sacraments are the lifeblood of the Church. With the shortage of priests, availability of the sacraments is declining drastically. Many women are theologically trained, are already doing the work of the traditional priest in many ways. Refusing to ordain women is a spiritual suicide in the Church."

Another WOC respondent stated: "The Eucharist is the center of the Catholic life. With not enough ordained persons some segments of the community can't have Eucharist."

On the surface, arguments that present women's ordination as a response to the shortage of priests may be viewed simply as an organizational solution to a personnel crisis. Yet as indicated by the above quotations, concern over the shortage of priests also points to an underlying doctrinal tension in church practices: the Vatican's prioritization of maintaining gender-based boundaries over the celebration of the Eucharist.

Overall, the majority of WOC respondents argue for consistency between Catholic doctrine and church practices. In the reasoning of the respondents quoted here, it is clear that a faith derived from the narrative of Christ's life cannot be used to defend any form of institutional inequality. Any doctrine therefore that is used to support women's exclusion from ordination must necessarily be contested regardless of its official authorization because it contravenes the exemplary practices of Christ as remembered and celebrated in the Catholic scriptural and institutional tradition.

Paralleling the WOC respondents' use of doctrinal reasoning, CFFC respondents also used the church's doctrinal and institutional tradition to justify their stance. CFFC respondents variously drew on the meanings of Christ's life (38%), conscience (53%), and the social justice tradition of Catholicism (59%) as a framework allowing a contextualist understanding of the morality of abortion and of pro-choice activism. One CFFC respondent explained her understanding of the links between being Catholic and pro-choice. She stated:

> "To be a Catholic means, to me, to be committed to the Gospel and to those with whom Christ stood. It is also to be committed to the resurrected Christ and His commands after the resurrection. (In other words I firmly believe in liberation theology.) I therefore believe that all adults are moral agents capable of making good, moral decisions. The decision to have an abortion is a moral one and I firmly believe that women make perfectly fine moral decisions. In being pro-choice, I feel that I am standing with the living, ensouled human being who has suffered through a terrible decision-making process. . . . Since 51 percent of the patients at clinics in [the region] are Catholics, it is my Catholic duty to stand by and with them. . . . This is, if you will excuse the expression, my ministry."

Also evident throughout the remarks of CFFC respondents was a stress on conscience, a theme evident in Catholic thought since at least the time of Saint Augustine and emphasized more recently by Vatican II. Over half of the CFFC sample (53%) discussed how the application of conscience supports their interpretation of Catholicism. One CFFC respondent elaborated:

> "I was raised as a Catholic and went through sixteen years of Catholic education. I was taught to follow my conscience. And to help others. I believe this includes helping women to achieve independent, fulfilling lives."

Other CFFC respondents stated:

> "Fidelity to conscience is the mark of a committed Catholic, not fidelity to hierarchical teaching on sexual ethics. If a Catholic's pro-choice position arises as a conscientious position arrived at

through reflection, then one can be both pro-choice and a 'committed' Catholic."

"Being Catholic must be freely chosen, not coercive. Conscience must be involved; after prayerful reflection this is where God sees my path to be."

As these quotations demonstrate, CFFC respondents locate conscience and its moral practical implications for human agency squarely within Catholic doctrine. In their view, the valuing of conscience within Catholicism means that a monopolistic interpretation of morality cannot be prescribed a priori as the authentic Catholic response to a particular situation. Rather, it provides the basis for moral pluralism.

CFFC respondents also evoked the church's people-centeredness and emphasis on social equality. They pointed to Catholic ethics of justice as the motivation for their pro-choice activism. CFFC respondents stated:

"From my late teens – I'm 51 now – I always saw the church as a source of and place to work for justice and dignity for people. 'Love thy neighbor as thyself.' First, the issues were poverty and racism. As my consciousness was raised it included women and gay men and lesbians."

"Commitment to many social justice issues, work with poor people – often leads Catholics to a different view about abortion than clergy often have. Catholics are often multi-issued, devoted to their parish or other religious community, and cultural and traditional aspects of church."

"I was born and raised a Catholic. I went to all Catholic schools – grade 1 to college. I believe God means love and justice. The Church is human and errs, and I have a moral responsibility to make my contribution to the life of the Church. How is it possible to be a committed Catholic and not work for the Church to stop committing the sin of sexism. Really! Most Catholics just ignore the bishops and the Pope. . . . Committed Catholics speak out. It's our Church and it has lost its way – and it's hurting women and their families."

"Catholicism stands for what I'm committed to: love of all
human beings, respect for individual conscience, and beliefs
based on both reason and faith. The Pope has strayed from these
principles, and so, under duress, have the bishops. I have not."

It is clear from the foregoing discussion that for WOC and CFFC
respondents doctrine is both personally sacred and a resource that can
be used to reason for doctrinal and institutional change. Respondents'
doctrinal contestation is empowered by their reflexive engagement
with different aspects of the Catholic tradition. Although not explicit
in respondents' remarks, it is apparent that respondents find the
authority to contest the church hierarchy's teaching in their own experiences of Catholicism. As in official church teaching, it is not scripture alone but tradition – respondents' understandings of scripture and
of the church's sacramental and social justice tradition – that mobilizes
and nurtures their commitment to building a transformed church. On
the one hand, respondents have a firsthand everyday knowledge of the
church's institutional routines that exclude and discriminate (e.g., the
celebration of the Mass by male priests only). At the same time, they
derive a contrasting belief from the scriptural narratives of pluralism,
equality, and justice celebrated in church liturgy and promoted by the
church's social justice activities. The perceived inconsistencies
between doctrine and practices which respondents witness in the
church allow them to challenge the doctrine that is offered as the
rationale for maintaining inequality. The respondents' doctrinal
"knowledge" supports their efforts to dismantle, rather than to maintain, the church's exclusionary boundaries. In their view, they cannot
be Catholic without contesting the inegalitarian institutional practices
justified by the church hierarchy.[7] The respondents thus engage in a
pro-change agenda that strives to give new practical meaning to the
values embodied by Christ. In this effort they seek to realize what the
theologian Francis Schüssler Fiorenza calls a "theology of praxis," in
which the meanings and actions associated with Christ are understood
creatively, carried forward, and given practical expression in contemporary contexts.[8]

7. It is noteworthy that Schneiders (1991: 87–89) and Winter et al. (1994:
    188–193) also stress the salience of social justice for women committed to insti-
    tutional transformation and the creation of a just church.
8. Francis Schüssler Fiorenza explains: "Theologians use the term 'praxis' to
    emphasize a configuration of meaning and action. The Christian belief in Jesus

POWER

The theme of power was also evident in the respondents' answers. Thirty-three percent of WOC respondents explicitly invoked arguments that framed women's exclusion from ordination as an expression of institutional power or oppression. These respondents challenged the structural and interpretive authority assumed by the church hierarchy in interpreting Catholic doctrine. For them, the Vatican's stance on ordination can be understood as the product of an historically and politically situated church hierarchy seeking to reproduce the exclusivity of the priesthood. A woman who is a nun and a clinical psychologist stated:

"I believe the real issue is power – priests, bishops, cardinals and Pope John Paul. The growing fear of women began after Vatican II when religious women became knowledgable about the Council documents and some clerics had not even read them, much less taught them."

Other respondents argued:

"To be a Catholic in full participation is to be a *man* today. Women are absent in image of God, in representation of priesthood, and from power – all going back to historical development."[emphasis in original]

"Women simply can no longer be subsumed into a humanity where maleness is considered the norm. A church where all power is in the hands of men (often very inferior in many ways) is lacking in simple justice."

"I know ordination will not in itself end sexism in the Church – one only need to look at Episcopalian women priests' struggle. It is part of a larger issue of how the Church uses, maintains power."

affirms Jesus as a configuration of God's meaning and action. This view of the presence and action of God in Christ as a specific configuration, or praxis, hinders the reduction of meaning of God's incarnation in Jesus to a specific teaching or a particular idea . . . to be Christian [is] not merely to adhere to a certain configuration of beliefs . . . but . . . to receive creatively, that is, to carry forward and to continue, the meaning and praxis of Jesus" (1994: 165).

"It is simply not right to exclude women and make them feel inferior. This suppresses their gifts and talents . . . and encourages the abuse of power, domination, and authoritarianism in the church."

"I strongly believe that the prohibition of women's ordination is a male defense of power in the church, whether consciously or subconsciously believed and practiced."

WOC respondents also answered a separate question probing their evaluation of Pope John Paul's declaration that women's ordination was a settled question. In response, almost half of the WOC sample (47%) imputed negative institutional power motives to John Paul. Respondents argued:

"He doesn't want to lose his power, and open many antiquated ideas to questioning by more intelligent beings [than himself]."

"The acceptance of a majority of Catholics of women's ordination – in a word, fear of losing power. This is a threat to a nearly 2,000 year old patriarchy. He is telling his sons and daughters not to pester him. We are adults now thanks to Vatican II and the evolution of consciousness. We are not minor children to be shushed."

"He is worried that the all-male power base and locus of control will have to be shared, when in fact, women who wish to be ordained want to be, not because they want power, but because they wish to serve more fully."

Other respondents framed John Paul's closure of debate as an institutional strategy to block the implementation of equality in the church. Specifically, the respondents remarked upon the Pope's fear of change (26%), his fear of dialogue (15%), and his sexism and fear of women (19%). The following quotations typify such comments:

"I believe that there is a strong fear of what would happen to and in the Church if women were considered equal enough to be ordained."

"Because that would be a dialogue of equals and to keep women's ordination out of the debate is to keep thinking women subservient to men."

"He cannot imagine a church in which women are treated equally with men. He and the men around him are unable to comprehend women as equal to men. Because they believe deep down that men are superior to women and are intended by the Divine to direct women. They fear allowing the discussion go on. The more openly the matter is discussed, the more logical women's ordination appears. Continued debate can only lead to universal consensus that women should be allowed ordination. That 'universal consensus' is the basic requisite for dogma. That is what the hierarchy fears most – reality!"

John Paul's recalcitrance in embracing equality in the church was also attributed to what respondents described as his conservative Polish Catholic cultural background (17%) and to various aspects of his personality (16%).[9] The remarks of one male respondent captured several of the negative themes prominent in the views of WOC members. He argued:

"Fear. Stubborness. A sense of Church that comes out of a suppressed Poland where the hierarchy had tremendous power in leading and galvanizing people. It's a style that will not work in 'governing the church universal' as hard as he/they try. Vatican II let the horse out of the barn and it ain't going back in! As long as you have bishops though who are willing to accept that kind of suppression of their own innate rights to teach, speak up, debate, the Pope will keep saying things like that because the bishops here let him. When you have no real theological argument, just tell them to 'shut up'!"

9. In addition to these reasons, less than one in ten respondents attributed John Paul II's closure of debate on women's ordination to the fact that he knows he has no theological reason for prohibiting women's ordination (6%) or to his commitment to preserving church tradition (6%). Only 6 percent attributed John Paul's stance to his sincere belief that women's ordination is simply not possible.

Sixty-six percent (n = 21) of CFFC respondents invoked power themes to explain their pro-choice stance on abortion. Some respondents emphasized a general commitment to dismantling the church hierarchy's power. One respondent did so by explaining her understanding of the links in official church teaching between abortion and other gender and sexual issues:

"My self-awareness as a woman has made me sensitive to the institutionalized sexism and misogyny of the Catholic Church. The Church's obsession with the issue of abortion simply demonstrates again the degree of sexism and misogyny. As in the secular world, the abortion war is a thinly disguised battle over who shall maintain control of women. Perhaps the only positive aspect of the 'abortion war' is that its very intensity reveals how threatened the traditional male order is."

Another CFFC respondent, a retired woman who has seven children, stated:

"There is absolutely no doubt in my mind that CFFC activities present a great threat to the majority of the R. C. hierarchy. Truth is always threatening. . . . We cannot outlaw the fact that this abortion struggle is the last hurrah for sexual politics in the church. . . . I believe there was a momentous happening in history when after much bitter wrangling, the 'primacy of conscience' was written into the Constitution of Vatican II. . . . For me, this represented the transfer of power – as well as the responsibility – for my conscience from the papacy to the individual. Awesome!"

Other respondents challenged the church hierarchy's power to define the Catholic position on abortion. Accordingly, some CFFC respondents highlighted CFFC's impact in confronting the church hierarchy with Catholics' diversity and pluralism, and cracking its representation of a monolithic Catholic voice. These respondents typically argued:

"The bishops cannot get away with the illusion that they speak for all Catholics."

"The American bishops can no longer get away with saying that this is how all Catholics think and frighten politicians to vote their way. It gives policy makers and politicians a way to talk back and stand up to the Roman Catholic hierarchy."

DOCTRINAL REASONING AND POWER

The quotations presented in the preceding two sections demonstrate WOC and CFFC respondents' ease in accessing doctrinal reasons and power-based arguments in discussing their claims for doctrinal and institutional change. Importantly, these themes were not exclusive of one another. My data show that pro-change respondents simultaneously maintain a critical engagement with Catholic doctrine and a critique of the church hierarchy's power. Thirty percent of the WOC respondents and 59 percent of CFFC respondents used both doctrinal reasoning and power-oriented arguments.[10] This thematic overlap confirms that reason and power exist side by side not only in people's understandings of institutional practices, but also in their justifications for the possible transformation in those practices. While Michel Foucault would argue that talking about power is inferior to engaging in inventive practices that unravel the status quo, WOC and CFFC respondents show that talk about power is itself an important dynamic in envisioning new institutional arrangements, and importantly, in anticipating new practices that can be carved from within an existing tradition. In parallel fashion, respondents' arguments show that notwithstanding Habermas's marginalization of the role of power in social relations, consciousness of power inequalities can nurture a critically reasoned stance. The following quotes from WOC respondents illustrate this understanding.

"The gospel needs to be proclaimed from different viewpoints and women need to add theirs to what is and has been a male-dominated church. Jesus, I don't think, would have wanted to be exclusive. He wanted the good news given to everyone and *by* everyone who believed it." [emphasis in original]

10. If CFFC respondents' social justice themes are excluded from the doctrinal category, there is an overlap between doctrinal (defined more narrowly as Christology and conscience) and power arguments evident in 47 percent of CFFC narratives.

"My belief is in Jesus Christ and the Church which developed from his teachings (this in my mind is a very different church from the Roman, hierarchical patriarchal church currently called the Catholic Church). The Church of Jesus Christ is inclusive, affirming, loving and supportive of everyone . . ."

"Only male arrogance relegates women to an inferior role despite their record of superiority. The church hierarchy is more concerned with their institution than its individuals. They contravene what Christ was all about. By the way, I am a male, senior citizen. Did God create second class beings in women? Not the God I know. Christ never excluded them. His choice of males was according to the times. Knowing Christ, how could he have meant to exclude them forever? The church makes self-serving statements and interpretations."

GENDER

Not surprisingly, given the gender-specific implications of both women's ordination and abortion, arguments about women featured prominently in respondents' answers. Many WOC respondents (39%) emphasized the interchangeability of gender roles and accordingly stated that women are entitled to the same recognition and opportunities long afforded men in the church and in other spheres. As one middle-aged woman physician observed:

"I find it ludicrous that a chromosome – which I have nothing to do with – keeps me from work I could do well and want to do very badly. As a pediatric surgeon I can have lives in my hands, but because I am a woman I can only save lives, not souls."

For some respondents the obligation to accord women equal participation in the church was driven by their knowledge of women's daily relevance in maintaining the church. These respondents linked the official recognition of priestly roles for women with recognition of their de facto roles in the church. One respondent, a psychotherapist, summarized the views of many of her WOC colleagues by noting:

"Women make this Church work. If all the women involved in ministry went on strike, the work of the church would stop. Women are as capable as men to be ordained priests."

Other respondents argued that the church had a moral obligation to be a leader in demonstrating women's equality. Typical of this sort of argument was that of an elderly married woman who stated:

"Women are striving for equality in all other areas of life. The Church should help, not hinder the struggle. The Church can help the cause by showing that women are equal in the Church."

Another respondent argued:

"Women are still victims of sexism, degradation, and discrimination. How can we hope to bring self-esteem to every woman if women are not deemed worthy of any and all types of participation in the church?"

CFFC respondents (41%) invoked women's equality to argue for the recognition of women's reasoned competence to make moral judgments about abortion. In their view, the church hierarchy's negation of moral pluralism devalues women's moral agency.

Of greater theoretical interest to this study, in view of official church teaching on the essentially different genius of women and men, was the emphasis by many WOC respondents on women's gender-specific positive qualities. Twenty-five percent of WOC respondents emphasized women's essential differences from men.[11] Distinctive to WOC respondents' discussion was, once again, the institutionally reflexive manner in which they applied the idea to the church. These respondents emphasized the positive, specifically feminine influence that women priests would have on the church:

"Women are more personal and sensitive (of course that is a generalization). I think that generally they are more suited to model Jesus than most men who are into power, wealth, status, etc."

11. Of course, Catholic women are not the only women who adhere to gender essentialist arguments, and gender essentialism can be used to support opposing visions of equality. For example, the women in Lynn Davidman's (1991: 130–135) study value the gender distinctions in Orthodox Judaism as a way of reclaiming recognition for women's traditional role. (In my study, there was an overlap in themes of role interchangeability and women's positive nature in the narratives of 6 percent of WOC respondents.)

"Women . . . may offer a different approach or insight in their counseling, teaching and in their homilies. Some women might find it easier to take their problems to another woman. The woman's touch has been found to be beneficial wherever it has been invited."

"Women will bring an embodied spirituality that has been largely missing."

"There is a crying need for the feminine approach to leadership, decision-making, and especially to pastoral guidance."

"I believe women would bring the Catholic religion a strength and the feminine view that we sorely need. The world needs a soft approach to life which only women can present."

"Many formerly male organizations have found that when women were admitted they brought a special kind of female rationale that softened, but also strengthened, the qualities of the organization."

Gender essentialist arguments that assign a distinctive feminine nature to women have been criticized by some feminists as comprising a weak base from which to launch egalitarian offensives (e.g., Ryan 1992). It may thus seem somewhat surprising that in the drive for women's equality in the church, a substantial proportion of WOC respondents stressed women's difference. Yet as in previous historical struggles over women's rights (cf. Ginsburg 1989; Ryan 1992), gender essentialist arguments can be used to mobilize institutional change. The essentialist arguments of Catholics challenging women's exclusion from ordination engage the Catholic tradition in ways that enhance their symbolic power in pushing for institutional change. On the one hand, the embrace of gender essentialism indicates the affinity of some Catholic feminists with official church teaching on women's "nature." This underscores that Catholic feminists are not by definition the "radical" post-Christian feminists depicted by some commentators (e.g., Bork 1996: 288). More important, the nurturing and life-giving values the church hierarchy associates with women's "essential genius" correspond to the values exemplified by Christ in Catholic theology as a God of love, understanding, and compassion. Consequently the use of gender-essentialist reasoning in favor of women's equality in the church exploits the doctrinal contradiction evinced by women's exclusion from reflecting Christ's image as priests. Such arguments challenge the gender-based reasoning of a church hierarchy that bars women from being priests while simultaneously celebrating their embodiment of the Christ-like "culture of life" (e.g., John Paul 1995a: 176–177). In short, while the church hierarchy uses gender differences to exclude women from being priests, some WOC respondents use gender differences to argue for women's fuller participation in and potential enhancement of the church.

The Emancipatory Power of Doctrinal Reflexivity

The respondents' doctrinal and gender essentialist arguments demonstrate a reflexive engagement with the Catholic tradition that both grounds their authority to contest doctrine and empowers them to challenge official church practices. It is evident, moreover, that the process of doctrinal contestation is one in which no one resource is privileged. For this study's respondents, faith, reason, and power are mutually nurturing of their pro-change project.

Respondents' participation in the Catholic tradition and their experience of its "higher truths" gives them a doctrinally informed authority to contest the church hierarchy's stance. By the same token, their commitment to what they experience as the "essential" meanings of Catholicism provides them with symbolic resources to which they apply their interpretive autonomy in a doctrinally reflexive manner. Contrary therefore to claims that American culture is impoverished by personalist, therapeutic, and hyperindividualistic vocabularies whose assertions are severed from languages of commitment (Bellah et al. 1985; Glendon 1991), for respondents in this study the authority of individual interpretive autonomy is derived and exercised from within an external communal tradition (Catholicism).

REASON AND FAITH

The respondents' reflexive use of doctrine in their push to eliminate inequality in the church illustrates that people can and do use religion in a critically reasoned manner. Jürgen Habermas, as noted earlier, dismisses the possibility that religious doctrine can play an emancipatory role in bringing about more egalitarian and participative social relations. Habermas sees reasoned dialogue as the basis for achieving a noncoerced consensus that can be used to effect institutional change. Yet his commitment to rescuing reason from its association with oppressive forces leads him to treat religious dogmas and traditions as enemies of reason. In Habermas's understanding, since faith is not open to a self-critical rationality (cf. 1984: 21–22, 397) and is associated with a pre-Enlightenment interpretive monopoly (cf. 1991: 36), all aspects of religion are seen to be beyond meaningful self-criticism. For Habermas, if religious argumentation is to be reflexively critical it must necessarily shed its religious component: it "is no longer borrowed from the language of a specific religious tradition, but from the universe of argumentative discourse that is uncoupled from the event of revelation" (1992: 233).

The findings presented in this chapter demonstrate that religion's critique of public values and secular institutions (see Casanova 1994; Wuthnow 1994a: 17) extends to how people reason when the egalitarian offensive is directed against institutional practices grounded in religious doctrine. It is evident that for those who are part of a shared "community of discourse" (F. Schüssler Fiorenza 1991; Wuthnow 1989b) or "community of memory" (Bellah et al. 1985), religion provides the language with which to contest doctrinal issues. For respondents in this study, religion, rather than demanding "a turning away from knowledge" and the "sacrifice of the intellect" (Weber 1918-20/1978: 567), provides the dominant "knowledge" grounding their drive to transform the church. As such, moreover, the doctrinal reasoning of pro-change Catholics shows that as Patricia Hill Collins (1990: 219) has argued, "values lie at the heart of the knowledge validation process such that inquiry always has an ethical aim."

While Habermas (1992: 233) might suggest that pro-change Catholics' doctrinal reasoning goes beyond religion into a sphere of critical discourse whereby it loses its theological distinctiveness, in my judgment respondents' critiques of church teaching and practices are firmly grounded in theology. The respondents' arguments integrate "the event of revelation" (cf. Habermas 1992: 233) and use meanings derived from it to justify change. In short, the respondents argue for "integrity" between Catholic doctrinal ethics and the church's institutional practices.[12] The institutional transformation advocated by res-

---

12. Quoting again, Francis Schüssler Fiorenza: "Integrity is narrower and stricter than coherence or consistency. It concerns priorities, principles, and paradigms.

pondents is thus expressed using the "first language" of the church itself. The symbols (e.g., Jesus) and ideas (e.g., "universality") that pro-change Catholics use to support their participative agenda not only come from within the church's doctrinal tradition but are central to it. The respondents contest what is "core" using doctrine to critique the doctrine offered by the church hierarchy to justify its interpretations.

THE DEMOCRATIZING POTENTIAL OF REASON

While this study's findings take issue with Habermas's negation of the possibility of a critical religious discourse, the data strongly support Habermas's faith in reason. In particular, the findings illuminate how Habermas's view of reason as the basis for communicative action has an egalitarian charge that is frequently overlooked in criticisms of Habermas. Critics of Habermas's accent on the emancipatory potential of the practical use of language tend to counter that differences among people in social experiences, vocabulary, and the use of language mean that an "ideal speech situation" will always be contaminated by power inequalities (e.g., Gould 1996; Mansbridge 1993; I. Young 1996). This point is well taken.

Yet it is also the case that, depending on the specific institutional context in which ideological contestation takes place, making reason the arbiter of competing claims can reduce the overarching hold of other, less democratic forms of authority. As seen in this study, the respondents' use of doctrine – the church's own language – allows them to challenge official church arguments in a way that lessens the power of the church hierarchy to make its interpretations the only legitimate interpretations possible. The resort to doctrinal reasoning recenters interpretive judgment on the "reasonableness" of the arguments offered, rather than on the authority of the church hierarchy and its invocation of the rule of tradition, dogma, or sacred office.

The articulation of doctrine, whether by church officials or nonordained Catholics, involves the contextualized interpretation of reli-

. . . To inquire about the integrity of a belief, tradition, or practice is to ask not how these cohere or correlate with one another but what critique, change, or expansion is required in the face of inconsistencies and conflicts. Integrity requires that one set priorities when there are conflicts and inconsistencies within the tradition, face squarely all the challenges to the tradition, include neglected and excluded voices, and take honestly and seriously changes in background assumptions" (1991: 138).

gious symbols and ideas and, therefore, cannot sustain an interpretive monopoly. The autonomous doctrinal interpretations of WOC and CFFC respondents (and of Dignity respondents in Chapter 5), highlight the relative diffuseness of interpretive activity that in my reading is central to Habermas's theory of communicative action. Since communicatively achieved agreement is a cooperative process of reciprocal critique, there can be no one fixed source but only multiple and shifting sites of interpretation. Accordingly, neither the church hierarchy nor this study's pro-change Catholics have a monopoly on doctrinal "truth."

Habermas notes that the rationality of reasons "makes them double-edged from the word go, because they can both reinforce and upset beliefs" (1996: 35). It may emerge from engagement in doctrinal critique, therefore, that both the contested definition of the situation and the counterposed claims cannot be reasonably defended. The stance taken by pro-change Catholics in making reason the arbiter of conflicting doctrinal claims thus does not guarantee that their alternative interpretations are right. What it does do, however, is open up doctrinal knowledge to the whole Catholic community and detach it from the privileged domain of the church hierarchy. It challenges the church hierarchy and all Catholics to examine the historical underpinnings, theological assumptions, and institutional power relations informing official church teaching and to consider the alternative reasons that pro-change Catholics (and others) offer. This exercise necessarily invites all Catholics as "audience" to the institutional debate to participate in the communal deliberation, which in itself contributes to strengthening Catholics' participative equality in the church. By thus opening up and reflexively critiquing the doctrinal reasons used to justify official church teaching, pro-change Catholics vindicate Habermas's emphasis on reason's emancipatory potential.

DOCTRINAL DIFFERENTIATION

The ability of this study's respondents to counter the church hierarchy's teaching with doctrinal reasons from within the same doctrinal tradition highlights the differentiated nature of doctrine and points to the fact that it is neither as dogmatic nor as static as Habermas, for example, assumes. The respondents' engagement with doctrinal ideas and how they apply to specific practical questions also highlights doctrinal reasoning as a processual activity. Religious believers are involved in a constant evaluation and reproduction of the objective meanings of religion in light of the specific social and cultural contexts of their individual lives. In view of respondents' ethical-practical understanding of faith, and contrary to Habermas and some other sociologists (e.g., Schluchter 1990), religion cannot be privatized but necessarily spills over into public and political activities. A critically reasoned involvement in a faith tradition that values human dignity and equality may result, as indicated by this study's respondents, in focusing attention on the ways in which religious and other institutional practices perpetuate inequality and how such processes might be changed.

CONFRONTING POWER

Just as faith commitments do not preclude people from using reason to critique their doctrinal tradition, neither does faith prevent people from perceiving institutional and doctrinal distortions stemming from structural power inequalities. Pro-change Catholics not only assume the authority to contest official church teaching, but in so doing they explicitly interrogate whether the church hierarchy's power interests subvert its interpretation of Catholic doctrine. As I have documented, many respondents interpret official church teaching on ordination or on abortion as manifestations of a church hierarchy committed to reproducing the supremacy of its interpretive authority.

Pro-change Catholics' doctrinal interpretive autonomy vis-à-vis the church hierarchy gives concrete expression to Foucault's (1978: 93–94) emphasis on the diffuse nature of power. Although doctrinal production in the church is officially controlled "from above" by the church hierarchy, pro-change respondents show that in practice there is a plurality of doctrinal standpoints and interpretations across the church. Further, their interpretation of an inclusive Catholicism in contrast to the exlusionary themes presented in official church teaching, reinforces their perception of what they consider to be the power-infused impurity of what the church hierarchy presents as divinely prescribed "truth."

Notwithstanding pro-change Catholics' illumination of Foucault's accent on the multiple "micro sites" of interpretive power, at the same time respondents' arguments challenge Foucault's claim that "power reduces one to silence" (1978: 60). Clearly, consciousness of the power behind official doctrinal teaching and of the obstacles to institutional

change presented by the church hierarchy does not prevent respondents from using doctrinal reasons to challenge the church hierarchy's
views. The respondents are able to hold a power-based critique of the
church's institutional practices and simultaneously present doctrinally
reasoned arguments supporting alternative practices. Pro-change
Catholics, therefore, experience the excitement derived from the identity experimentation advised by Foucault (1984b/1997: 172–173) *within* rather than outside the bounds of an institutional tradition. Equally
important, this transformation can be modeled discursively rather than
realized solely through behavior (ibid. 165).

The respondents' participation in the Catholic tradition sensitizes
them to the social and institutional bases of the church hierarchy's
power and to the various ways in which official interpretations of
Catholicism deviate from what respondents have come to know as its
"higher" meanings. It is this same institutional tradition nonetheless
that also facilitates pro-change Catholics' doctrinally reflexive critique
of church practices. Pro-change respondents thus combine reason,
faith, and power in articulating the possibilities for institutional
change. They find doctrinal reasons within the Catholic tradition to
challenge their marginalization by church officials and, further, to
"conquer new territory" (Habermas 1987: 393) by demonstrating the
doctrinal validity of a church in which their pluralistic claims are
affirmed.

Of course, Foucault might challenge the idea that people can escape
the power of the church by staying in the church; but the respondents
in this study show that one can do that at least in a piecemeal fashion.
While discursive challenges do not necessarily lead to changes in institutional practices, I would argue that the doctrinal engagement of
WOC and CFFC respondents is itself changing the parameters of the
church's institutional conversation, even in the absence of any change
in official church policies. The respondents offer alternative ways of
talking about the interpretive possibilities of Catholicism and in the
process also articulate the practical compatibility of an identity that is
Catholic and pro-women's ordination, or Catholic and pro-choice (or
in the case of Dignity, Catholic and gay or lesbian). The public evoca-
tion of these identities and their grounding in the same doctrinal tradition from which the church hierarchy pronounces their incompati-
bility opens up for critique the whole system of "doctrinal production"
in the church. It destabilizes the assumed immutability of official
church teaching on the contested questions by focusing Catholic com-

munal attention on the fact that the church hierarchy is an "interpreter" of the Catholic faith tradition rather than a "source" of revelation (cf. Congar 1967: 336–337) and as such is institutionally free, but constrained by its own power interests, to change its doctrinal stance in response to shifts in historical and cultural consciousness.

REVITALIZING COMMUNAL PARTICIPATION

Through their doctrinal and power-based critique of church practices, pro-change Catholics show how their quest for affirmation in the church does not necessitate the abandonment of participation in the tradition being critiqued. The respondents did not use their arguments defensively as a form of resistance or institutional withdrawal (Habermas 1987: 393–395), but as a re-valuation of the differences invalidated by the church hierarchy. In the respondents' vision, the practical affirmation of differences revitalizes rather than fragments the church's broader communality (cf. Habermas 1987: 393). Thus pro-change Catholics, thinking of the church in Vatican II's language as the communal People of God rather than as the church hierarchy, do not see their disagreement with the Vatican as undermining the cohesiveness of Catholic communality.[13]

Insofar as talk is a "moral expression" (Fine 1995: 130) of how people construe their individual and collective identities, the doctrinal arguments of pro-change Catholics underscore respondents' integration with the larger Catholic community. The respondents' views show a dynamic reciprocity between their own reinterpretations and broadly accessible doctrinal and institutional symbols (including the symbolism of the church hierarchy); they thus keep the Catholic commu-

---

13. Dignity, WOC, and CFFC respondents were asked: "What do you usually think of when you hear the word 'Church' mentioned?" and were given three closed response categories: (1) The place where you go to Mass; (2) The Pope and the bishops; (3) The people "ourselves as the People of God." Substantial majorities of WOC (82%), CFFC (86%), and Dignity (70%) respondents said that they think of the church as the People of God and not as the church hierarchy or a physical location. The fact that a substantial minority of Dignity respondents (19%) thought of the church as the physical Mass location would seem to reflect Dignity members' strong identification with their weekly community Mass gathering. It is also noteworthy that in response to a follow-up question, the majority of the respondents in each group said that the idea of the church as the People of God fitted with their own local experience of being Catholic (WOC, 68%; CFFC, 64%; Dignity, 58%).

nity of memory alive. Catholicism can continue to act therefore as an obligatory moral tradition instead of being relegated to a past that no longer has relevance or coherence (cf. Bellah et al. 1985: 281–283). Contrary to Ronald Inglehart's assertion (1990: 179), traditional religious symbols can continue to be persuasive outside their "original setting." Pro-change Catholics are empowered to "conquer new territory" not by abandoning their communal tradition but by reworking its symbolic resources.

Like their peers in Dignity, WOC and CFFC respondents are tied to communities larger than themselves by their Catholicism and by other identities (being gay/lesbian, an advocate of women's ordination, or pro-choice on abortion) of which they are self-consciously aware. The mutuality of these identities provides respondents with an objective ethical framework for evaluating institutional practices, constructing transformative visions, and mobilizing for change. In other words, the respondents' Catholicism has to be egalitarian, and their egalitarianism has to be consistent with Catholic ethics of justice. For the participants in this study, therefore, multicommunity membership derived from what may appear as multiple "incongruous" identities, rather than weakening the moral expression of values as suggested by some communitarians (e.g., Etzioni 1997: 128), grounds and may in fact amplify their expression.

If postmodernity is, as Craig Calhoun suggests (1995: 108), "the era of the sign," it might seem that the symbolic manipulation and reinterpretation engaged in by pro-change Catholics typifies them as postmodern. In producing new "signs" or new interpretations, respondents reject the view of Catholic identity promulgated in official church teaching. Yet, as I have documented, the new models of Catholic identity and the church put forward by pro-change respondents derive their meaningfulness in large part from the fact that they maintain continuity with the Catholic doctrinal tradition. While the postmodern ethos rejects universalizing arguments, and calls for the construction of new interpretive stances derived from an array of fragmented and contradictory sources (cf. Rosenau 1992: 6–8), pro-change Catholics carve an emancipatory framework from within Catholicism. This enables them to remain Catholic without abandoning their quest for pluralism and equality. Their reasoned critique of the Catholic tradition supports the possibility of a future church that in practice is inclusive, participative, and which gives positive recognition to differences. Since the

Catholic Church is not immutable but, as seen throughout its history and underscored by Vatican II, is open to reformulating doctrine and changing institutional practices, it is both institutionally and doctrinally possible for the church at some future time to embrace some or all of the changes advocated by this study's Catholics.

CHAPTER SEVEN

PLURALISM IN COMMUNITY

As documented in the preceding two chapters, this study's pro-change Catholics envision a transformed church in which differences empower rather than threaten communal solidarity. For them, integration with the larger Catholic tradition does not demand adherence to a uniform identity. This chapter underlines the point that differences characterize community and do so without necessarily fragmenting communal cohesiveness. I focus both on the pluralism that exists among pro-change Catholics and the commonalities that exist between them and conservative Catholics. The findings will contribute to dispelling three popular assumptions: one, that there is a monolithic pro-change bloc or "culturally progressive" worldview (Hunter 1991: 44); two, that pro-change projects in the church represent a "neo-pagan" sensibility rather than a commitment to core Christian symbols (cf. Bork 1996: 288); and three, that pro-change groups are so culturally disconnected from their conservative coreligionists (cf. Hunter 1991: 86–95; Wuthnow 1988: 133, 218–225) that among Catholics, "polarization" has put the church "in jeopardy."[1] This chapter's findings will thus fur-

1. Robert Bork (1996: 288) states that ". . . logic is not what the feminist assault on scripture and liturgy is about. What it is about is sweeping change in the Roman Catholic Church – the ordination of women as priests, and acceptance of gay and lesbian sexual practices, for example. But the motivation may go deeper than that as one suspects from hearing that the feminists within the church engage in neo-pagan ritual magic and the worship of pagan goddesses." Some Catholic commentators interpret the doctrinal differences among Catholics as threatening the cohesion of the church, arguing that "the situation has reached such an alarming state that something has to be done about it soon or the survival of the American Catholic Church will be in jeopardy" (Tripole 1996: 9).

ther show the complexity of identity and of religion as a meaning system in late modernity.

DIVERSITY AND CULTURAL COHESION

Descriptive statistical data based on the questionnaires completed by
Dignity, WOC, and CFFC respondents will highlight differences
among the three groups on specific questions of faith, conscience, sexuality, abortion, and other politically controversial questions in
American society. This chapter also uses survey data from respondents
who are members of the Catholic League for Religious and Civil
Rights. As noted in Chapter 1, data from this relatively conservative
and older group of American Catholics provides a useful counterpoint
to the book's primary focus on pro-change Catholics. Incorporating the
Catholic League data facilitates exploring whether contemporary
American Catholicism is as divided into two cultures as is claimed to
characterize both Catholicism (Kennedy 1988: 3, 19) and American
society more generally (Hunter 1991: 42–46).[2] Influenced by a more
positive heuristic, the comparative analysis also probes whether cultural differences offer the possibility of cohesiveness and conversation
across ideological divisions. The Catholic League data will highlight
differences between conservative and pro-change Catholics, and more
important, it will illustrate their commitment to a shared, although
contested, doctrinal tradition. I will suggest that the pluralism evident
among Catholics is not a source of communal fragmentation. It is contained by commitment to overarching symbols and traditions that can
be used to facilitate both the bridging and validation of differences.

By illustrating differences among pro-change Catholics who comprise a relatively homogeneous group, this chapter will underscore the

---

2. Kennedy (1988: xiii) argues that there are two cultures of American
   Catholicism. He differentiates the institutional "organizational church" (culture one) from the church as "mystery," the people of God, "a community of
   vital believers" (culture two). Kennedy argues that "culture two Catholicism
   has developed to remind the institutional leaders of culture one of the true
   nature of the church" (ibid. xv). On the surface, therefore, it might seem that
   according to this model my pro-change Catholics belong to culture two. Yet,
   since Kennedy maintains that groups who "seek to prove that they belong firmly and fully" to the institutional church belong to culture one, the strategies
   and institutional focus of pro-change Catholics would seem to place them in
   culture one, even though they also clearly comprise culture two.

presence of pluralism in everyday life. At the same time, the valuing of shared symbols among groups who are different points to the fact that pluralism does not inevitably threaten communal solidarity. It suggests rather that unity can be forged out of diversity whether in a local or more global communal context without necessarily suppressing the antagonisms that frequently accompany contested differences.

CULTURAL PLURALISM AMONG PRO-CHANGE CATHOLICS

Previous chapters have pointed to the pluralism that exists among pro-change Catholics. Most obviously, there are differences in the purposes of pro-change Catholic organizations as highlighted by the range of activist groups that exist. Each group included in this study pursues a specific agenda notwithstanding the aim common to all three of constructing a more inclusive church. For Dignity, the recognition of gay and lesbian sexuality is paramount; for WOC respondents, it is women's ordination, and for CFFC it is a moral pluralism that validates differences on abortion. Nonetheless, participants in each of these groups are united by their participation in a symbolic community of pro-change Catholics, indicated by their affiliation with the Call to Action lay reform movement in the church.

Since respondents in this study comprise a group committed to achieving participative equality in the church, it seems reasonable to think of them as embracing a "culturally progressive" worldview. James Hunter argues that "cultural progressives" have a rational, subjective, contextual, and processual view of morality, and he contrasts this orientation with that of the "culturally orthodox," who are committed to an external and transcendent authority (1991: 44). According to Hunter, these "fundamentally different conceptions of moral authority" account for what he sees as a "culture war" over not just specific issues such as abortion, sexuality, or women's roles, but more fundamentally, "over different ideas and beliefs about truth, the good, obligation to one another, the nature of community and so on" (ibid: 49).

Many studies have challenged the empirical validity of claims for the existence of polarizing liberal and conservative worldviews (e.g., Davis and Robinson 1996a, 1996b; Dillon 1996b; DiMaggio, Evans, and Bryson 1996; Williams 1997). These critiques variously demonstrate that while liberals and conservatives take opposing views on many issues, there is also a substantial amount of disagreement among relatively homogeneous groups, and of similarity among opponents on specific moral, theological, and sociopolitical questions. It is evident moreover that an individual's commitment to one set of values (e.g., Christian morality) can be moderated by an equally strong commitment to what might appear as opposing values (e.g., individualism and altruism) (cf. Hart 1992).[3]

Although the data in this book are confined to a very specific sample of pro-change Catholics, they allow me to explore whether as a group committed to the sort of institutional change that James Hunter would label culturally progressive, they share the undifferentiated sensibility toward pluralism and diversity which his thesis maintains (1991: 114–115). In other words, we should expect not attitudinal differences among pro-change Catholics, but a shared commitment to the discrete issues that comprise the pro-change agenda. Irrespective of whether they are drawn from Dignity, WOC, or CFFC we should, on Hunter's thesis, expect respondents to express similarly accepting attitudes toward homosexuality, women's ordination, and abortion. This pattern should demonstrate, as Amitai Etzioni (1997: 197) might suspect, the rejection of a limited or qualified diversity. In this view, calling for the elimination of institutional prohibitions regarding sexuality or gender, for example, would extend to favoring the elimination of restrictions regarding abortion.

In order to investigate whether there was internal cultural variation among pro-change Catholics, I included several Likert-type rating scales and other closed-ended questions in the Dignity, WOC, and CFFC self-administered questionnaires. Respondents were asked about their religious beliefs and church participation, and about their views on morality, conscience, sexual behavior, women's ordination, abortion, economic issues, and the death penalty. Since the respondents in

3. Hunter's thesis is clearly controversial on a number of fronts (see, for example, Williams 1997). Hunter repeatedly states that his critics do not understand the complex understanding of culture he posits, in which "we become separated from our own speech," compelled by the constraints and expectations of public culture to accentuate our views (1996: 247). Hunter thus seems to embrace a reified understanding of culture that fails to recognize the agency and moral authorship of individual and collective actors in everyday life. While Hunter (1994: 122–149) is rather pointed in his critique of Americans' inability to draw on "languages of conviction," in his understanding of a coercive public culture such languages would seem to be irrelevant, since in his view they become disembodied from the people speaking.

this study were not a statistically representative sample of American "pro-change" Catholics, and since the sizes of the Dignity, WOC, and CFFC samples varied, the findings are not generalizable to a larger population and are limited in their statistical reliability. Nevertheless, in view of the differences that characterize this relatively homogenous group of pro-change Catholics, it is important to give them due consideration.

RELIGIOUS BELIEFS AND MORALITY

Pro-change respondents differ significantly from one another with respect to some core faith beliefs and practices.[4] It is noteworthy that CFFC respondents were comparatively less involved in the institutional church. For example, only one-third (32%) of CFFC respondents, unlike the majority of WOC (74%) and Dignity (88%) respondents, attended weekly Mass. Similarly, whereas the majority of WOC (63%) and Dignity (56%) respondents believe in transubstantiation (i.e., that during the Mass the consecration changes the bread and wine into the body and blood of Christ), this was true for only 23 percent of CFFC respondents.

There are also differences among pro-change Catholics in their overarching view of morality. The majority of the respondents in each of the three groups endorsed a contextualist understanding of morality, agreeing with the statement that "what is morally right depends on the particular situation and circumstances of the individual." WOC respondents (39%), however, were significantly more likely than either Dignity (17%) or CFFC (19%) respondents to sanction a universal view of morality, believing that "moral norms exist which are valid for all people." WOC respondents were also significantly more

4. In this chapter, significance refers to statistical significance. All the differences reported are statistically significant using the Chi-square test (x^2) that measures the relationship between two categorical variables. The significance level used was less than, or equal to, .05. This means that the likelihood of obtaining the same result by chance alone is less than one in twenty. Since x^2 is sensitive to sample size, the comparative smallness in size of this study's sample of pro-change Catholics (n = 310) compared to typical national survey samples of 1,000 respondents, and the differences in the size of the three specific groups who comprise the sample (WOC, n = 214; Dignity, n = 64; CFFC, n = 32) call for a certain amount of caution in making inferences from the statistical differences observed. Nonetheless, the statistical exercise remains substantively useful in that it allows us to explore whether there are patterned differences among this relatively homogeneous group of pro-change Catholics.

likely (51%) than their Dignity (30%) and CFFC (36%) counterparts to state that they "usually give a lot of thought to Catholic teaching" in informing their conscience.

In light of these differences in respondents' views of morality it is not surprising that differences emerged among WOC and CFFC respondents in their attitudes toward homosexuality. Similar to the consensus among Dignity participants regarding sexuality, substantial majorities from both CFFC (77%) and WOC (74%) agreed that people are born rather than choose or are brought up to be gay. Nevertheless, 61 percent of WOC respondents compared to 23 percent of their CFFC counterparts said that same-sex sexual relations were "sometimes wrong." Even allowing for the ambiguity contained in such standard survey questions and their failure to distinguish the source or nature of the moral wrong, and for the fact that any sexual relationship can be wrong "sometimes" if it is exploitative in some way, the proportion of WOC respondents who took a negative stance is still quite high. Further, 14 percent of WOC respondents in contrast to none of the CFFC respondents said that the church is right to disapprove of homosexual behavior.

ABORTION

Differences among respondents are more clearly evident over abortion. Predictably, all but two of the thirty-two CFFC respondents described their views on abortion as "strongly" rather than "moderately" pro-choice. All the CFFC respondents stated that abortion should be legal in cases of rape and economic hardship; and all but one agreed that it should be legal in the case of a serious fetal defect. Three respondents expressed reservations about abortion in objectively less pressing circumstances (e.g., abortion for any reason), with one respondent emphasizing that there should be more extensive pre-abortion counseling in such cases. All of the CFFC respondents disagreed with legally requiring parental notification for teenagers; one respondent agreed with spousal notification; and three agreed with the imposition of a twenty-four-hour waiting requirement.

By contrast with their CFFC peers, there was quite a substantial amount of variation within the WOC group in abortion attitudes. WOC respondents were equally likely to describe their abortion views as either "strongly pro-life" (24%) or "strongly pro-choice" (24%). Somewhat more respondents described themselves as "moderately pro-choice" (30%), and somewhat fewer as "moderately pro-life" (22%).

Just over half (52%) of the WOC sample agreed with the statement that "the church should relax its stance on abortion." Whereas the majority (68%) of WOC respondents agreed that abortion should be legal in the case of rape, just under half (47%) agreed that it should be legal in the case of a serious fetal defect. Smaller minorities agreed that abortion should be legal in cases of economic hardship (36%) and for any unwanted pregnancy (25%). Substantial majorities of WOC respondents also agreed with required counseling concerning the effects of abortion (89%), a twenty-four-hour waiting period (77%), and parental (65%) and spousal (55%) notification.

Dignity respondents also showed internal variation in attitudes toward abortion. Over half (56%) of the Dignity sample, somewhat similar to WOC, stated that the church should relax its opposition to abortion. Overall, however, Dignity participants were somewhat more likely than WOC respondents to endorse a liberal view of abortion. A substantial majority of Dignity participants agreed that abortion should be legal in cases of rape (66%) and fetal defect (61%). Although they were still minority views, Dignity respondents were more likely than WOC respondents to agree that abortion should be legal in cases of economic hardship (44%) and for any unwanted pregnancy (38%). Among Dignity participants, women were more likely than men to say that the church should relax its abortion stance and to favor legal abortion in the case of economic hardship, although these gender differences were significant at the trend level only. In sum, there were differences on abortion both within WOC and Dignity and between the two groups. At the same time, the WOC and Dignity samples differed significantly from the CFFC respondents in their abortion views.

SOCIOPOLITICAL ATTITUDES

There was also variation in pro-change respondents' self-described political orientations and sociopolitical attitudes. It is noteworthy that although the majority of Dignity (66%), WOC (69%), and CFFC (90%) respondents described their political orientation as liberal or very liberal, a substantial proportion of Dignity (31%) and WOC (27%) respondents described themselves as moderate.[5] Given the self-

5. Dignity, WOC, and CFFC respondents were asked: "Overall, how would you describe your political views?" and given five closed response categories: very conservative, conservative, moderate, liberal, very liberal. While somewhat

described overall political liberalism of respondents, it is not surprising that almost all of the respondents in each group agreed that the government should take either "a great deal" or a "fair amount" of responsibility for providing health and medical care (WOC, 96%; Dignity, 96%; CFFC, 100%) and providing jobs for all who want them (WOC, 87%; Dignity, 87%; CFFC, 97%). Substantial majorities also agreed that the government should take responsibility for reducing income differences between the rich and the poor (WOC, 81%; Dignity, 67%; CFFC, 91%), and providing welfare benefits for teenage mothers (WOC, 76%; Dignity, 69%; CFFC, 88%). Overall, only a small minority of respondents favored the death penalty for people convicted of murder.

Yet once again, as on the abortion and morality items, there were significant differences among respondents in their attitudes toward specific issues. CFFC respondents, for example, were more liberal than WOC respondents regarding government responsibility for health care, with 88 percent of the former compared to 53 percent of the latter stating that the government should take a "great deal" of responsibility for providing health care. Dignity respondents, on the other hand – notwithstanding women members' significantly greater liberalism on economic inequality – were more conservative overall than their CFFC and WOC counterparts in their attitudes toward reducing economic differences between rich and poor, and in their attitudes toward welfare benefits for teenage mothers.[6]

These findings highlight the significant differences among pro-change Catholics in their attitudes toward a wide range of issues. Some of the differences observed among WOC, Dignity, and CFFC respondents are obviously related to the differences in the specific institu-

similar majorities in each group described their political orientations as liberal (WOC, 57%; CFFC, 53%; Dignity, 47%), a larger proportion of CFFC (37%) compared to Dignity (19%) and WOC (12%) respondents said they were very liberal.

6. For example, 33 percent of Dignity respondents, compared to 68 percent of CFFC respondents and 51 percent of WOC respondents, said that the government should take a "great deal" of responsibility for reducing income inequalities. Similarly, only 11 percent of Dignity respondents, compared to 47 percent of CFFC respondents and 30 percent of WOC respondents, said that the government should take a "great deal" of responsibility for providing welfare benefits for teenage mothers. Dignity respondents (25%) were also more likely than CFFC (0%) or WOC (13%) respondents to agree with the death penalty.

tional agendas of the respective groups. Thus, for example, it is not surprising that CFFC respondents demonstrated a strong commitment to
choice on abortion, and that Dignity respondents were more sympathetic than WOC respondents to a contextual understanding of personal morality. By the same token, CFFC respondents' less frequent
Mass attendance may be related to the fact that their pro-choice agenda is further removed from the church's sacramental life than are either
WOC's or Dignity's aims.

Notwithstanding differences in their respective organizational
agendas, all of the respondents are Catholics committed to institutionalizing change in the church. In line with the "culturally progressive" worldview identified by Hunter (1991: 44), they favor a contextual approach to doctrinal interpretation. Yet it is evident that commitment to church reform, although it may be a good predictor of a
disposition toward a "progressive" multi-issue ideological package, does
not mean that there is cultural uniformity among those who envision
change. As seen in Chapter 5, even the relative focus and cohesiveness
of the Dignity/Boston community does not preclude internal communal differentiation as to what strategies and values should be prioritized
in devising practices that seek to be inclusive. Contrary to the idea of
a monolithic, culturally progressive moral sensibility (Hunter 1991:
115), this study indicates that at least among pro-change Catholics,
there is internal cultural differentiation. Commitment to institutional
change does not coincide with an overarching political liberalism.
Liberalism on abortion cannot be inferred a priori from liberalism on
issues of gender equality such as women's ordination, for instance, and
liberalism on homosexuality does not necessarily translate into liberalism on women's issues or on economic equality. The fact that people
may share an egalitarian agenda in the Catholic Church, as in secular
political movements, but construe its practical limits differently,
underscores the point that in practice people who are committed to
pluralism are also constrained by their own moral and ideological
boundaries.

Dignity's, WOC's, and CFFC's organizational affinity with each
other's agendas and their alliance as members of the Call to Action
coalition for church reform is not sufficient to override important attitudinal differences among members. It is evident that the interpretive
autonomy displayed by the respondents in regard to the church hierarchy's authority is also present in their disposition toward discrete issues
on the pro-change agenda. It is not surprising, perhaps, that people

who emphasize the need for pluralism in institutional practices, themselves demonstrate a plurality of views on issues that might on the surface appear to comprise a coherent agenda.

In sum, pro-change respondents' internal pluralism highlights the extent to which differences can characterize relatively like-minded symbolic communities. The multiple differences that comprise any individual identity have practical effects in daily life. Being a member of WOC, for example, in contrast to Dignity or CFFC, matters with regard to how some WOC respondents evaluate specific issues such as abortion or homosexuality. The fact that there are attitudinal differences among pro-change respondents highlights the challenge associated with enacting interpretive pluralism and forging coalitions among groups that, while sharing overarching commitments, have discrete interests.

MAINTAINING THE SACRED AND REAFFIRMING CORE SYMBOLS

The preceding section highlighted the attitudinal differences among Dignity, WOC, and CFFC respondents and showed that being a pro-change Catholic is not determinant of a multi-issue moral liberalism. This section dispels a second myth, namely that Catholics who are committed to a more egalitarian church eschew traditional Catholic symbols in their pro-change offensive. Dignity's reconstruction of the Mass liturgy (Chapter 5) and WOC and CFFC respondents' doctrinal reasoning (Chapter 6) served to illustrate that while pro-change Catholics understand doctrine as contextually dependent, they retain the sanctity of important symbols in the Catholic tradition. This section will use questionnaire survey data from Dignity, WOC, and CFFC respondents to clarify further what pro-change respondents see as core and peripheral in Catholicism.

In response to an open-ended question, respondents were asked to list any three aspects of Catholicism that they considered to be so central to their personal understanding of Catholicism that they would not want to see them changed. The majority of WOC (56%), almost half of Dignity (46%), and somewhat fewer of the CFFC (41%) respondents identified the church's sacramental and liturgical symbol system as personally core. This finding accords with other studies (Redmont 1992: 230–232; Winter et al. 1994: 152–153) that stress the importance of the church's sacramental life especially for Catholic women. In addition, somewhat similar proportions in each of the three groups identified the redemptive and incarnate meanings of Jesus's life (Dignity, 26%; WOC, 16%; CFFC, 22%), the church's social justice tradition (Dignity, 11%; WOC, 14%; CFFC, 24%), and Catholic global communality (Dignity, 16%; WOC, 14%; CFFC, 13%).[7]

The responses to this question thus revealed a relatively strong consensus among respondents in their subjective mapping of the core aspects of Catholicism. At the same time, of course, the statistical variation across the three groups in the symbols identified as core suggests a pluralism that may lead pro-change Catholics to focus on different priorities. Nonetheless, the data clearly reinforce the findings presented in Chapters 5 and 6 that Catholics who are committed to changes in the church's institutional practices are deeply attached to core symbols and values in the tradition. It may be argued, indeed, that it is their valuing of those symbols and the meanings they ascribe to them that mobilizes their identity and institutional projects, even if, as suggested by some CFFC respondents' infrequent Mass attendance, they sometimes restrict their sacramental participation in protest against the inegalitarian ways in which core symbols are currently institutionalized (e.g., the ban on women priests).

The importance of "core" Catholic symbols to pro-change Catholics is also manifested in respondents' disposition toward the papacy. Although the majority of pro-change Catholics see the church as the communal People of God[8] and disagree with the church hierarchy's use of authority, it is not the case that they are opposed to the most visible manifestation of the church's hierarchical structure, the papacy. Almost all pro-change respondents reject the idea of an equivalence between the church hierarchy's teaching and divine law, and not surprisingly, a substantial majority disagree with the church hierarchy's self-understanding of its right to articulate universally applicable moral principles.[9] Yet substantial majorities of WOC (81%) and

---

7. In addition, 1 percent of Dignity respondents mentioned the church's hierarchical tradition as core to their understanding of Catholicism. This open-ended question was answered by 174 WOC, 50 Dignity, and 27 CFFC respondents. Winter et al. (1994: 152) suggest that Catholic women "have a greater love of liturgy than is ordinarily typical of women in other denominations."

8. As noted in Chapter 6, 82 percent of WOC, 86 percent of CFFC, and 70 percent of Dignity respondents think of the church as the People of God.

9. Using a five-point scale (1 = strongly agree to 5 = strongly disagree), respondents' level of agreement with the following two statements was ascertained:

Dignity (78%) respondents, and over half (54%) of the CFFC respondents, stated that it was important for the Catholic Church to have a Pope. Lending support to the argument that "the principle of hierarchy remains deeply rooted in the Catholic imagination" (Coleman 1989: 269), pro-change Catholics are clearly not averse to papal symbolism. In their view, however, the Pope's role should be to provide what they consider to be socially responsive moral leadership. Pro-change Catholics thus value the charisma of papal office but see it as representing the unity of a global and pluralistic communal tradition rather than signaling a monopolistic interpretation of Catholicism.[10]

It is evident from the preceding discussion, and from the data presented in Chapters 5 and 6, that pro-change Catholics are critically engaged with the church's sacramental and institutional dimensions simultaneously. For them, Catholicism as a "way of life" means that there is a mutuality, rather than the polarity suggested by Kennedy (1988: 4), between focusing on the church's institutional life and celebrating the faith mysteries within the tradition. This study's findings also demonstrate that the contestation of doctrinal knowledge and interpretive authority in the church is not accompanied by an erosion of the power of "traditional" Catholic symbols.[11] These symbols, rather, have a "depth" and a diffuseness that allows them to be linked with personal identities in many diverse ways (Coleman 1989: 262). Clearly, all symbols and traditions are open to multiple interpretations (Hall 1973), and the meanings of particular symbols in specific contexts can be the source of antagonism and conflict even in the most

(1) "Church teaching and God's law are basically one and the same thing because Church teaching is inspired by God's law"; (2) "The Pope and the bishops have the right to state moral principles that apply to all people regardless of their religious beliefs."

10. On a 1 (strongly agree) to 5 (strongly disagree) point scale, respondents strongly agreed with the following important qualities for a Pope to have in order to carry out the church's mission in the world today: open to new ideas: WOC, 95 percent; Dignity, 98 percent; CFFC, 96 percent; responsive to diverse Catholic voices: WOC, 92 percent; Dignity, 95 percent; CFFC, 97 percent; provide strong moral leadership: WOC, 82 percent; Dignity, 67 percent; CFFC, 76 percent.

11. Roger Finke and Rodney Stark (1992: 268) argue that the crisis in Catholic vocations "reflects a crisis of faith and the deep erosion of the power of traditional Catholic symbols and practices." Contrary to this claim, and similar to my findings, Patrick McNamara's (1992) study suggests that "beliefs and values central to the Catholic tradition" are still important for late adolescent American Catholics.

cooperative of communities (recall, for example, the issue of co-presiding for Dignity/Boston). It would seem nevertheless that for those who are part of a specific religious or other cultural tradition, some symbols can have an enduring and unifying power that transcends the context of their articulation; they are frequently reworked but not necessarily abandoned.

This study's pro-change Catholics, therefore, unlike those who embrace a post-Christian consciousness (e.g., Daly 1996), do not find it necessary to either eschew traditional Catholic symbols or to acquire new symbols from outside Catholicism (cf. Weaver 1985: 182–186) to realize their multiple identities. While clearly critical of the Catholic tradition, they also value its positive resources (see also Schneiders 1991: 39). In the postmodern era of decontextualized signs (cf. Rosenau 1992: 34–39), pro-change Catholics retain symbols whose significance derives from a remembered tradition. As this study's overall findings show, pro-change respondents inject traditional Catholic symbols with meanings that serve their emancipatory purposes at the same time that their use of those symbols demonstrates their integration with the tradition. In reworking the symbols of Catholicism, pro-change Catholics show that critiquing a tradition's narratives, and discrediting some of the ways in which those symbols have been used to perpetuate inequality, does not weaken the hold of the tradition on participants' identities. As this book demonstrates, people do not view grand narratives in all-or-nothing terms; while critique of any tradition will (hopefully) lead to repentance for injustices committed, it does not mean that the tradition can no longer function as a source of personal and collective esteem. Most traditions contain multiple strands, and the bad strands do not necessarily contaminate the good with which they are intertwined.[12]

SACRED CANOPIES

The findings presented thus far underline the fact that pro-change Catholics are neither monolithic nor "post-Christian." This section presents data which suggest that a third related assumption – that

12. Discussing collective memory and how Abraham Lincoln's memory "embodied a universal cultural presence that constituted common models for acting" in America during the Second World War, Barry Schwartz asks: "Is the nation not weakened when its grand narratives are discredited, when its citizens conceive the past as something to be repented rather than embraced?" (1996: 923, 925).

there is a cultural lacuna between pro-change and conservative Catholics that threatens the church's unity and cohesiveness – may also be a distortion of the actual situation. Here I compare pro-change Catholics with their more conservative coreligionists from the Catholic League for Religious and Civil Rights (n = 213), an organization that defends official church teaching. Once again, if the "culture war" thesis is right, the polarized moral orientations and attendant understandings of community attributed to liberals and conservatives (Hunter 1991: 42-50) should lessen the grounds for communality between pro-change and conservative Catholics. On the other hand, if identities are more complex and multifaceted, pro-change and conservative Catholics' objectively shared religious identity should provide them with common subjectively experienced attachments and memories that facilitate communal integration notwithstanding doctrinal differences. In addition, these same symbolic attachments may also, perhaps, be critical to the forging of new institutional practices.

Almost all of the Catholic League respondents attended Mass at least once a week (98%); were opposed to abortion (98%), homosexuality (93%), and women priests (92%); accepted the special authority of papal teaching on faith (99%) and morality (97%); and endorsed the universal applicability (90%) and divinely inspired nature (81%) of papal teaching. Quite clearly, their views on the doctrinal questions contested by pro-change Catholics and their attitudes toward papal authority show them to be starkly at odds with the understanding of doctrine demonstrated by this study's pro-change respondents.

Yet despite their different doctrinal attitudes, there is remarkable overlap between Catholic League and pro-change respondents in the features identified as core to their personal understandings of Catholicism. Similar to Dignity, WOC, and CFFC respondents, a substantial proportion of Catholic League respondents (61%) prioritized the church's sacramental-liturgical tradition. The attachment shared by conservative and pro-change Catholics to the church's sacramental tradition would seem to offer a bridge over some of the doctrinal differences between these divergent groups. It is evident, for instance, that independent of their different perspectives on women's ordination, both groups value the Mass as a core sacramental ritual of Catho-

Contrary to Schwartz, this book's findings indicate that people can both critique and remain committed to a communal tradition, and indeed, that commitment may be strengthened as a result of critique.

licism. Some of the symbols and meanings associated with the Mass, therefore, may function as sources of communal integration for those who might otherwise inhabit discrete symbolic universes. Since what is doctrinally core in the Catholic tradition is not as fixed as one might assume from Vatican pronouncements, attitudinal differences between conservative and pro-change Catholics on women's ordination, for example, inevitably raise the question as to whether the consecration of the Eucharist is more core to Catholicism than the assumption that the consecration should be performed by a male priest. Such a question would seem to provide a critical opening for conversation between Catholics who, on the surface, appear to have opposing doctrinal views.

The possibility of maintaining pluralism and cohesiveness within the broader Catholic community is further enhanced by participants' shared subjectively meaningful experiences as Catholics. Pro-change (Dignity, WOC, and CFFC) and conservative (Catholic League) respondents were asked to identify events or occasions during their lives when they felt particularly proud to be Catholic. Once again, there was significant overlap across the groups in what they identified as personal sources of Catholic pride. The pull of Catholic communal identity was strikingly evident for a substantial minority of both pro-change and conservative respondents. Relatively similar proportions of respondents from each of the pro-change groups (24%) and from the conservative Catholic League (21%) mentioned events or occasions that affirmed for them the personal importance of various aspects of their Catholic roots and identity. Among specific identity subthemes were respondents' pride in Catholic public figures (e.g., John F. Kennedy), the shared recognition and global presence of Catholicism in foreign settings, and respondents' pride in seeing their children continue the Catholic faith

The following quotations provide a sense of the communal pride shared by respondents from all four groups:

"When Pope John XXIII died, people of varied faiths gave me their condolences, as if I was family. When, as army chaplain in Germany, 1976, Bernard Haring spoke to Army Medical Professionals on *Humanae Vitae* and answered all questions relating to Catholic ethics – he was soundly applauded." (WOC man, retired Catholic priest)

"Our family did not stress ethnic heritage because we were of German descent and this was unpopular during World War II. Rather, our Catholic heritage was our primary identity." (WOC woman over 65)

"When a Catholic was found to have led France's anti-Nazi underground during World War II. When John XXIII presided over Vatican II. When Catholic priests in Central and South America stood up for social justice. When John Kennedy explained his Catholicism in the Bible Belt." (CFFC woman)

"Christmas 1960. I was in Korea. Several Americans joined with a Korean choir to sing the Christmas Mass. We had little in common with those people. We spoke no Korean. They spoke little English. But when we began to sing the Latin of the Mass, we became one. We looked at each other differently. We felt close to those Korean Catholics, our brothers and sisters in Christ." (Catholic League man)

"I'm always proud to be part of the community and Church, and Catholicism is my most comfortable expression of that sense. I always use Mario Cuomo's words 'The Catholic church is my spiritual home and my life.' " (CFFC woman)

"When I see my children living their faith, I am happy that my Catholic faith has given me a solid foundation to pass on to them." (WOC woman)

In addition, sacramental occasions marking life events including family funerals, celebrations, and college reunion Masses were commonly salient for respondents, and a small proportion in each group mentioned conversions to Catholicism – of themselves, family members, or of parishioners during the Easter Vigil Mass – as sources of pride.[13] The relational significance of the Mass and other liturgies was variously expressed by the following respondents:

13. The percentage distribution was special Masses: WOC, 11 percent; Dignity, 13 percent; CFFC, 2 percent; Catholic League, 21 percent; conversions: WOC, 3 percent; Dignity, 3 percent; CFFC, 5 percent; Catholic League, 5 percent; papal visits: WOC, 5 percent; Dignity, 8 percent; CFFC, 5 percent; Catholic League, 5 percent.

"My father's funeral. My brother's ordination. The ritual is comforting and assuring. It gives one a historical and social perspective absent in contemporary life." (Dignity man)

"My wedding day. The baptism of our children, our son's funeral." (Catholic League man)

"I feel it when I return to my Catholic College for an extraordinary event and everyone joins in the liturgy – they don't have to. The singing is joyous, the responses thunderous from people of all ages, from all over the country. I feel it at my husband's Catholic alma mater when people leave the football festivities to join in the Mass – again with thunderous response. And at our vacation parish which has four daily Masses with several hundred people at each. I think to myself, 'These are the people of God, coming together in worship.' " (WOC woman)

Pointing to Catholics' valuing of the pope as a global public symbol of Catholicism, it was notable that approximately five percent of respondents from each of the four groups identified John Paul II's various visits to the U.S. and elsewhere as sources of pride:

"I think I was rather proud of John Paul II in his address to the U.N. and others on social justice and the need for the U.N." (CFFC woman)

"Pope John Paul's visit to Boston in 1979." (Catholic League man)

"Believe it or not, when John Paul II first came to Boston in 1979. He was the first non-Italian and Polish (my heritage) who had experienced oppression in World War II. I thought he was a sign (gift) from God . . ."(Dignity woman)

"When the Pope came to San Francisco and ministered to those with AIDS." (Dignity man)

How pro-change Catholics construe what it means to be Catholic clearly has a different accent compared to the meanings upheld by conservative Catholics. Most obviously, as underscored by their projects of institutional change, the former subscribe to a radically different understanding of interpretive authority, historical consciousness, and the mutability of doctrine. Given the Catholic League's organizational commitment to upholding Catholic "orthodoxy," it is not surprising that in contrast to pro-change Catholics, a substantial minority of league respondents (27%) emphasized the church's hierarchical tradition as core to Catholicism. There were also some differences between pro-change and conservative respondents in what they remembered as occasions of Catholic pride. Pro-change respondents invoked illustrative examples of social justice, religious memories from their childhood, past adulthood experiences, and the Vatican II era as sources of pride. Catholic League respondents by contrast were more likely to mention specific papal pronouncements and what they considered to be the enduring stability of Catholic moral standards.[14]

Notwithstanding these differences, the overlap between pro-change and conservative respondents in their personal attachment to the church's sacramental tradition and the common themes identified as sources of pride suggest that there are substantially more grounds for their joint sharing of a meaningful Catholic identity than is suggested by the attitudinal differences between them. Although pro-change and conservative Catholics present polarized views on many doctrinal issues, they share a committed attachment to core symbols, meanings, and memories in the Catholic tradition.

Being Catholic appears to have a communal significance that transcends the liberalism or conservatism of its adherents. There seems to be something about socialization in the "remembered trajectory" of the Catholic tradition that anchors Catholics as a group, notwithstanding the participants' contestation of its practical meanings and interpretations. While many Catholics leave the church, the Catholic Church's institutional origin as a church rather than a sect (Weber 1978: 1164–1166) provides a historically continuous (although not a monolithic) narrative (cf. Tracy 1987: 68–69) that may attenuate the tendency toward fragmentation more associated with Protestantism.

The historical roots of Protestantism and its spawning of various dis-

14. Social justice (WOC, 23%; Dignity, 23%; CFFC, 30%), childhood experiences (WOC, 18%; Dignity, 25%; CFFC, 18%), and Vatican II (WOC, 9%; Dignity, 0%, CFFC, 16%) were identified by pro-change Catholics as personal occasions of Catholic pride. Catholic League respondents emphasized papal teaching/statements (25%) and the church's stable moral values (19%). A small minority in each group identified miscellaneous events and memories.

senting sects, originating with Calvin's split from Luther in the six-teenth century (Elton 1963: 210–238), validate the formation of new traditions rather than containing doctrinal or cultural diversity within the existing tradition. In this sense, the evolution of Protestantism is in part a history of the organizational structuring of particular claims. Division has characterized Protestantism since its inception, especial-ly in the United States, where conflicts over theology and social issues have caused several denominational splits (Hoge 1976: 19–42). Of course Protestant denominations are also able to contain dissent among members over controversial doctrinal and political questions. As Nancy Ammerman (1990: 271) has observed, for example, in re-gard to the Southern Baptist Convention (SBC), the lack of tight hier-archical control means that both fundamentalist and moderate con-gregations can remain within the bounds of the SBC while maintain-ing distance from official policies. On the other hand, the overall weakness of denominational identity among some Protestants (e.g., Presbyterians studied by Hoge et al. 1994: 118–119; 211) may make religious mobility a more readily acceptable option for Protestants.[15]

By contrast with Protestantism, the Catholic Church's institutional self-understanding is one of historical continuity with the early pre-Reformation church. Its attendant accent on unity and catholicity rather than factionalism seems to make staying rather than leaving the "natural" or more "meaningful" option for Catholics who disagree with official church teachings. The historical motif of continuity appears to confer upon Catholics ownership rights that motivate them to deal with interpretive differences by reconstructing the church from within rather than leaving it. The actual interpretive differences within the church, even though they are frequently delegitimated in official church teaching, may push the transformative possibility of discover-ing what the Catholic theologian David Tracy calls "similarity in dif-ference" (1981: 408; 1987: 20, 93). Tracy's (1981) hermeneutical anal-ysis of "classic" narratives, events, and symbols in Catholic theology leads him to argue for a Catholic analogical imagination that empha-sizes the ultimate trustworthiness and wonder of people and society; it thus sees "the entire world, the ordinary in all its variety . . . theologi-

---

15. It is of interest here that Troy Perry, who founded the nondenominational "gay" Metropolitan Community Church, recounts a childhood and early adult-hood that for various personal reasons was characterized by quite a bit of denominational switching. See Perry (1990: 8–15, 22–23).

cally envisioned as sacrament" (ibid. 413). This theological imagination provides Catholics with preconscious symbols and images that encourage belief in the redeemability of "sinful" or unjust institutional practices and social relations, and attitudes that seek to preserve rather than fragment community (see Greeley 1989b).[16]

As expressed by many pro-change respondents in this study, Catholicism is understood as a "birthright" (see also Hout and Greeley 1987: 325) that can neither be given up nor taken away; it must be refashioned. It is perhaps this entitled sense of church ownership that nurtures pro-change Catholics' use of voice (cf. Hirschman 1970: 96–98) as a powerful strategy in the remaking of the church. As previous chapters have documented, pro-change Catholics are not just voicing opposition; they are reinterpreting Catholic doctrine, using doctrine to legitimate a transformed church. This reinterpretive activity, moreover, in accord with their project of maintaining connection with the Catholic community, is not perceived by pro-change respondents as greatly threatening the "unity" of the church, but as preserving its communality through the reconstruction of a more just and inclusively participative church. Thus, for example, in response to the survey question, "Do you think that the unity of the Catholic Church is lessened by the fact that Catholics differ in their interpretation of what it means to be Catholic?" only a small minority of respondents said that it was lessened "a lot" (Dignity, 13%; WOC, 9%; CFFC, 17%). Respondents were more likely to say that it was lessened "not at all" (Dignity, 35%; WOC, 47%; CFFC, 45%), or "somewhat" (Dignity, 52%; WOC, 44%; CFFC, 38%).

The integrating pull of the church's "universalism" and its historical continuity exert a strong claim on pro-change Catholics' collective communal memory. Almost all of this study's respondents do not see the Catholic Church as the "one true church." Dignity (84%), WOC (77%), and CFFC (91%) respondents see Catholicism rather as one of many equally true faiths.[17] The pluralistic view of faith they endorse is

---

16. Andrew Greeley (1989b) provides extensive cross-national empirical evidence that these differences in religious symbols and images continue to statistically differentiate the values and attitudes of Catholics (communal) and Protestants (individualist), leading him to conclude that "[t]he Protestant ethic and the Catholic ethic are alive and well . . ." (ibid. 500). For a critically appreciative discussion of David Tracy's understanding of theological "method" and his construal of a religious "classic," see Sanks 1993.

17. In the Dignity, WOC, and CFFC surveys, the closed response question asked

nonetheless accompanied by a deep personal attachment to the specificity of the Catholic Church's historical roots and global presence. These themes emerged as important markers of Catholicism in pro-change respondents' explanations of what for them personally makes being a Catholic different from being a Protestant.[18] Consider the following illustrative quotes from WOC respondents:

> "It is one of the only truly worldwide religions. I'm proud that I look to the same Pope as an impoverished person from Central America or Asia."

> "The universality of belief and rite."

> "International unity and scope of membership. 2000+ years of history."

> "I like the 'unity,' the feeling of extended community – a diverse people under one umbrella."

> "Direct relationship to Jesus founding a Church."

> "Tradition of unity back to the Apostles."

> "The rich tradition which goes back 2000 years, the continuity, the willingness to take a stand on issues."

> "Consistent line of growth/struggle in the faith – remaining with the struggle, not dissociating."

> "The possibility of drawing on a longer, richer, more multidimensional tradition and history."

was: "Do you think of Catholicism as being the one true faith, or as one among a number of equally true faiths?" In response, a minority of respondents said that it was the one true faith (Dignity, 5%; WOC, 12%; CFFC, 3%), or that they did not know (Dignity, 11%; WOC, 11%; CFFC, 6%).

18. WOC and CFFC respondents were asked the following open-ended question: "What for you makes being a Catholic different, for instance, from being a Protestant?" Themes of historical continuity and global communality were prevalent in the responses of 29 percent of WOC and 35 percent of CFFC respondents. Other aspects identified by the respondents included specific sacraments, doctrinal beliefs, saints, mysticism, and biblical nonliteralism. On account of space constraints, this question was not included in the Dignity questionnaire.

"Universality; continuity in the apostolic tradition (which includes women in my view); respect for the value of tradition with
all its imperfections and human sinfulness; centrality of Eucharist
. . ."

The globalism and the historically continuous rather than fragmenting tradition of Catholicism were also distinguishing characteristics identified by CFFC respondents. One respondent highlighted the
church's "sweeping global perspective," and another its "deep historical roots." Other CFFC respondents stated:

"The Catholic Church is universal. I enjoy visiting a church in
different parts of the world."

"There is . . . depth to the structure of the Church that's allowed
it to endure and survive (even through things like the abortion
debate)."

The motifs of historical continuity and global communality appear
to bolster pro-change respondents' commitment to remaining connected to Catholicism. Their appreciation of the church's historical
trajectory also functions in an objective, collectively unself-conscious
manner to link them with doctrinally conservative Catholics. Thirty-
seven percent of the Catholic League respondents, for example, highlighted historical continuity as a distinguishing feature of Catholicism
for them. The subjectively experienced meaningfulness of continuity,
although it may differ in emphasis between pro-change and conservative Catholics, thus contributes to reproducing the symbolic cohesion
of the larger Catholic community notwithstanding doctrinal differences among its participants.

Overall, the findings presented in this section point to significant
sources of communality between pro-change and doctrinally conservative Catholics. The church's sacramental and liturgical symbol system,
felt pride in public affirmations of Catholic identity, and respondents'
investment in the church's globalism and historical continuity serve
both to integrate doctrinally diverse Catholics and to demarcate some
of the distinct features of Catholicism. These dimensions of
Catholicism comprise, in a sense, a "sacred canopy" (Berger 1967) that
integrates Catholics and gives meaning to their objectively shared
Catholic identity. But as emphasized throughout this book, symbols

(including doctrinal symbols) are neither static nor historically deter-
mining. The "culture" of Catholicism is not something that automatically reproduces Catholic identities and Catholic practices. As the
findings presented in the previous two chapters illustrate, producing
Catholicism is a critical, reflexive, and collectively contested activity
whereby the plurality of symbols and traditions within Catholicism are
appropriated and reinterpreted in multiple ways. Change happens, and
although as difficult to accomplish in the Catholic Church as in other
institutional spheres, it remains an eternally present possibility.

The findings in this section suggest that change may spring not just
from localized sites of pro-change Catholic activity, but also from the
bridges that could be constructed between doctrinally opposed Catholics. The overlap in commitments, memories, and understandings
among pro-change and conservative Catholics suggests that the very
symbols that integrate these Catholics may also be strategic in contributing to a future redrawing of the boundaries of Catholicism. The
symbolic significance of the Eucharist for Catholics serves as a case in
point. As the data indicate, the Eucharist is core to doctrinally conservative (and pro-change) Catholics, is personally salient to their
major life events (weddings, funerals, reunion Masses, war experiences), and is *the* public and geographically global celebration of
Catholicism which enacts the historical continuity of today's
Catholics with an "unbroken" (but multifaceted) tradition. Notwithstanding conservative Catholics' respect for the church hierarchy's
teaching, they may accept, or at least be open to accepting, the idea
that the strength of their faith and of the Catholic sacramental tradition would be better served by the celebration of the Eucharist (by
women or men) than by its absence in Catholic life (due to a shortage
of male priests). This conjecture may or may not be true; what it does
suggest, however, is that seeds of change can find a fruitful furrow in
what on the surface is a very practical but deeply sacramental consideration.[19]

19. Fueling this conjecture, although 92 percent of the Catholic League respon-
    dents expressed opposition to women's ordination in a closed, Likert-type ques-
    tion, a substantial minority of the same sample took a more positive view of
    women's ordination in response to an open-ended question seeking their views
    of possible futures for the church. The question asked: "Some people say that
    the issue of women's ordination is, in a sense, the tip of the iceberg – that if the
    Church allowed women to be priests, then all kinds of other changes would
    happen in the Church. What do you think about this?" Of those who answered

ENGAGING PLURALISM

Although there are significant doctrinal differences between pro-change and conservative Catholics, this study suggests that these differences do not necessarily indicate a fractured church. Since the differences that are divisive are informed by participants' shared commitment to a common but contested doctrinal tradition, there is always the possibility of forging new institutional practices that can reproduce the sacred meanings Catholics inject into their identity. As observed by Emile Durkheim, "when a sacred thing is subdivided, each of its parts remain equal to the thing itself" (1912/1976: 229). Accordingly, the construction of a plurality of Catholic identities does not necessarily weaken the collective solidarity attendant on being Catholic. Rather, as some feminist scholars recognize (e.g., Farley 1995: 139), it is the practical recognition of diversity and pluralism wherein lies the possibility of a lived community. The symbolic bases shared by pro-change and conservative Catholics and the church hierarchy alike, thus offer hope that the multiple voices of Catholicism can be in conversation with one another in ways that empower the church to be a vibrant community.

This hope is not grounded in the illusion, as Jane Mansbridge cautions (1993: 374), that common interests derive from participation in a shared communal tradition. It is obvious from the doctrinal differences between pro-change and conservative Catholics and from the Vatican's teaching on sexuality, women's ordination, abortion, and the role of the theologian, that different Catholics have different visions of the institutional expression of Catholicism. Nor is the hope for dialogue grounded in the sexist assumption that since women appear to value community more than men, pro-change women in particular might be persuaded to drop their demands for equality in the church in order to preserve what some might postulate to be the greater common good of the Catholic community.

The hope for dialogue across differences emerges rather from pro-change respondents' reflexive engagement with Catholic doctrine in validating their claims. As noted throughout this book, the Catholic tradition stresses the coupling of faith and reason. This emphasis received renewed institutional attention with Vatican II's vision of Ca-

this question (n = 126), 30 percent took a positive view of change (for further discussion, see Dillon 1999).

tholicism as a dialogical community wherein disagreements would be resolved by honest and reasoned discussion among members. In the church as in other domains, it would be sociologically naïve to think that contested issues could be easily discussed in a way that mimics Habermas's ideal speech situation. Nonetheless, the Catholic doctrinal and institutional tradition embodies the expectation that rather than silencing differences, Catholics will talk to one another about their differences. This is a communicative burden that all Catholics bear, irrespective of their doctrinal or ideological commitments. Thus even when Catholics associate in relatively like-minded groups, such as Dignity/Boston, there is the expectation that differences will be talked about with a view toward understanding them and possibly moving toward a resolution which responds to rather than denies differences.

Currently, the Catholic Common Ground Initiative has established a formal structure for facilitating discussion of the doctrinal differences that characterize American Catholics. Initiated by Cardinal Bernardin of Chicago in the summer of 1996, and coordinated by the National Pastoral Life Center, the project was designed to "redress polarization" and encourage dialogue among Catholics to address "differences constructively – a common ground centered on faith in Jesus, marked by accountability to the living Catholic tradition, and ruled by a renewed spirit of civility, dialogue, generosity, and broad and serious consultation."[20] The national and local conferences organized by the Common Ground Initiative so far point to the possibility that Catholics who hold doctrinally opposed views can discuss their different positions and begin exploring their similarities in difference. While the Catholic Church is not, of course, a democracy wherein the opinions of the majority hold sway, neither is it a premodern encrustation closed to an institutionally self-critical, cultural and historical consciousness. As most publicly demonstrated by Vatican II, official church teaching is mutable. Dialogue across differences in a deliberative institutional environment can only contribute to articulating the doctrinal possi-

20. The quotation is from the statement "Called to Be Catholic" published in *America* (August 31, 1996): 5–8. The Common Ground initiative is not without controversy. Some of Cardinal Bernardin's fellow bishops rejected "dialogue as a path to common ground," arguing instead that "the church already has common ground. It is found in Sacred Scripture and Tradition" (see Reese 1996b: 6). For details on the activities of the Catholic Common Ground Initiative, see its quarterly Initiative Reports.

bilities that may exist for legitimating change while maintaining continuity with the Catholic tradition.

The divisions between pro-change and conservative Catholics are obviously greater than those within and between the pro-change groups in this study. Pro-change and conservative Catholics take very different approaches to interpretive authority and to the substance of specific doctrinal questions. Nevertheless, people who are opposed to change in general are often quite accepting of a specific change once it is contextualized with respect to prominent concerns in their own lives.[21] Pro-change Catholics' grounding of their institutional projects in the same doctrinal tradition that is so important to conservative Catholics, rather than in a less religiously salient language of equal rights, for instance, may facilitate conservative Catholics' reflection about and possible acceptance of changes in select church practices (e.g., women's ordination).

In sum, the threat posed by interpretive pluralism to the cohesiveness of Catholic communality is lessened by the symbolic resources that exist for dialogue across differences. Pro-change and conservative Catholics' shared "objective" tradition, with its emphasis on continuity, reflexivity, and the coupling of faith and reason, demands that they talk, while their shared subjective commitments to particular aspects of the tradition can provide talking points that enhance their practical ability to engage in meaningful conversation. With Catholics' common symbolic and institutional framework providing the base for dialogue, pro-change Catholics' doctrinally reflexive arguments offer hope that the presence of differences can be used with a view toward the construction of a Catholic community that is more inclusive of difference. Whether in the church or in the larger society, unless there is "sustained discourse about the human good," as David Hollenbach (1994: 333) warns us, "shared meaning, understanding, and therefore community become even harder to achieve." Differences, then, should

21. For example, in her study of women working as pastoral administrators of priestless Catholic churches, Ruth Wallace (1992) found that parishioners initially opposed to "women pastors" gradually came to accept and value them. It would seem that conservative parishioners' commitment to the sacramental and communal life of the church, in addition to the competence of the women themselves, was sufficient to override their initial misgivings about having women as pastoral administrators. Similar findings are reported in Winter, Lummis, and Stokes (1994: 112–113).

not be used to maintain silence. It is through talk that people can discover shared experiences, attachments, and commitments. Most important, communal engagement across differences contributes to humanizing rather than dehumanizing and stigmatizing the Other. If this occurs, it matters less whether some programmatic "common ground" can be forged so long as people recognize that differences are inherently human and communal, part of who we are as social beings.

CHAPTER EIGHT

REASONED THEOLOGY:
LEGITIMATING EMANCIPATORY
POSSIBILITIES

The preceding three chapters have focused on pro-change Catholics whose activism within the church seeks the institutional affirmation of the differences that comprise Catholic communality. The community practices of Dignity/Boston, the arguments presented by WOC and CFFC respondents, and the internal pluralism evident among pro-change respondents themselves underscore the challenge posed to the church hierarchy's attempt to demarcate a universal and uniform Catholic identity. At the same time, pro-change Catholics demonstrate their commitment to maintaining their connection with Catholicism, and rather than fracturing the tradition, seek a greater integrity between its doctrinal values and institutional practices. Since interpretive authority and the doctrinal possibilities of Catholicism are central concerns of this study, I also include interviews with Catholic theologians. Theologians are interesting for two reasons. As professional experts committed to the understanding of faith, they are steeped in and have a deep knowledge of the Catholic tradition. At the same time, despite their formal institutional status in the church as interpreters of the faith, they are subordinate to the church hierarchy.

In the Vatican's understanding of the church as a divinely prescribed hierarchical institution wherein magisterial authority is supreme, the task of the theologian is seen as elaborating official church teaching rather than being autonomous of it. Thus the doctrinal interpretations theologians offer based on appeals to disciplinary knowledge must, if the case arises, defer to alternative interpretations supported by the authority of sacred office. Although the autonomy of professional experts in any organization is curtailed by varied bureaucratic interests, the interpretive autonomy of Catholic theologians is constrained a priori by their commitment to a religious tradition whose official institutional practices privilege the primacy of the Pope and the bishops.[1] Theologians, therefore, are objectively marginal relative to the church hierarchy's power.[2] Given their institutional location in the church as experts whose intellectual autonomy is curtailed by the Vatican, it is interesting to know how theologians interpret Catholicism. Does their understanding of Catholic identity bear a close affinity to official church teaching as elaborated in Chapter 3, or does it approximate more closely with the views of pro-change Catholics documented in the intervening chapters?

In order to explore how theologians understand Catholicism, I conducted in-depth personal interviews with twenty Catholic theologians randomly drawn from the theological faculties of the Boston Theological Institute and the Graduate Theological Union at Berkeley, two major geographical centers of theological education in the United States. The interviews lasted approximately one hour and followed a loosely structured format. Although some questions were tailored to the particular expertise and interests of the interviewee, I asked all of the theologians questions about what constitutes a "good" Catholic; questions pertaining to the church's sacramental tradition, sexuality, and women's ordination; and questions about their understanding of morality, conscience formation, and papal authority.

Almost all of the theologians adopted what might be called a "progressive" theological stance.[3] While there were nuanced differences

1. Although theologians played a highly visible role in influencing the doctrinal reforms endorsed during Vatican II, their subsidiary teaching role vis-à-vis the magisterium was upheld. Thus the Pope and the bishops remained as the sole "authentic" teachers — in other words, as "teachers endowed with the authority of Christ" (Abbott 1966: 47). Problematic, therefore, at the conclusion of Vatican II was the question accentuated by Vatican II's doctrinal reforms, of how the process of legitimating doctrinal change worked in practice, and central to this was the legitimacy of theological "dissent" from the magisterium. The authority crisis that marked Catholic theologians response to Paul VI's *Humanae Vitae* (1968) underscored that this was not simply an abstract concern.

2. As is evident from the proceedings of the CTSA, theologians frequently discuss the dilemmas of being a Catholic theologian and, in particular, query their role in the church vis-à-vis the magisterium. See, for example, Dulles (1976), Haight (1995), Hellwig (1987), Komonchak (1985), and McCormick (1969).

3. Theological "progressivism" is the term recently used by the U.S. National Conference of Catholic Bishops' Committee on Doctrine (U.S. Bishops 1996a) in detailing their criticisms of certain points in a bestselling book, *Catholicism*, by Richard McBrien, a professor of theology at the University of Notre Dame.

among the theologians in how they expressed and contextualized various points, most of them tended toward a view of Catholicism that was quite strikingly at odds with that presented by the Vatican. Their views of Catholic identity bore a remarkable similarity to those of this study's pro-change Catholics. The sample clearly is not a representative sample of American Catholic theological faculty. The progressivism of the theologians interviewed may well be a reflection of the fact that they were chosen from geographical areas renowned for their academic and political liberalism. At the same time, nonetheless, their views are closely aligned with the collective positions taken by the Catholic Theological Society of America (CTSA), the largest and oldest association of American Catholic theologians.

Specifically, the CTSA has evaluated the two issues of sexuality and women's ordination. As noted in Chapter 3, the CTSA commissioned a theological study on sexuality in the 1970s (Kosnik et al. 1977). In that study the CTSA emphasized an understanding of sexuality that, contrary to official church teaching, focused on the morality of whole relationships rather than on specific (homosexual or heterosexual) sexual acts. More recently, the CTSA has addressed the question of women's ordination. At its 1997 convention the association overwhelmingly approved a report by its members that challenged the Vatican's opposition to women priests. In addition to critiquing the substance of the church hierarchy's arguments, the CTSA concluded that there are "serious doubts" that opposition to women's ordination should be considered part of the deposit of faith. Indeed, the CTSA questioned whether women's exclusion from the priesthood is in fact a moral practice, and if immoral whether it is thus "foreign to the deposit of the faith" (1997: 78, 79).[4]

Although the CTSA has not undertaken a study on the morality of

The bishops critique relates primarily to issues stemming from McBrien's representation of the validity of Catholic theological pluralism. They interpret his discussion as undermining the authority of magisterial teaching, reflecting a minimalist creedal essentialism, and overstating the significance of post–Vatican II theological "progressivism" in the church.

4. The CTSA document (CTSA 1997) cites biblical evidence documenting women's visibility in the early Christian ministry and emphasizes the lack of scriptural reasons for women's exclusion from the priesthood. The CTSA acknowledges that church traditions should not be lightly dismissed. It nonetheless argues that since the primary reason offered by medieval theologians, including Thomas Aquinas, against women priests was women's supposed inferiority, the Vatican's continued opposition needs to be carefully evaluated.

abortion, the writings of some prominent Catholic theologians (not interviewed for this study) indicate that the Vatican's absolute opposition to abortion is not shared by all Catholic theologians. For example, Richard McCormick, Professor of Christian Ethics at the University of Notre Dame, takes issue with Pope John Paul's rejection of moral proportionality. He argues that critiques of proportionalism fail to distinguish intentions from motives in postulating abortion (and other acts) as "intrinsically evil."[5]

McCormick (1995: 16) argues that the apparent clarity of John Paul's (1995a) condemnation of "direct abortion" is ambiguous if consideration is given to philosophical and traditional understandings of what is meant by "direct." He argues that an abortion may be "indirect" if there is a commensurate reason for it. McCormick suggests that all Catholic moral theologians would accept the principle "that there is always a strong presumption against taking human life." He notes, nevertheless, that theologians might well disagree over the application of this principle and accordingly might differ over "whether a particular termination . . . should be called an abortion in the moral sense" (1995: 16).

The theological positions expressed by the CTSA on sexuality and on women's ordination, and the view of abortion outlined by Richard McCormick, are not unanimously shared by all Catholic theologians. It seems nonetheless that many American and European Catholic theologians lean toward progressivism rather than conservatism on the questions contested by this study's participants.[6] Consequently, the

5. As McCormick explains, it is "the intention that makes the act what it is" (1994: 495). Using as contrasting examples self-defense versus killing, and an organ transplant versus body mutilation, McCormick states that these distinctions refer to different acts and are not the same actions with different motives (1994: 495).

6. Despite the overwhelming endorsement given by conference participants to the CTSA position on women's ordination, it is evident that some Catholic theologians understand the issue and the exercise of papal authority very differently. Avery Dulles, a Jesuit professor of religion and society at Fordham University, for instance, has defended John Paul's stance precisely on grounds of magisterial authority. Dulles argues that where "plausible arguments can be made for contrary views, it is imperative to have a doctrinal authority capable of settling the matter" (1996: 782). Dulles's position nonetheless seems to be a minority view among Catholic theologians who have entered the public debate on ordination. Several have argued that the diversity of reasoned opinion not only among the laity but among bishops on women's ordination challenges the invocation of

views elaborated by the theologians I interviewed may be considered substantively although not statistically representative of many of their colleagues.

Redrawing the Boundaries of Catholic Identity

There was a strong consensus among the theologians that being Catholic transcended specific behavioral acts to encompass a person's whole life. All but two of the interviewees said that a person could be a "good" Catholic and still engage in various behaviors that are condemned as morally wrong by the Vatican. One of the theologians who disagreed said that while people could, for instance, use artificial contraception or engage in same-sex sexual relations and still be "good human beings," it was "not helpful to call them good Catholics." In his view, being a good Catholic required that people agree with important aspects of official church teaching. Although this theologian stressed his belief in "original sin," he stated, nevertheless, that "the division between the good guys and the bad guys is not so clear cut – everyone is burdened; lifestyles get in the way of our moral judgments."

Other theologians emphasized that being a good Catholic was much more complex than could be captured by a checklist approach even if, as one averred, this is the approach preferred by the Vatican. Catholicism was not, as one theologian stressed, "a model of isolated doctrines on the table." Several thus argued that the frequently voiced characterization of dissenting Catholics as "cafeteria Catholics" who are not serious about their religion was a misrepresentation. These theologians pointed out that Catholicism was a life-centered, Christocentric vision. Thus one theologian, quoting Thomas Aquinas, described a good Catholic as "one who tries to do good and avoid evil; who tries to integrate the teachings of Jesus in their lives." Another theologian echoed this view, stating that what was important was "being a good Christian, living out a sense of vocation, personal faith in Christ, listening to and following the voice of Christ; having a vision of His expectations."

One theologian expressed his understanding in terms of an "interrelated vision of God, of human persons, and of society." In this view

---

papal infallibility since it does not reflect a "universal consensus" in the church, one of the criteria recognized as validating papal teaching as infallible. See, for example, Freyne 1996, Orsy 1996, F. Sullivan 1995, and Surlis 1996.

"one's whole life and relationships," including sexual, social, and economic relationships, should be guided by and testament to this "ultimate vision." Others stressed that belief in Jesus Christ was core to the
faith, and that sexual-moral issues were not as central. In one theologian's view, a person's "attitude toward the poor is more central than
sex in discerning what is a good Catholic." Accordingly, he wondered
why people don't feel they have to leave the church if they don't give
their money to the poor. For this theologian the "first thing for a
Christian to do was love God, pray to God, worship and sense his presence." He emphasized moreover that this love for God should be self-
consciously present and should manifest itself in people's routine activities.

Several theologians highlighted the difficulty and questioned the
relevance of drawing boundaries between "good" and "not-good"
Catholics. They stressed that what matters is how faith impacts on a
person's everyday life. This understanding, they argued, means that
faith should not and cannot be reduced, as it frequently is both by the
church hierarchy and by some Catholics, to official church teaching
on sexual morality. Issues pertaining to sexual morality, these theologians stated, should be evaluated within the overall direction and
moral context of a person's life. Thus one theologian argued that while
sexual morality was not central to faith, it was "not unimportant. It is
important insofar as it concerns justice issues." Demonstrating the
complex and multidimensional nature of the relation between faith
and morality which was highlighted in several interviews, one theologian elaborated:

> "The easy answer is to say that it [faith and morality] is all one
> piece. And if you don't agree with this position on abortion or
> contraception, then you reject the God of Christianity. Or if you
> don't agree with what the bishops say about the appropriate
> approach to welfare reform, then you're rejecting the God of
> Christianity. I think it's not quite that simple. One tendency is to
> say that these moral questions that are behavioral in their orien-
> tation is really one sphere, and then the domain of belief in God
> and faith is completely separate. That's wrong too. You don't col-
> lapse morality and faith into each other but they're not separate
> from each other either. That's why the issue becomes so compli-
> cated, I think. Because they're related but not identical. . . . I
> think the issue of drawing boundaries is a very, very hard ques-

tion. The present Pope thinks he knows how to draw those boundaries very clearly. I don't think they're as clear as the Pope does. And I, on the other hand, I'm not of a mind to say that more or less everything and anything goes. At some point, the issue is how do I think about the relationship between faith and behavior . . . the most interesting questions for ethics is not what should I do and what should I not do. The most interesting questions are what kind of a person should I be and what kinds of a community should we be."

In discussing the meanings of Catholic identity, the theologians voiced expectations that to a remarkable degree fitted with the identity negotiations demonstrated by Dignity, WOC, and CFFC respondents. The theologians' construal of Catholic identity strongly corresponded to the themes evident in pro-change respondents' Catholicism. The theologians variously emphasized themes of communality, reason and doctrinal engagement, and interpretive pluralism as dynamic aspects of Catholicism. In elevating the significance of these strands in the Catholic tradition, it was noteworthy that the theologians offered a more restrictive understanding of the exercise of papal authority than that which in their view is assumed by the Vatican.

COMMUNITY

The emphasis on community in the Catholic tradition expressed itself in several different ways in the theologians' arguments. All of the theologians stressed the importance of shared sacramental and liturgical practices. They argued that being a Catholic requires self-identification with the Catholic tradition and participation in the church's sacramental and communal life. One theologian argued that being a Catholic is "not purely cultural." In his view, "someone who doesn't practice at all or only very infrequently is not a Catholic. There doesn't have to be assent to every doctrine, but there should be a serious involvement with the sacraments." In addition to sacramental participation and regular Mass attendance, other theologians emphasized the importance of having, as it was phrased by one interviewee, a "sense of the liturgical seasons."

The importance of Catholic communality was also discussed regarding the important role it should play in informing and constraining Catholics' values and behavior. One theologian highlighted the communal dimension of conscience formation. He argued that the "community of Catholics" has authority in discerning what is right. In this view, for dissent to be "conscientious" it must "bear some relation to what the community of Catholics believe on an issue or otherwise it runs the risk of constituting 'individualism' and not Catholicism." While stating that he would not judge people's consciences, this theologian was firm, nonetheless, that there can be "erroneous conscience," if for various reasons a person's "mind was not in touch with the Catholic community" and thus, for example, ignored the church's pro-life ethic. Another theologian stated that people who are active in militias or who are racists can have "erroneous consciences."

A third way in which the Catholic valuing of community was invoked was in how theologians talked about some of the currently contested issues in the church. Several theologians who disagreed with the theological arguments used by the Vatican suggested instead that cultural arguments emphasizing different aspects of societal and religious communality could have greater weight. In the area of sexuality, for instance, four theologians who rejected some of the Vatican's conclusions about sexual behavior nonetheless expressed their high regard for its substantive emphasis that relationships should be generative rather than exploitative. They argued that what is valuable about official church teaching on sex is that, as one theologian stated, "it has always stressed its relational importance and has always been sensitive to the way that sex can be used to dehumanize." One middle-aged theologian commented, "my generation was sexually repressed but today sex is all screwed up in the U.S." In his view, the church hierarchy's overall teaching on sexuality "makes good societal sense."

Two other theologians similarly focused on the societal relevance of official church teaching. They stated, for example, that rather than using natural law reasoning to oppose artificial contraception, Paul VI in his 1968 papal encyclical *Humanae Vitae* should have defended the ban on contraception by appealing to the church's concern that a "contraceptive culture" was demeaning personal and social relationships. They suggested that the Vatican should emphasize how "permissiveness" and uncontrolled sexuality lead to communal fragmentation, as indicated by problems such as divorce. Another theologian suggested that cross-cultural differences in the legal status and cultural acceptability of gay and lesbian rights could be used by the Vatican to defend the upholding of its conservative stance on homosexuality.

Similarly on women's ordination, theologians who themselves

favored women priests suggested that because there were no good theological reasons for excluding women from the priesthood, the Pope
could defend his view by appealing to the communal unity of the global church rather than by using "unsound" theology. One theologian,
for instance, suggested that the fact that women's roles in the West are
different to their roles in African and Latin American countries might
allow the Pope to state that the "church as a whole is not ready for
women priests." Another theologian elaborated on the persuasiveness
of communal over theological reasoning:

> "I think and believe after having thought about this that women
> should be ordained. I don't think there are good reasons theolog-
> ically for not ordaining women. And when the Pope says that
> Jesus didn't ordain women, therefore, I don't have the authority
> to legitimate the ordination of women, I think his theology is all
> wrong. If he were to say 'We live in a complex multi-cultural
> world where the relation of the sexes or the genders is very dif-
> ferent from one culture to the other, this community of the
> Roman Catholic Church lives in multiple cultures and therefore
> the unity of the church around this issue demands that we pro-
> ceed very slowly and with prudence before making a change,' I
> would be willing to grant him the argument."

Notwithstanding the theologians' accent on the cultural importance of maintaining community, they were also aware of the tensions
posed by using cultural rationales to defend specific church practices.
Observing the differences in women's equality cross-nationally, two
theologians emphasized the "enormously prophetic" leadership role
the Vatican could play by "just stimulating dialogue across cultural
boundaries." On the other hand, two different theologians suggested
that the great disparities in women's experiences cross-culturally
meant that, as one stated, "listening to bishops in Africa and Third
World countries [talk about their social problems], the Pope is not
going to sympathize with bourgeois women's ideology."

REASON AND DOCTRINAL ENGAGEMENT

All of the theologians emphasized the importance of Catholics according respect to official church teaching in informing their consciences.
They argued, however, that people have to judge for themselves what

is morally right. This moral judgment, the theologians variously stressed, should not be "flippant" or "whimsical" or simply "about one's choices" but should be grounded in solid reasons. Observing that "conscience today is usually protest language," one theologian argued that people "should always appeal to conscience – for doing right and not just for 'disagreeing'." He offered three criteria which should be followed in discerning one's conscience: "(a) Know what the church's official teaching is; (b) know why it teaches what it teaches; and (c) have solid reasons why you disagree with that position." In his view, people could then live as they do but, as he noted, with a certain sense of "sadness" (but not necessarily resignation) on account of the gap between their own and the Vatican's understanding of Catholicism.

Several theologians reiterated the importance of having sound reasons for behavior. As one stated, "if you are going to argue against the bishops or the Pope, you have to have good reasons for going against them; you have to have sound reasons for your argument." These reasons, as many of the theologians explained, could be grounded in a variety of sources. Legitimate reasons could draw on knowledge of social science or history, for instance, notwithstanding how, as one theologian pointed out, "we can be victims of particular kinds of historiography." Other theologians stressed the value of personal experience and the resources it provides in moral decision-making processes.

Many theologians pointed to the importance of knowing the motivational context for Catholics' disagreement with official church teaching. One theologian stated that "we have to ask whether the dissent is misinformed and what motivates it." While personally in favor of women's ordination and critical of the church hierarchy's sexism, this theologian suggested that the drive for ordination should not be motivated by cultural rights or power; Catholic dissent on women's ordination for these reasons, he felt, would be misinformed. Others similarly argued that judging an abortion to be moral must be based on sounder reasons than "simple individual rights language."

Theologians' emphasis on the importance of people being able to offer sound reasons for their views was also echoed in how some interviewees denounced what they saw as the religious inarticulateness of Catholics in general. One theologian said:

> "I am disappointed with Catholics – they can't talk about Christ, the Holy Spirit, the sacraments in the most simple terms. They

can talk about cars, sports and lots of other issues, but they are not reflective about their faith. If they felt the Bible was the word of God, then you think they would read it. . . . Much of Catholics' understanding is ignorance. I am bothered by Catholic laziness. There is an anti-intellectualism."

Two other theologians commented that Robert Bellah and his coauthors in *Habits of the Heart* (1985) are right in characterizing Americans as inarticulate about their religious values. One theologian who argued that it was "important to ask 'What do people give to their church?' rather than always asking what it does for them," suggested that "we don't have the language to articulate our contribution." It was this theologian's view that "Catholics have not been able to find a way to express [verbally] their faith. . . . they can't talk about God." While some theologians pointed to the individualism and privatization of religion in American culture as reasons for this, they also noted that it was, as one stated, at odds with the Catholic Church's "really good history of reflecting on issues and having a valuable and open-ended conversation" about various questions. Expressing a positive view of Catholics' ability to connect their values to a religious base, another theologian argued that "if you push people hard enough they are usually aware of the source of their behavior, that it is Catholic motivated and driven, even if they are not active Catholics."

INTERPRETIVE PLURALISM

Interpretive pluralism was a third prominent theme in the interviews with the theologians. Many emphasized the validity of interpretive diversity in the Catholic tradition and the necessity for recognizing the historical and cultural variability in church practices. One theologian pointed to the multiple meanings that might legitimately be associated with the core faith beliefs of Catholicism. Specifically highlighting the Trinity, the redemptive incarnation of Christ, the Eucharist, and the communion of saints, this theologian argued that rather than being static in their meanings, "there are lots of ways of formulating those doctrines; there is a lot of variation in the tradition concerning their meanings."

In particular, this theologian stressed that faith had to be given a practical understanding that would both nurture and reflect the diversity of actual communities. It was this person's view that "we need living Catholic communities" which reflect "all sorts of diversity" in accord with the "cast the wide net" metaphor of Matthew's gospel. This theologian regretted that many parishes do not meet the spiritual and religious needs of the people due in part to the elitist theology of priesthood that prevails. Another theologian stated that "we live in the present moment and its incarnation; but it has not and does not have to be this way." In this view, understanding variability "enriches our imagination" as to what is possible both morally and in terms of the church's institutional life.

Underscoring the legitimacy of moral pluralism, several of the theologians invoked Thomas Aquinas's thesis that the more specific and concrete a situation, the greater the room for variation in applying a moral principle. These theologians were thus wary of prescribing definite ways in which broad principles should apply in particular situations. One theologian stated:

> ". . . one of the basic principles is to have real respect for the dignity and worth of every human being. But when you get into the details of whether this means that under no circumstances should a married couple use an artificially aided form of reproduction like in vitro fertilization like the Vatican has said, I think Aquinas would be of the mind to say 'Well maybe we don't have enough experience to know whether that's true yet or not.' Is it really the case that this is dehumanizing, or is it the case that this is a possible way of enhancing people's humanity?"

Some theologians took a similarly nuanced approach to abortion. While emphasizing the difficult moral challenges the issue of abortion raises, these theologians did not adopt the absolute anti-abortion stand of official church teaching. One theologian stated:

> "Abortion, although much touchier [than artificial contraception], is an area where there's a lot of biological issues that have to be sorted through about what is a fetus and all of that. And there's enough ambiguity there for me to say that I'm not sure that I want to write out of the church somebody who disagrees with the official position on abortion. I don't think that should be done. On the other hand, somebody who thinks this is not a

big deal, and what's the difference, then you begin to raise questions. So I think it's a complicated set of issues."

Paralleling theologians' emphasis on the interpretive pluralism appropriate to understanding the church's sacramental tradition and the application of moral principles, some also discussed the possibility of diversity in global church practices. These theologians recognized the importance of global unity for the church but suggested that unity does not require uniformity. They argued that there was no reason why there could not be cross-cultural flexibility with respect to contested questions. Thus, for example, one theologian suggested the legitimacy of having women priests in societies where women have equal rights. Another theologian similarly argued that while not all cultural options were equally good, "you cannot enforce universality." He suggested that in speaking about the common good on family policy, for instance, the Vatican should recognize that while "people do things differently, similar benefits, such as stability and commitment, can come out of the differences."

THE CHURCH HIERARCHY'S AUTHORITY

Many of the theologians suggested that John Paul's interpretation of papal authority undermined the values of community, reason, and pluralism in the Catholic tradition. All of the theologians expressed a strong respect for the papal office and stressed that it has many good features. In particular they highlighted its potential to offer a coherent voice on behalf of the whole church and to mobilize people around good causes. Some theologians nonetheless emphasized the importance of having a contextualized understanding of the papacy that recognized the limits to papal authority in the Catholic tradition.

One theologian stressed the historical variation in understandings of the papacy. He argued that while "the Petrine ministry is an integral part of being a Christian, it is not essential." Another theologian similarly emphasized that the accent on papal power was a late development in Catholicism. He argued that "adherence to the exact strictures of the modern papacy . . . is a miniscule piece of the distinctiveness of Catholicism. The papacy as it exists today has really only been in existence for about 150 years. This means 1,850 years went by without that as part of the Catholic tradition. It would be a mistake to identify Catholicism with a late-modern form of authority structure."

Several theologians argued that John Paul exercises his authority in a "legal and authoritarian" way that contravenes a communal understanding of church. One theologian argued that rather than being "a symbol of unity, facilitation, and a privileged spokesperson in dialogue with the People of God," the Pope demonstrates a certain "juridical understanding of the papacy and a rather naive understanding of the Catholic tradition." In this theologian's view, John Paul's papacy has been "disastrous" for the church. In particular, he emphasized what he considered to be John Paul's didacticism, as evidenced by the number and tone of the papal encyclicals and statements issued, the Vatican's retaliation against dissent, and the selection of doctrinally conservative bishops.

Another theologian suggested that there has been "an overemphasis on authority in John Paul's papacy," extending what he labeled as the "unhealthy creeping infallibilism" present in the church before Vatican II. Similarly, another interviewee commented that John Paul has "claimed greater authority than he has" in his position, for instance, on the question of women's ordination. Arguing that the "church cannot operate by formal authority," this theologian stressed that "authority must be respected." Presenting an analogy between the relationship of the Pope to the laity and the parent-child relationship, he suggested that parents who are respected by their children are more effective.

By contrast to John Paul's magisterial understanding of the papacy, many interviewees favored a more dialogical process of reasoned communication within the church. As one commented, the only way we can establish the "essentials" of our tradition is if "we keep talking, and try to establish the meanings behind people's divergent views." Another stated, "an institutional church that keeps saying 'no, no, no', cannot get very far. It has to have decent reasons for the positions it advocates." Another theologian expressed appreciation for the "cultural and faith difficulties people have with changing symbols" (as, for example, with the idea of women priests). In this theologian's view, nonetheless, it was better for the Vatican to talk about these cultural difficulties than "to say we can't talk about it, which is the worst thing to do."

One theologian characterized John Paul's attitude toward pluralism in the church as an attempt to "silence the voices of those who speak without the grace of hierarchical office," thus showing a "distrust of the Holy Spirit and of the faithful." This theologian emphasized Catholics' obligation to respect the church hierarchy's authority, but argued that authority must be "exercised legitimately." It was this interviewee's opinion that "the voice that speaks for the community of faith has jeopardized its authority because it does not listen to the faithful."

Several of the theologians invoked Thomas Aquinas's admonition that all those in authority should be faithful to their role in the church. Other theologians drew on Vatican II's affirmation of collegial unity and lay expertise to similarly argue that unless appropriate means are used to teach particular doctrines, Catholics are not obliged to accept what is proclaimed. These theologians stressed that what is taught must be reasonable and must "make sense." Others echoed this view, variously emphasizing that, as one theologian stated, "the hierarchy which is supposed to be in the service of the community, cannot posit doctrine and force its acceptance."

In view of the tension between theologians and church officials it is noteworthy that many interviewees underscored the mutuality of the roles of theologian and bishop. Several commented that it was very important for theologians and bishops to be in dialogue. As one theologian elaborated:

> ". . . the hierarchy and the theologians really need each other. I think the bishops need the theologians because the theologians have done a lot of study about the tradition and Scripture and so forth. I think the theologians need to be plugged into the world that the bishops are playing a key role in because if you sit around in an office like this . . . your world can get very small if you don't encounter the world that the church is involved in day by day. And if you're trying to figure out or think more about or understand more about what's going on in terms of God's involvement in human history, you have to know something about what's going on. You can't just sit here and cogitate it."

Theologians' appreciation for the importance of interaction between bishops and theologians is clearly not in itself sufficient to make the relationship work in practice. In the assessment of the theologian quoted above, the relation between bishops and theologians currently "is not in good shape," on account of the church hierarchy's vigilance in monitoring what it considers to be "authentic" theology. Several interviewees discussed what they characterized as theologians' comparatively "greater marginalization" by Pope John Paul II; in particular, they highlighted the exclusion of liberal theological voices from the writing of papal statements and encyclicals. As one theologian stated, the Vatican's policy of bringing in like-minded theologians as consultants means that the Pope's advisors are "like a Greek chorus, all singing in unison."

Although many of the theologians commented on the distant relationship between theologians and bishops, most of them were not personally bothered by the lack of consultation. One theologian contextualized his lack of access to official power by stating, "while I am marginal to the lines of authority in the church, I am just as marginal to the military industrial complex" (but even so, the military industrial complex is not the subject of his work). Another suggested that if theologians are marginalized in the church, this may be good insofar as it "helps them to identify with others who are marginalized, and in this way, do good theology." Other theologians pointedly noted that they were "glad to be left alone" since, as one suggested, "contact" with the bishops may risk "interference" from them.

Theologians' awareness of the consequences of attention from the church hierarchy contributes to self-censorship. One theologian stated that while theologians had "a moral obligation to speak out," pragmatic considerations including the "time-consuming hassle of getting into trouble with the hierarchy" made it difficult to do so. Many of the theologians were more explicit in discussing what they saw as the "chilling effect" on theological inquiry of the "fear of retaliation and reprisals" occasioned by the denial of promotions or of academic awards to themselves or their colleagues. One theologian argued that "freedom of speech is not really valued in a Catholic university environment." In his view, and that of one of his colleagues, one consequence of self-censorship was the neglect of scholarship on controversial questions. He stated that "any problematic area of ethics is being ignored, or being done by older people who are not afraid of not getting tenure."

These same theologians, nonetheless, were sympathetic toward bishops, noting as one stated that "any bishop's job is difficult" because of the multiple pressures they confront from the Vatican and from diverse constituencies within their own diocese's. At the same time, some were critical of the bishops, both individually and collectively, for not taking their obligation to be "authentic" teachers more seriously and standing up to the Pope when they held a view contrary to that expressed by the Vatican.

Some interviewees interpreted the church hierarchy's vigilance toward doctrinal inquiry as evidence that theologians were being successful in challenging it. One theologian argued that the fact that the Vatican was so focused on controlling theologians was a response to their "not falling into line," and that "many more were disagreeing than agreeing with the Vatican." Another theologian whose views differed from official church teaching on several questions said that he felt "aligned with the tradition of the church." This theologian emphasized that in his judgment he was "living in terms of what the church has historically stood for." He argued, moreover, that the prevalence of so many dissenting Catholics throughout the church made him "feel part of the community, part of the consensus about what it means to be Catholic."

EMANCIPATORY CATHOLICISM

The understandings of Catholicism articulated by the theologians provide strong support for the transformative agendas pursued by pro-change Catholics. Many pro-change Catholics are aware of the theological legitimacy given to their projects by the writings of a few well-known theologians including Mary Hunt, Rosemary Ruether, and Elisabeth Schüssler Fiorenza (none of whom I interviewed), who are frequent contributors to the newsletters and journals of the various pro-change organizations. What is striking here is that theologians who are not publicly involved in the issue-specific agendas of this study's pro-change Catholics, nonetheless share to a large extent their interpretation of Catholicism.

Rather than suggesting that pro-change projects are driven by localized interests that threaten the cohesiveness of the Catholic tradition, the theologians' mapping of Catholicism validates an emancipatory Catholicism. At the level of individual Catholic behavior and identity, the theologians' rejection of an act-centered sexual morality provides gay and lesbian Catholics, for example, with an "expert" opinion that it is legitimate to be gay or lesbian and Catholic. Contrary to official church teaching on the contradictions presented by these identities, in the theologians' framing Catholic identities only become contradictory when they violate relational and communal ethics of justice and care. In this understanding, as argued by the theologians, all Catholics run the risk of offending Catholic communality if their lives disconnect from the meanings illuminated by the practices of Christ's life.

Theologians' rejection of a checklist approach to Catholicism appears on the surface to give credence to the American bishops' negative view of "progressive" theology as minimalist. According to the bishops, progressive theologians reduce to an "absolute minimum the church teachings and beliefs that are to be considered essential to the Catholic faith and to which one must adhere in order to consider oneself Catholic" (U.S. Bishops 1996a: 742). As seen by the bishops, this minimalism is aimed toward accommodating the diverse and contradictory intellectual positions in the church, and toward reducing the significance of certain traditional beliefs that contemporary Catholics might have difficulty accepting.

Yet the minimalism articulated by this study's theologians confronts Catholics with an expansive task. It challenges them to know and to publicly manifest and engage with the meanings of a dynamically evolving Catholic faith tradition. In the theologians' understanding, a living faith must be evident in Catholics' personal and public commitments. Being Catholic, therefore, is invariably the public enactment of multiple cross-cutting ("private" and "public") identities. Faith, as the theologians emphasized, cannot be separated from the justice imperatives of personal and communal relations. The mutuality of faith and morality means that all domains of life are infused with a theology of praxis. In this view, theology is political, and it strives to be emancipatory. It provides the symbolic resources motivating and nurturing the personal and collective transformation of unjust practices into moral practices identified by the extent to which they realize inclusivity and equality. Theology is thus engaged with everyday life in its diverse and overlapping "private" and "public" spheres.

Theologians' emphasis on the interpretive diversity within the Catholic tradition and the fact that the practical expression of faith changes in response to historical and cultural exigencies further bolsters the identity negotiation of pro-change Catholics. At the same time, contrary to the negative view expressed by some of the theologians toward Catholics' vocabulary of faith, this study's pro-change Catholics clearly demonstrate doctrinal competence and articulateness. As advised by the theologians, they show the thoughtfulness and soundness of their reasons for disagreeing with official church teaching and, more emancipatory in its possible consequences, the doctrinal rationales for creating an inclusive and pluralist church. Equally important, in tune with the theologians' understanding of conscience formation, the respondents demonstrate a deliberative, self-conscious connection with the larger Catholic community and a commitment to calibrating their current practical interpretations of Catholicism with the tradition.

Finally, the theologians' restrictive understanding of the church hierarchy's authority supports the interpretive autonomy demonstrated by pro-change Catholics in choosing to stay Catholic and to reconstruct a Catholicism that recognizes multiple differences. The respondents' critical probing of the Catholic tradition illustrates the kind of reasoned deliberative communality preferred by the theologians over John Paul's closure of communal dialogue, and what theologians regard as his expansive interpretation of papal power.

One area of difference between theologians and pro-change respondents was the theologians' greater sensitivity to the global demands and constraints of Catholicism. Theologians demonstrated their professional obligation to the church as a cross-national entity, in contrast to the more particular concerns of the pro-change respondents. Thus, as we saw, some of the theologians tempered their opinions on women's ordination, for example, by highlighting the difficulties women priests would present in non-Western contexts. Overall, however, as the preceding discussion has underscored, the theologians spoke of a Catholicism that was remarkably similar to that construed by Dignity, WOC, and CFFC respondents.

THE MEDIATING IMPORTANCE OF INSTITUTIONAL LOCATION

The theologians' interpretation of Catholicism provides further evidence that as discussed in Chapter 6, reason, faith, and power are interrelated resources that can be simultaneously drawn upon in institutional critique. Clearly, theologians' faith commitment to Catholicism does not preclude them from taking a critical disposition toward official church teaching and using reasons from within the Catholic tradition to validate an emancipatory Catholicism. It is evident that their role, as stated by one theologian, in "sorting out good expressions of the faith from inadequate ones," involves them adopting a power-based critique of the church hierarchy's use of authority. By the same token, they also query Catholics' motivation in dissenting from official church teaching. It is through this dual-edged critique of the church as both hierarchy and community that theologians, in the words of one of their number, try to "keep the church honest and more faithful to its spirit." The doctrinal "progressivism" of theologians is thus constrained by their commitment to maintaining their own and the church's Catholic identity.

Theologians are an "oddity," as one stated, in the sense that they are "always on the verge of speaking *for* the church, just like bishops." Yet the relative marginality of being on the verge as opposed to within hierarchical office clearly gives a different tone and substance to their understanding of Catholicism. As documented in this study, theologians present a Catholicism that, contrary to official church teaching, validates the identities and institutional projects of pro-change Catholics. Although the theologians interviewed are not statistically representative of Catholic theologians in general, it is nonetheless the case that as noted at the outset of this chapter, progressivism appears to be a dominant strand in American and European theology. It may be that the marginality of theologians relative to the church hierarchy gives theologians a standpoint that may encourage them to identify, as one interviewee stated, with the community of dissenting Catholics. In the interest of diluting the exclusive interpretive power of the Pope and the bishops, theologians may perceive a strategic advantage in validating more communal and local understandings of the practical meanings of Catholicism.

On the other hand, the intellectual task of theologians is to develop a self-conscious historical understanding of what the Catholic tradition is and what it can legitimately contain, as theologians engage, according to one interviewee, in "rediscovering and renewing the essentials of the Christian tradition." In this view, then, it is not so surprising that in critiquing the church the theologians tap into the prominence of reason and of "faith and reason" in the Catholic tradition. For the church hierarchy, by contrast, the standpoint of official authority gives their historical consciousness a different orientation. The accent on magisterial authority legitimated by the thesis of apostolic succession favors an emphasis on historical continuity, and of stemming institutional and doctrinal changes that may undermine what the church hierarchy sees as the "constancy" of its teaching. Moreover, as official church teachers, responsible for maintaining church "unity" and the "orthodoxy of faith," and out of loyalty to the Pope, many bishops apparently feel that they cannot openly discuss some of the issues currently contested in the church (Quinn 1996: 16).

From their different institutional locations, therefore, it is the power of reason as opposed to the power of sacred office that pushes theologians rather than bishops to articulate the emancipatory possibilities of Catholicism.

During "unsettled" times (cf. Swidler 1986) when competing understandings of what is doctrinally possible dominate the evaluation of institutional practices, theologians' reasoned engagement with the Catholic tradition may be especially salient. In view of the individual and institutional reflexivity of contemporary society (cf. Giddens 1991: 20), it is evident that for doctrinal claims to be persuasive they must be able to sustain their reasonableness against doctrinally grounded counterclaims. Through participating in current doctrinal debates, therefore, theologians can play a significant role in both adjudicating doctrinal disputes and legitimating pro-change institutional projects.[7] In this way, theologians stoke the spiral of possibility implicitly expressed in the attitudes of all Catholics who endorse changes in the church and explicitly demonstrated by this study's pro-change Catholics.

7. An adjudicatory role for theologians has historical precedence. Although the medieval university originated as a church institution, the adjudicatory role of the university theological faculty in doctrinal disputes was "an important one" (Boyle 1985: 173).

CHAPTER NINE

CATHOLIC OPTIONS

This study has focused on a select group of Americans: pro-change Catholics and theologians who articulate a Catholic identity that challenges the official church view. Catholics who are openly gay or lesbian, advocates of women's ordination, or pro-choice on abortion are delegitimated in official church teaching and practices. Theologians' interpretive autonomy is similarly restricted by the church hierarchy. Nonetheless, pro-change Catholics and many theologians contest the boundaries of Catholic identity delineated by the Vatican and reconstruct what it means for individuals, collectivities, and the church to be Catholic.

The commitment of pro-change Catholics to the church and the resources they use to affirm a plural identity engage important sociological debates. This book's findings illustrate the complex and multifaceted nature of individual experiences, the importance of shared group membership in both anchoring and mobilizing individuals, and the differentiated nature of the Catholic Church as both a doctrinal tradition and an institutional environment.

VALUING COMMUNITY AND PLURALISM

Communitarians (e.g., Etzioni 1997: 128, 197) worry that the celebration of individual and group differences may lessen people's willingness to acknowledge the ties that link them to others, thus resulting in a fragmentation of societal cohesiveness and moral order. This concern is bolstered by recent studies emphasizing Americans' inability to define themselves using a moral vocabulary that recognizes their participation in an ongoing web of obligatory social relationships (Bellah et al. 1985; Glendon 1991). From a different perspective, the pessimistic strand in communitarian thinking is nurtured by the postmodern accent on the rootless, fractured, and socially saturated nature of the "multiphrenic" self (e.g., Gergen 1991: 48–80), and by neo-Marxist scholars who see tradition negatively as a defensive force (e.g., Castells 1997: 59–67).

The empirical findings presented in this book point to the practical and moral compatibility of diversity and community, and therefore challenge the assumption (cf. Etzioni 1997: 64, 131) that cultural differences lead to social anarchy. The sociological significance of the pro-change Catholics I chose to study lies in the fact that they attempt to create an identity by embracing rather than denying the tension associated with belonging to seemingly incompatible groups. Their identity is self-consciously integrated with participation in the more global Catholic tradition. In so doing, they combine a need for membership in a larger community with a stress on individual differences, and illustrate the feasibility of grafting new ways of being onto old traditions.

Pro-change Catholics demonstrate that the affirmation of cultural differences does not invariably lead to social segmentation. This contrasts with the public expression of difference indicated, for example, by the construction of self-segregating, particularistic enclaves or subcultures (Bellah et al. 1985: 71–75; Habermas 1987: 393). Ethnic subcultures have long been a feature of America's immigrant history as different groups have sought to preserve the distinctions of their country of origin while simultaneously struggling to be recognized for their "similarity" as loyal Americans. Today, differences in life stage and socioeconomic status are demarcated by the increasing popularity of gated communities for retired and upper-middle-class groups. Lifestyle differences similarly comprise relatively bounded cultural communities, as seen for example in San Francisco's gay Castro district. Such enclaves clearly serve important functions for their respective participants.

Like many other people, Catholics who choose to stay in the church demonstrate the search for community. But, unlike some Americans who appear to find fulfillment in relatively ad hoc or single-issue communal groups (cf. Wuthnow 1994b), pro-change Catholics value belonging to a historically grounded community of memory. They find that for their "new" identity to be meaningful, it must be integrated with their attachment to the larger Catholic tradition. In this melding process, the respondents underscore, as Stephen Hart (1992: 84) has observed, that mixing the languages of individualism and community is not indicative of "intellectual confusion," but rather of the fact that "both individualistic and communal concerns are valid and important."

As documented, this study's participants relied primarily upon Catholic doctrine to argue for the legitimacy of their identities and the construction of an inclusive and participative church. Further, they situated their personal sense of Catholic identity squarely in the church's transhistorical and global presence. Overall, it was apparent that a privatized self-oriented identity (cf. "Sheilaism" as discussed by Bellah et al. 1985: 221) or a communal commitment that diverted them from Catholicism was not really a practical option. Contrary to emphases on the anchorless nature of spiritual seekers (e.g., Wuthnow 1998: 3–10), pro-change Catholics seek change by dwelling within their home tradition. For them, emancipatory ideals are advanced not by severing links with the institution whose official teaching marginalizes them, but by reinterpreting the tradition in ways that validate a more inclusive Catholicism.

This study's findings thus offer a more optimistic view of people's search for and commitment to participating in a community of memory, as opposed to a lifestyle or therapeutic community, than that suggested by other studies of middle-class life in America (e.g. Bellah et al. 1985; Wuthnow 1994b). Pro-change Catholics seek an identity that derives its meaningfulness from the continuity they are able to maintain with an external communal tradition. Their decision to remain Catholic as opposed to taking on some other identity suggests that they experience a "debt" (cf. Schudson 1992: 51) to the Catholic tradition that lessens the plausibility for them of alternative, ad hoc identities. As other studies have documented (e.g., Davidman 1991: 83; Neitz 1987: 257–258), the availability of religious and other options does not undercut the conviction with which individual choices are made. For this study's respondents, the choice to remain Catholic is empowered by Catholicism and by an appreciative collective memory of the many diverse strands that comprise it. It is not, as Peter Berger (1967: 152–153) might argue, a tentative or subjectively idiosyncratic response. Rather, there continues to be a "givenness" (Bellah et al. 1985: 227) about being Catholic that makes sense to pro-change Catholics notwithstanding their critique of aspects of the tradition.

This study's respondents also show that participation in a theological tradition is not limited to a depoliticized, self-oriented spiritual

(Schluchter 1990) or therapeutic (Bellah et al. 1985; Berger 1967) endeavor. Rather, for pro-change Catholics, the search for an authentic spirituality compels their engagement in the emancipation of self, which is necessarily a social and collective project. For them, religion becomes, in part, a public and political activity, focused on effecting change in institutional practices that undermine equality. Pro-change Catholics' practical interpretation of religion as a reasoned theology challenges the imposition of a dichotomy between faith and reason, and by extension, between putatively private and public spheres, whether in individual or institutional practices. They demonstrate and the theologians in this study affirm that, as observed regarding other aspects of "private" life (Calhoun 1995: 217), religion is not a settled or prepolitical identity that one might then draw on in the public sphere. Instead, "being Catholic" is negotiated in public, as people "become" and live out the multiple identities that they experience, which in the process nurtures institutional change.

Pro-change Catholics show that doctrinal questions can form the basis for public conversations in which "meanings" as opposed to "facts" are contested (cf. Gouldner 1976: 93–96). People deliberate about the practical implications of assigning particular meanings to various religious symbols and traditions. The goal is not to prove or disprove redemptive beliefs, but to unpack how specific doctrinal tenets might be given practical interpretation in current times. These conversations are in principle accessible to anyone irrespective of faith who wants to participate, and they are conducted in public. In this view, theological ideas are not the monopoly of any one faith tradition but are accessible for public discussion by believers and nonbelievers alike (Tracy 1981: 28–31), just as, for example, the Declaration of Independence contains distinctly American cultural ideas that can be used and critiqued by those who are not American. While, as previously emphasized, the meanings derived will vary depending on the context of their interpretation, symbols are too rich and too important to be monopolized by any one interpretive community.[1] Doctrinal debate, rather, can contribute to the vibrancy of the public sphere and

1. In arguing for the public accessibility of doctrinal ideas, I am endorsing David Tracy's emphasis on "theology as public discourse" (1981: 28–31). He argues that engagement with religious symbols and narratives is not just for religious believers; as "classic" cultural texts, they can also become "testimonies to possibility" and of "resistance and hope" for nonbelieving interpreters (1987: 88). Tracy's emphasis on a public theology is challenged by other theologians, most

elaborate, as shown by pro-change Catholics, how religious ideas can advance our practical understanding of pluralism and community.[2]

HUMANIZING PLURALISM

Although pro-change Catholics as members of Dignity, WOC, or CFFC are united in their decision to remain Catholic and in their progressive emancipatory agenda, they also have differences of opinion. Members of the Women's Ordination Conference (WOC), for example, are clearly committed to the participatory equality of women in the church. For a substantial number of WOC respondents, however, as documented in Chapter 7, this view of equality does not extend to a woman's right to choose abortion. Similarly, while participants in Dignity share the goal of eliminating the marginal status of gays and lesbians in the church, gay men as a group are less likely than their lesbian coparticipants to see gender discrimination as inextricably linked to their broader project of communal inclusivity. Just as there are attitudinal differences among pro-change Catholics, there are also significant cultural commonalities between them and conservative Catholics who, as members of the Catholic League, are committed to defending official church teaching on the issues contested by pro-change Catholics. Both groups, for example, value the Catholic sacramental tradition and find common personal meanings in the church's global presence.

These are important findings because some scholars (e.g., Hunter 1991) claim that progressives and conservatives have polarized moral visions that render the cultural differences between them unbridgeable. Yet, as seen in this study, the heterogeneity among pro-change Catholics, and the shared commitments between them and conservative Catholics, suggest a more complex picture of individual and group identity. As Edward Said argues, we must recognize that despite differences, identities "have always overlapped one another" in various ways (1993: 330–331; see also Hall 1992). If we want to eliminate inequal-

---

notably Lindbeck (1984), who argues that religion as a cultural system is accessible only to those within a specific religious discursive community.

2. For discussion of the contributions of Catholic social thought to American public debates, see, for example, Douglass and Hollenbach (1994) and Shannon (1995b). For an historical overview of the development of a "public Catholicism" in American society, see O'Brien (1989).

ity we have to recognize that the differences institutionalized in particular domains of life (whether, for example, in gender relations or in geopolitics) have histories, but that these histories do not justify or determine the continuation of inegalitarian practices. We thus need to move away from conceptualizations that stereotype individuals and groups in monolithic terms, and instead recognize (cf. Wink 1997) that in daily life, groups are usually more differentiated than is assumed by convenient categorizations.

Once we recognize the humanity of those who are not like us, the pluralism that is part of everyday life may be seen as enriching rather than undermining community. It is our social task to live with social diversity and thus to find ways to harness diversity in the service of enhancing the vibrancy of community. Cultural diversity, as we saw, for example, with Dignity/Boston, does not preclude the possibility of conversation across differences; as David Tracy (1981: 363) reminds us, "we understand one another, if at all, only through analogies," through recognizing the authenticity of the Other and our similarities in difference.

REVALUING REASON

It is apparent that the theoretical contribution of Habermas in focusing on communicative reason and of Foucault in alerting us to the ubiquitousness of power are critical to our appreciation of the complexities and possibilities of social life in late modernity. At the same time, both demonstrate an idealism that is somewhat removed from the empirical realities confronted in specific contexts. In this study, pro-change Catholics show that the pursuit of an emancipatory agenda does not proceed by the march of reason alone (contrary to Habermas) but is accompanied by faith and power. They also highlight the fact that an emancipatory project is not necessarily undermined (contrary to Foucault) by its attempt to forge new meanings and practices that remain in continuity with an institutional tradition.

This study emphasizes reason's meshing with tradition and religion, and challenges the assumption that reason alone is the critical resource in emancipatory projects. Pro-change Catholics combine faith and reason in their push for identity and institutional transformation. They use doctrinal reasoning to contest the inegalitarian institutional practices of the church and to present alternative interpretations of how doctrine validates more inclusive practices. As argued in Chapter 6,

pro-change Catholics' use of doctrinal reasoning exerts a democratiz-
ing effect in the context of the hierarchically structured church to the
extent that it opens up official church arguments for scrutiny and
counterargument by all Catholics. Respondents' reasoning challenges
not only the validity of the theology used by the church hierarchy to
defend its positions on specific questions; it also probes the nature of
interpretive authority in the church. In both tasks, moreover, pro-
change Catholics necessarily invite the whole Catholic community to
deliberate about the doctrinal questions at issue.

In the Catholic Church, despite the openness ushered in by Vatican
II, the Vatican tries to maintain theological discussion as a protected
space from which ordinary Catholics are excluded.[3] It is the public
nature of dissent, whether among theologians or ordinary Catholics,
that the Vatican abhors, believing rightly that when its doctrinal positions are publicly contested people may hear reasons that lead them to
question the reasonableness of the official arguments. Therefore, while
many scholars note the importance of "protected" or "subaltern"
enclaves in which people are empowered to develop their consciousness of inequality (e.g., Collins 1990: 95; Fraser 1992: 123; Mansbridge 1996: 58), in the institutional context of Catholicism "unpro-
tected" public debate would seem to play a critical role in alerting
ordinary Catholics to the "unreasonableness" of some of the arguments in official church teachings. Such openness may bring participants to the conversation who otherwise would not necessarily be
included.

Critics of Habermas argue that the emphasis on reason is a compet-
itive strategy designed to reproduce the status quo because its rules of
deliberation favor dominant groups and privilege male speaking styles
(I. Young 1996: 123). This claim is difficult to sustain in the context
of this study. The vast majority of pro-change respondents were wo-

---

3. Although Vatican II encouraged Catholics to deepen their understanding of the
   "sacred sciences" (Abbott 1966: 270), the Vatican is concerned that "theological opinions" (e.g., moral proportionality) may not be fully understood by the
   "people of God" (John Paul 1993: 331; CDF 1990: 120), whom the U.S.
   Bishops have, in the McBrien controversy, referred to as "theological begin-
   ners" (1996a: 739). The church hierarchy thus denounces the use of mass
   media and other public forums by theologians or organized groups who present
   alternate opinions (CDF 1990: 123–124).

men, and a substantial proportion of the remainder were gay men.[4] Yet being outside of the heterosexual male hermeneutic does not inhibit respondents' ability to engage in doctrinal reasoning. This finding takes on added significance in view of the historical and contemporary fear that the "feminization" of religion, whether derived from women's comparatively greater involvement than men in religion or from the increased popularity of feminine images of God (see Douglas 1977: 80-117; Greeley 1989a; McDannell 1995), serves to lessen its "universal" (that is, male inclusive) appeal.

The doctrinal reasoning of pro-change Catholics effectively challenges such sexist and homophobic assumptions. They demonstrate that communicative reason is not the prerogative of men alone, and equally important, that its use by women does not sabotage the presentation of rationally defensible arguments in favor of, for example, gender or sexual equality. While Foucault, for example, might suggest that pro-change respondents' recourse to reason was strategically compelled by their exclusion from the official power structure in the church, it is nonetheless the case that they used reason to challenge that power structure by explicating the rationale for a transformed church. In this study, therefore, rather than seeing reason as affirming the status quo, we see evidence of its emancipatory use.

The outcome of any reasoned deliberative process, as Habermas (1996: 35) has stressed, does not guarantee the adoption of a shared working consensus committed to the elimination of inequality. Yet, as the communal deliberations of gay and lesbian participants in Dignity/Boston underscore, reasoned conversation about issues of gender conflict, for instance, enables participants to "listen for" and achieve a better understanding of the reasons for differences and why they emerge and in some instances persist. Reason, as emphasized earlier, never stands alone but coexists with power inequalities, and with the hold of tradition and affective ties. Accordingly, no matter how objectively compelling the reasons for action may be, the social context in which change is discussed invariably means that not everyone will want to embrace change.

Notwithstanding reason's imperfections, what is nonetheless striking is people's openness to and desire for deliberative processes in

---

4. As noted in the Appendix, 87 percent of WOC and 88 percent of CFFC respondents are women.

which they can talk about their differences. Pro-change Catholics and the theologians interviewed crave a "deliberative" church. This is not a subterfuge for making the church into a "democracy"; as Habermas (1996: 35) emphasizes, reasons are not simply "dispositions to have opinions." Following Habermas's concept of "deliberative politics" (1996: 287–328), a deliberative church or any deliberative community is one in which people reason about contested differences with a view toward reaching understanding about a future course of action. Consensus can only prevail as a "claim to truth," however, if, as the Catholic theologian David Tracy (1994: 211) argues, it derives from an "arguing community of inquiry and . . . interpretation." It is through reasoned conversation as illuminated, for example, by Dignity/Boston's consensus-building "listening nights," that the diversity that comprises a community may be engaged, and in the process used to build a community that is (or becomes) more pluralistic in practice.

In short, this study highlights the emancipatory power of reason, and its integration with faith, community attachments, and power inequalities. As depicted in the etchings of the Spanish painter Francisco Goya, the sleep of reason may release the monsters of the night. Conversely, of course, as argued by Max Weber, an overreliance on technical reason leads to disenchantment and the ascendancy of "specialists without spirit, sensualists without heart" (1904-05/1958: 182).

CATHOLIC IDENTITY

Unlike earlier understandings of identity as fixed and immutable, there is increasing awareness today that identity is an evolving process of "becoming" rather than simply "being." As Stuart Hall argues,

> we should think of identity as a 'production,' which is never complete, always in process. . . . Cultural identity is a matter of becoming as well as of being. It belongs to the future as much as to the past. It is not something which already exists, transcending place, time, history and culture. Cultural identities come from somewhere, have histories. But, like everything which is historical, they undergo constant transformation. (1992: 222, 225)

In this dynamic understanding of identity, the identities being forged by Dignity, WOC, and CFFC participants make sense and do not appear incongruous. They demonstrate that "being Catholic" is an ongoing personal and collective project paralleling the construction of gender, sexual, class, ethnic, nationalist, and other identities (cf. Calhoun 1995: 222). For this study's Catholics, being Catholic involves the public affirmation of an identity that integrates claims deemed contradictory in official church teaching. Importantly, however, it is primarily Catholicism and not some other frame of reference that empowers pro-change Catholics to carve out the validity of their Catholicism.

INSTITUTIONAL REPRODUCTION

Although the Catholic Church is a hierarchical institution with a tightly controlled power structure consolidated in the Vatican (Reese 1996a), the fluidity of interpretive authority in contemporary Catholicism means that institutional reproduction is, in part, a diffuse, communal activity not confined to authorization by the church hierarchy. Similar to other institutional contexts (Friedland and Alford 1991: 256), Catholicism constrains but does not determine how its symbols and routines are interpreted in daily life. The church hierarchy can refuse, for instance, to allow women priests, but as this study demonstrates, it cannot prevent Catholics from questioning whether this is an immoral practice and collectively mobilizing to change it. Similarly, the church hierarchy can refuse to allow gay and lesbian Catholics to worship collectively on Catholic Church property, but it cannot prevent them from experiencing the charisma of Catholic communality or from worshipping together as gay and lesbian Catholics at alternate sites. Nor can it prevent pro-choice Catholics from arguing for the morality of judgments that contravene the church hierarchy's understanding of a universal morality.

It is thus evident that resistance or withdrawal are not the only options available to Catholics who disagree with official church teachings. As this book has documented, pro-change Catholics are institutionalizing new ways of speaking about and being Catholic, by expressing what it means to be (or become) Catholic *and* gay, or lesbian, or an advocate of women's ordination, or pro-choice. Their public presence in the church and their doctrinal engagement with the Catholic tradition mean that the church hierarchy and other Catholics must confront, or at least cannot silence, the doctrinal and institutional possibilities which their redrawing of Catholicism presents. This challenge may not lead to sweeping institutional changes, but in my judgment, its articulation in itself enhances the reflexivity and deliberativeness of the church as a whole, and illuminates the opportunities for future doctrinal and institutional change. History, as William Sewell argues, is not shaped solely by anonymous social forces but also by the ways in which cultural redefinitions "significantly reconstitute . . . the possibilities for collective action" (1990: 534, 541). Since pro-change Catholics are institutionalizing new understandings of Catholic identity, perhaps they can reshape the future of the Catholic Church by disseminating new doctrinal meanings which may connect with and transform the lives of Catholics (and others) in the twenty-first century.

INTERPRETIVE CONFLICT.

By contrast with the depiction of institutional routines as habitual and pre-given (e.g, Meyer and Rowan 1977/1991; Zucker 1991), this study's findings demonstrate that institutional schemas are also actively critiqued and reworked. Pro-change Catholics illustrate that interpretive conflicts are an ongoing and critical component of institutional life. While not discounting the impact of social movements in bringing about institutional change, it is important also to pay attention to the ongoing interpretive differences within institutions that may contribute to processes of change.

Institutional identity is more complicated and open-ended than it may appear on the surface. As Richard Scott (1991: 181) argues, it is important to recognize that most organizations make choices in selecting the cultural resources with which they connect. It is evident that in the case of the Catholic Church, there are many diverse institutional strands all legitimately comprising the Catholic tradition, and pro-change Catholics variously draw on these resources. In the Catholic Church, an institution established to enact remembrance (traced to Christ's exhortation at the Last Supper, "Do this in memory of me"), it is evident that the memories to be retained and the meanings injected into those memories are not without interpretive conflict. Discerning whose memory and which memories get reproduced in institutional practices can thus highlight the power interests that underpin particular routines (see Powell 1987). This in turn opens up the possibility that alternative practices and new interpretations of existing doctrines may make better sense than what is purported to be the "constant" tradition.

At the same time, in light of the importance of institutional tradition in validating specific practices, the prospects for successfully achieving change may be enhanced if the initiatives proposed are in continuity with the tradition. What makes the claims of pro-change Catholics potentially persuasive is their solid grounding in the Catholic tradition rather than, for example, in appeals to individual or group rights. As emphasized, contrary to claims that Americans are unable to access "languages of conviction" in articulating their values (e.g., Hunter 1994), it is the church's own tradition that pro-change Catholics use to validate institutional transformation.

SUSTAINING CATHOLIC IDENTITY

Finally, let me conclude with some observations about contemporary Catholicism. The evidence of widespread disagreement with official church teaching among American and other Catholics is frequently characterized as indicating a selective "cafeteria-style" Catholicism or the Protestantization of Catholicism. My study leads me to conclude that rather than signaling the dilution of Catholicism, it may be more helpful to regard the interpretive autonomy demonstrated by Catholics as indicative of the seriousness with which some of them, at least, engage their doctrinal tradition.

The interpretive reasoning of pro-change Catholics underscores the idea that the Catholic doctrinal tradition is not something that is uncritically taken for granted. Its symbols and meanings are not "naturally" or invisibly reproduced transgenerationally, but are evaluated and recast by Catholics themselves to ensure their ethical-practical relevance. Since these symbols have their visibility in Catholic sacramental rituals and theology, it is evident that if the vibrancy of the tradition is to be sustained, each generation of Catholics must discover Catholicism by experiencing the rituals and knowing the multifaceted doctrine.

As Catholics committed to change in the church, it is likely that Dignity, WOC, and CFFC respondents are more deliberately involved with Catholicism than some of their coreligionists. How this study's respondents understand Catholicism is not necessarily reflective of the disposition taken by other Catholics. Different Catholics manifest their Catholic identities in different ways, and individual Catholics who choose to stay Catholic likely do so for a variety of socio-biographical reasons. Irrespective of the uniqueness of the reasons for staying Catholic, this study has identified resources within Catholicism that enable Catholics to carve out an identity that is relatively autonomous of the church hierarchy's authority: the valuing of community, doctrinal reflexivity, pluralism, and a reasoned theology. Together these interrelated strands mobilize pro-change Catholics' interrogation of the Catholic tradition for reasons supporting the reconstruction of a more inclusive church.

Religious identity for pro-change Catholics is an achieved identity, but the achievement involves creating new identities and practices within Catholicism. Thus, unlike what Stephen Warner (1993: 1078) observed to be true for members of the "gay" Metropolitan Community Church, it is not liberation from, but reconstruction of, the "old" religion that this study's pro-change Catholics find both self-affirming and collectively empowering. The findings here suggest that pro-change Catholics act rationally by staying Catholic, but the rationality of their decision has little to do with the supply-side religious economy model (e.g., Iannaccone, Finke, and Stark 1997: 350). It is a critical rationality derived from the interpretive authority of their doctrinal reasoning, and informed by their commitment to and memories of the Catholic doctrinal and communal tradition, notwithstanding their awareness of the power inequalities it contains.

Although the Catholic Church is a hierarchical organization where the line between doctrinal producers and consumers might seem to be relatively rigid, the church hierarchy is not the sole or primary producer of Catholicism. The view that the church hierarchy alone is the privileged producer of doctrine is very much the result of papal reforms which culminated with the declaration of papal infallibility at Vatican I. To marginalize the laity's influence in the production of Catholic doctrine is to take a relatively restricted view of church history, and further, to privilege official doctrine as *the* doctrine.

In contemporary times, being Catholic is both dependent on the church hierarchy's interpretation of Catholicism and simultaneously independent of it. It means being both the consumer and the producer of doctrine. Religious doctrines and practices are cultural products and thus have to be scrutinized in order to unpack the diverse meanings they hold for different people in various social contexts. The example of pro-change Catholics' interpretive autonomy cautions against assuming that the meanings contained in religious traditions are uncontested by believers. As is well documented (e.g., D'Antonio et al. 1996; Greeley 1985), many Catholics reject official church teaching on many issues and continue to be actively involved in the church. Contrary to Chaves's (1994: 769) restricted view which makes submission to official religious authority the measure of "effective religious authority," the context in which doctrine is interpreted clearly influences the ways in which the content is used and injected with new meanings that may well be at odds with official definitions. The fact that Catholics who disagree with official church teaching continue to participate in Catholicism suggests that meaningful religious identity cannot be reduced to behaviorist indicators of the acceptance of official religious authority. Rather, religion also derives its authority and its meanings from the practical, lived contexts in which people interpret and use religion.

For pro-change Catholics and for most of the theologians interviewed, "heresy" lies not in a critical disposition toward doctrine but in its unquestioned acceptance. They present an understanding of Catholicism that sees its relevance as derived from a reflective theology of praxis rather than from blind submission to official church teaching. For them, at both the institutional and the personal levels, faith and reason do not have to be contradictory. It is thus not conformity to the church hierarchy's authority but an authoritative engagement with the doctrinal tradition that enables individual Catholics to maintain the relevance of Catholicism today. It is faith in the vibrancy of a pluralistic community grounded in the seamlessness of faith and reason, that makes pro-change Catholics deliberatively choose to stay Catholic and to use their interpretive autonomy to affirm an identity that validates differences.

CONCLUSION

What makes pro-change Catholics interesting is that they try to forge a new identity while retaining connections to a larger tradition. They chart new symbolic territory that integrates apparently incongruous identities while maintaining links to Catholicism as a community of memory. The temptation to risk new identities while retaining the security offered by established cultural frameworks would appear to be a core dilemma for many people in this age of rapid globalization, with its loosening of boundaries and the proliferation of life choices (Giddens 1991). This quest, of necessity, raises the question of how one can embrace change while retaining cultural anchors. Although the strategies for accomplishing communality amid diversity will vary from one site to another, pro-change Catholics are exemplars that this is possible.

I would like to think that the way pro-change Catholics deal with identity may serve as a model for some of the possibilities that are more broadly accessible (such as the critical use of tradition, and communal deliberation) as we individually and collectively embark on a new century. While Catholicism has unique symbolic resources, all societies are rich in symbols and ideas derived from an array of (contested) religious, political, and cultural traditions. The challenge is to reconstruct those resources to strive toward realizing the emancipatory promises buried within them. If modernity is a "risk society" (Beck 1992), where restraining differences may seem less risky than trusting in cultural diversity, pro-change Catholics suggest otherwise. They demonstrate a critical trust in tradition, in community, in pluralism, in reason, and in the emancipatory power of a faith, or culture, that is public and not just private.

Appendix

Research Methodology

This methodological appendix explains the study's research design, including how the sample was chosen, the data gathering methods used, and the kinds of questions asked of each group. It also provides a sketch of respondents' sociodemographic characteristics. As documented by the *Encyclopedia of Associations* (Gale Research Company 1995: 2259–2282), there are many Catholic organizations whose purpose is to lobby for changes in official church teachings and institutional practices. Since the theoretical interest of this study lay in investigating why institutionally marginalized Catholics stay Catholic, I selected single-issue groups whose pro-change activities aim to make the church more inclusive, participatory, and pluralistic. I chose organizations identified with the culturally and institutionally salient issues of homosexuality, women's ordination, and abortion, respectively, rather than with narrower intrachurch issues such as celibacy, or multi-issue Catholic organizations whose purposes are more diffuse.[1] Dignity, WOC, and CFFC are the sole organizations representing the respective interests of gay and lesbian Catholics, advocates of women's ordination, and pro-choice Catholics.[2] I also included professional Catho-

---

1. While all of the pro-change groups comprise a pro-change Call to Action coalition, WOC, Dignity, and CFFC each has a primary concern with a single issue. I thus excluded, for example, the Association for the Rights of Catholics in the Church, and Catholics Speak Out, on account of the breadth of their agendas.
2. There is an alternative association for Catholic lesbians called the Conference for Catholic Lesbians. Since it excludes gay Catholic men, I chose to focus on Dignity on account of its gender-inclusivity.

lic theologians because their subordinate relation to the church hierarchy gives them a relatively marginalized position from which, as doctrinal experts, they interpret Catholicism.

In order to explore why marginalized Catholics stay Catholic, I used a combination of research methods including content analysis of organizational documents, ethnographic observation, self-administered mail questionnaire surveys, and in-depth personal interviews. Common to the study of Dignity, WOC, and CFFC was (1) a systematic content analysis of their organizational literature, including promotional materials and regular newsletters or journals; and (2) a self-administered questionnaire survey of participants in each group investigating several common issues, and questions tailored to the specific focus of each group. Further, I did a nonparticipant observation study of Dignity/Boston, and conducted personal in-depth interviews with twenty-six active members of the chapter. I also personally interviewed twenty Catholic theologians sampled from centers of theological scholarship in Boston, Massachusetts, and Berkeley, California.

CONTENT ANALYSIS OF ORGANIZATIONAL MATERIALS

Beginning in the early spring of 1995, I collated the organizational materials of Dignity, WOC, and CFFC. The materials consisted primarily of promotional literature, policy statements and memoranda, and organizational newsletters and journals. I conducted an exhaustive analysis of the contents of each group's newsletter or journal from the time of the organization's founding up until the summer of 1996. Thus I examined all issues of Dignity's national monthly newsletter, all issues of WOC's quarterly newspaper, *New Woman, New Church*, and all issues of CFFC's quarterly journal, *Conscience*. The purpose of the content analysis was to familiarize myself with the dynamics and evolution of each organization's history, and to get a sense of how each group defined its collective self-identity. In particular, I focused on the framing of each group's organizational objectives, their relations with church officials, and evidence of intraorganizational tensions.

PRIMARY DATA: SAMPLING PROCEDURES AND DATA GATHERING

DIGNITY/BOSTON.

Dignity/USA's nationwide network of local chapters or faith communities suggested that an ethnographic study of one of its chapters would be an appropriate method by which to investigate the practical ways in which members negotiate identity. Beginning in April 1995, I conducted a five-month ethnographic study of Dignity's Boston chapter. I selected the Boston chapter for practical and substantive reasons. Boston's geographical convenience enhanced the feasibility of my spending time attending the chapter's Masses and various community activities, and interviewing its members. Equally important, Dignity/Boston is one of the largest of the Dignity chapters. It has approximately 100 members, compared to an overall average of 45 members for other chapters. Its prominence is reflected in the fact that many of Dignity/USA's current or previous national officers, board members, and regional representatives are members of the Boston chapter. The chapter was also the host committee for Dignity's 1997 national convention, held in Boston.

I began my ethnographic study of Dignity/Boston by regularly attending its weekly Mass as an anonymous observer, during and after which I took detailed notes. After four weeks of visiting, I contacted the chapter's president, introduced myself, and told her about my research project. She was very enthusiastic about my choice to include Dignity in the study, and over lunch one day, in what was the first of many conversations, gave me an outline of the chapter's structure, history, personalities, and activities. I continued regular attendance and note-taking at Dignity's weekly Sunday evening Mass. Having made my purpose known to the chapter's president and to others who introduced themselves to me at Mass, I also attended Dignity's after-Mass coffee hour, at which I had informal conversations with many of the members. In addition to weekly Masses and coffee hours, I attended two "listening evenings" organized by the chapter to discuss members' views on issues to be voted upon by delegates to the 1995 national convention. I also attended two evening meetings of the liturgy committee, an elected committee charged with planning and overseeing the chapter's liturgical events.

In addition to the observation research, I also conducted a survey of Dignity/Boston participants. Prior to doing the survey, I met collectively with Dignity/Boston's member-elected board as part of one of its regularly scheduled meetings, during which I spoke about my study and board members reviewed my proposed questionnaire. The board gave me permission to conduct a survey, but on account of issues of confidentiality I did not get access to Dignity/Boston's mailing list of members. I was thus unable to contact every member of Dignity/Boston to ask them to participate in the survey. I therefore decided to distribute survey packets to members as they left church after the weekly Mass. After Mass on two consecutive Sundays in June 1995, I distributed a survey packet containing a letter introducing myself and the study, the questionnaire, and a return stamped envelope addressed to me for the completed questionnaire. In all, of the 90 questionnaires distributed, 64 respondents subsequently returned fully completed questionnaires. I was impressed by the large number of completed questionnaires. In addition to participants' enthusiasm for the research topic (which many personally indicated), my ongoing research at Dignity Masses and events and verbal reminders concerning the questionnaire during interviews and in informal personal conversations with Dignity members likely contributed to the high return rate.

The Dignity questionnaire was nine pages long, with several open-ended and closed-ended questions. Part one focused on members' participation in Dignity. Using open-ended questions, I asked respondents to elaborate their reasons for joining and continuing to participate in Dignity, the relevance of Catholicism to their understanding of their sexuality, how their experiences as Catholics influenced their coming-out process as gays or lesbians, their views of official church teaching on homosexuality, and the ways in which they would like official church teaching to change. Part two of the questionnaire focused on Dignity respondents' faith beliefs, sociopolitical attitudes, and their views of various contested issues in the church. Likert-type rating scales elicited opinions on women's ordination, celibacy, abortion, the death penalty and government spending on health care and welfare for the poor. In part three, open-ended questions asked respondents about the personal relevance and meanings of the church and Catholicism to them and about times in their life when they felt particularly proud to be Catholic. Part four used a series of closed-ended questions asking respondents their views of the church hierarchy's teaching authority, the influence of official church teaching in the formation of personal conscience, and their views of papal authority and of the papal office. This section concluded with open-ended questions asking respondents to list whatever aspects of Catholicism they personally considered to be so central to Catholicism that they would not want them changed, and those aspects that in their opinion could be changed. The final section of the questionnaire focused on respondents sociodemographic characteristics.

The Dignity survey sample (n = 64) was predominantly male (75%). The modal age category was 26 to 44 years, although a substantial minority of respondents (22%) were between 45 and 54 years old. Over one-third of the respondents lived alone (38%), and another one-third (35%) lived with their partner. The remainder of the sample shared a house or apartment with friends or with family members. The vast majority of Dignity respondents were college-educated (93%), with 60 percent having completed either graduate school or some form of postgraduate training. Just over one-third of the sample had attended Catholic colleges (36%). Occupationally, the majority of the respondents (51%) were lower professionals. Others were evenly divided among higher professional (14%), managerial/executive (11%), and clerical or sales occupations (14%). A further 10 percent of respondents were not working full-time. Dignity respondents were most likely to affiliate with the Democratic party (64%), although a substantial 29 percent said that they were independent. The majority described their overall political views as either liberal (47%) or very liberal (19%), and one-third described their views as moderate (31%).

I conducted personal in-depth interviews with twenty-six members of Dignity/Boston whom I selected based on observation of their frequent attendance at and/or active involvement in Dignity's activities. Thirteen were women and thirteen were men; some had joined Dignity within the previous three or four years, whereas others had been active in the chapter for several years. Most of the interviewees were in their late twenties or thirties, and a few were older. At the time of the interview, most of the interviewees were involved in a couple relationship and living with their partner, who in most cases was also an active member of Dignity/Boston. Almost all of the interviewees held professional occupational positions. Following a loosely structured format, I used the personal interviews to explore in greater detail the Catholic identity-related questions included in the self-administered questionnaire. Most of the interviews lasted for approximately ninety minutes. All but one of the interviews were taped and later transcribed.

In the spring of 1995, I contacted WOC's national headquarters by telephone and spoke with its national coordinator about my proposed study. I intimated my desire to survey a sample of WOC members as part of the study and discussed the possibility of gaining access to WOC's membership list. As agreed, I mailed WOC a copy of a draft of the proposed questionnaire. Soon thereafter, WOC sent me a comprehensive set of members' mailing labels.

After receiving WOC's mailing labels I proceeded to select a sample. In order to facilitate the conduct of meaningful statistical analyses of the anticipated returned questionnaire data, I estimated that a sample size of 200 would be necessary. In anticipation of a 50 percent response rate associated with mail questionnaire surveys, I drew a representative random sample of 400 names from WOC's list of 3,705 members. In early October 1995, I mailed a self-administered questionnaire to the 400 selected names. I also enclosed a letter explaining the broad purpose of the study and a return stamped envelope addressed to me. Of the 400 questionnaires sent out, 214 completed questionnaires were returned, yielding a response rate of 54 percent.

The WOC questionnaire was a ten-page document that included several open-ended and closed-ended questions. Part one focused on respondents' membership in WOC. It used open-ended questions asking respondents to elaborate on their reasons for joining WOC, the importance of women's ordination to their understanding of Catholicism, the theological and sociocultural reasons that they believed favored women's ordination, their views on why debate on the issue was foreclosed by the Vatican, and their vision of a future church that ordains women.

Part two focused on respondents' faith beliefs and sociopolitical attitudes. Closed-ended Likert-type scales asked respondents their views on celibacy, gay rights, abortion, the death penalty, and government funding of health and welfare benefits. Part three focused on the personal relevance and meaning of Catholicism to the respondents. Open-ended questions were used to establish respondents' understandings of the church and the reasons why respondents remain Catholic.

Respondents were asked to write about special times or occasions in their lives when they felt particularly proud to be Catholic, and to discuss what made being Catholic different for them than, for example, being Protestant. Similar to the Dignity questionnaire, WOC members were also asked their views of the church hierarchy's authority, and open-ended questions on which aspects of Catholicism they personally value as core to the tradition and which they regard as less central. The questionnaire concluded with sociodemographic questions.

The vast majority (87%) of WOC respondents were women. Almost all had college degrees (97%), with 79 percent having completed graduate or professional school. Seventy-two percent had attended Catholic colleges. Occupationally, a substantial proportion of the WOC sample was engaged in expressive-therapeutic occupations, including religious or pastoral work (26%), education (18%), psychology or social work (9%), and creative art or writing (6%). An additional 16 perent of the respondents were engaged in upper professional or managerial occupations (e.g., attorneys, CEOs), and 15 percent were lower professionals (e.g., nurses). Only 2 percent of the respondents were in clerical-type occupations, and less than one in ten (8%) were at home full-time. In terms of other sociodemographic characteristics, the typical WOC respondent was married (51%), between 45 and 64 years old (62%), and supported the Democratic Party (70%). While the majority of WOC respondents described their overall political views as liberal (57%) or very liberal (12%), a substantial proportion (30%) said that they were political moderates.

CATHOLICS FOR A FREE CHOICE (CFFC).

CFFC is neither a membership nor a local community-based organization. Since CFFC's select group of a total of about seventy-five highly committed volunteer activists live in different parts of the United States, it was not feasible to interview them face-to-face. I thus decided to use a mail questionnaire survey to probe how they justify a pro-choice Catholic identity. In the spring of 1995, I contacted CFFC's coordinator of regional activism and explained my interest in including CFFC volunteer activists in the proposed study of pro-change Catholics. From the outset he was cooperative, but he cautioned that the anonymity of the volunteers was a paramount concern in light of sporadic reprisals by church officials against activist pro-choice Catholics. After I forwarded CFFC a draft of the proposed self-administered mail questionnaire, CFFC consented to mail the questionnaire

to its volunteer activists on my behalf. I subsequently sent CFFC seventy-five survey packets that included the questionnaire, an accompanying letter explaining my study's purpose, and a return stamped envelope addressed to me.

Of the seventy-five questionnaires that were mailed, thirty-two
completed questionnaires were returned, yielding a response rate of 43
percent. This response rate is higher than the 20 percent response rate
typically found in mail questionnaire surveys of the general population
(Bourque and Fielder 1995), and although it was lower than the WOC
response rate (54%), compares favorably with the response rates in
other studies addressing controversial issues at the interface of religion
and politics.[3]

The CFFC questionnaire was thirteen pages long. Part one focused
on respondents' abortion activism. Respondents were asked open-
ended questions about their reasons for joining CFFC, how they relate
their pro-choice activism to their Catholicism, what makes it possible
to be pro-choice and a committed Catholic, the theological, social,
and cultural reasons they deem relevant to a pro-choice stand, the
ways in which they would like the church to change its teaching on
abortion, and their perceptions of the impact of CFFC on the church
hierarchy's position.

The format and substance of the remainder of the questionnaire was
similar to that of the Dignity and WOC questionnaires. Thus, in addition to sociodemographic questions, respondents were asked about
their faith beliefs, sociopolitical attitudes, views on women's ordination, gay rights, and celibacy, the personal relevance and meaning of
Catholicism to them, questions designed to elicit the reasons why they
remain Catholic, their views of official church authority, and what
they consider to be core and less central in the Catholic tradition.

The CFFC sample was comprised primarily of women (88%). Over
one-third of the sample was between 45 and 54 years of age, and an
additional 41 percent were age 55 or over. The majority of the respondents were married (57%). Nineteen percent were separated or
divorced, 12 percent were single, and 12 percent described their marital status as other. Almost all of the CFFC respondents had college
degrees (94%), with 63 percent having completed graduate or profes-

3. For example, Demerath and Williams's (1992: 17) mail questionnaire survey of
   Springfield, Mass., residents' attitudes toward local religious and political issues
   yielded a 47 percent response rate.

sional school. Over half of the CFFC sample reported that they had attended Catholic colleges (58%). The majority were engaged in lower professional occupations (56%), although substantial minorities were involved in either higher professional (16%), or managerial/executive (16%) occupations. Three percent of CFFC respondents had clerical occupations, and nine percent were at home full-time. Most of the CFFC respondents were Democrats (78%), and the remainder described themselves as independent. Almost all described their overall political views as either liberal (53%) or very liberal (37%).

CATHOLIC THEOLOGIANS.

Catholic theologians were included in order to investigate their evaluation of the theological legitimacy of pro-change Catholics and to explore their understanding of Catholicism more generally. Rather than surveying a representative sample of American Catholic theologians, my research purposes suggested that in-depth interviews with a select number of theologians would be more appropriate. I thus concentrated my data gathering among theological faculty at two major centers of theological education in the United States, the Boston Theological Institute and the Graduate Theological Union at Berkeley, California.

The Boston Theological Institute (BTI) is a consortium of theological schools in the Boston area, including among others, Boston College, Boston University, Harvard Divinity School, the Weston School of Theology, and Saint John's (diocesan) Seminary. Participating schools in Berkeley's Graduate Theological Union (GTU) include, among others, the Dominican School of Philosophy and Theology, the Franciscan School of Theology, and the Jesuit School of Theology at Berkeley. Having decided on these two geographical centers, in April 1995 I used the academic prospectus and course schedule for each participating school to compile a list of faculty teaching in the areas of interest to my study – specifically, Catholic moral theology, Catholic ethics, and church history. During the summer of 1995, I conducted in-depth interviews with thirteen members of the theological faculty associated with schools participating in the BTI, and with one additional theologian chosen from an adjacent geographic area. In early fall 1995, I initiated contact with the GTU faculty, and subsequently conducted in-depth personal interviews with six GTU faculty members during the 1995–1996 academic year. Of the twenty theologians interviewed, four were women. My interviews with the theologians followed a loosely structured format. I focused the interview primarily around their understandings of what constitutes a "good" Catholic, the constraints, bounds, and limits of the church hierarchy's authority, the formation of individual conscience, the possibilities for change in the church's institutional practices, and the theologians' personal views of what is core in the Catholic tradition.

As is evident from this information, this study's sample of pro-change Catholics represents a relatively homogeneous and elite group. Participants are well educated and employed in relatively high-status occupations that enhance access to the elaborated linguistic codes and cultural capital (e.g., Bourdieu 1984) sociologists associate with the middle and upper classes. Clearly, the pro-change Catholics in this study are not representative of religiously involved American Catholics in general, or of Americans whose identities are derived in part from a minority racial and/or lower social class location.

COMPARATIVE ANALYSES USING DOCTRINALLY CONSERVATIVE CATHOLICS

This study also incorporates supplementary survey data collected from doctrinally conservative Catholics. I conducted a self-administered mail questionnaire survey among a randomly chosen representative sample of members of the Catholic League for Religious and Civil Rights. Founded in 1973, the Catholic League is a lay organization and is the largest Catholic civil rights association in America. Its head-quarters is in New York, and it has several chapters across the United States. One of the league's main purposes is to defend the right of the church hierarchy to "publicly teach and proclaim Catholic dogma and moral doctrine" (Catholic League organizational literature). The league's organizational literature and monthly journal, *Catalyst*, reflect its commitment to upholding the primacy of the church hierarchy's teaching; in the view of the Catholic League, "to be a Catholic is to acknowledge the authority of the magisterium of the Catholic Church" (Catholic League organizational literature). Much of its organizational activity revolves around counteracting what it regards as the inauthenticity of the Catholicism of pro-change groups in the church, especially Dignity and Catholics for a Free Choice.

Paralleling concerns about anonymity and confidentiality at Dignity and CFFC, I did not receive direct access to the Catholic League's mailing list of members. Accordingly, on my behalf, the

Catholic League's publications' office sent a mail questionnaire survey to 400 randomly selected league members chosen from the league's membership list.[4] The Catholic League questionnaire was nine pages long. The questionnaire asked respondents questions relating to their faith and religious beliefs, their attitudes toward various contested issues in the church including women's ordination, celibacy, abortion, and gay rights, and their general political views; the personal relevance and meaning of Catholicism, personal occasions of Catholic pride, and the aspects of Catholicism they personally consider core and less central; their attitudes toward conscience and the church hierarchy's authority, and their sociodemographic background.

A total of 213 completed questionnaires were returned, yielding a response rate of 53 percent. Fifty-nine percent of the respondents were male and 41 percent were female. The majority of the respondents were college-educated (75%) and age 55 or over (75%). Seventy-five percent described their political views as conservative, including 14 percent who said they were very conservative, and 22 percent identified themselves as moderate. Only 3 percent of league respondents identified themselves as liberal. Fifty-five percent of respondents supported the Republican Party, 13 percent the Democrats, and a substantial 32 percent said they were independent. In Chapter 7, I use data from the Catholic League survey to present comparative analyses documenting differences and commonalities between conservative and pro-change Catholics.

4. I am grateful to John Pantuso and his staff at the Catholic League publications office.

REFERENCES

Abbott, Walter, ed. 1966. *The Documents of Vatican II*. New York: Herder and
    Herder.
Ahlstrom, Sydney. 1972. *A Religious History of the American People*. New Haven:
    Yale University Press.
Ammerman, Nancy. 1990. *Baptist Battles: Social Change and Religious Conflict in the
    Southern Baptist Convention*. New Brunswick, NJ: Rutgers University Press.
Ammerman, Nancy. 1997. *Congregation and Community*. New Brunswick, NJ:
    Rutgers University Press.
Apter, David. 1995. "Foucault's Paradox: From Inversionary Discourse to
    Hegemonic Power in 'Mao's Republic.' " *The Copenhagen Journal of Asian
    Studies* 10:6-39.
Aquinas, Thomas. 1948/1991. "Summa Theologiae: Question 94. Of the Natural
    Law." Pages 101–113 in Charles Curran and Richard McCormick eds.
    Readings in Moral Theology No. 7. New York: Paulist Press.
Beck, Ulrich. 1992. *Risk Society: Toward a New Modernity*. Translated by Mark
    Ritter. London: Sage.
Bell, Wendell. 1994. "The World as a Moral Community." *Society* (July/August):
    17-22.
Bellah, Robert, Richard Madsen, William Sullivan, Ann Swidler, and Steven
    Tipton. 1985. *Habits of the Heart: Individualism and Commitment in American
    Life*. Berkeley: University of California Press.
Bellah, Robert, Richard Madsen, William Sullivan, Ann Swidler, and Steven
    Tipton. 1991. *The Good Society*. New York: Knopf.
Berger, Peter. 1967. *The Sacred Canopy: Elements of a Sociological Theory of Religion*.
    Garden City, NY: Doubleday.
Berger, Peter. 1992. *A Far Glory: The Quest for Faith in an Age of Credulity*. New
    York: Free Press
Berger, Peter, and Thomas Luckmann. 1966. *The Social Construction of Reality: A
    Treatise in the Sociology of Knowledge*. Garden City, NY: Doubleday.
Berger, Peter, Brigitte Berger, and Hansfried Kellner. 1973. *The Homeless Mind*.
    New York: Penguin.
Bernstein, Mary. 1997. "Celebration and Suppression: The Strategic Uses of
    Identity by the Lesbian and Gay Movement." *American Journal of Sociology*
    103: 531-565.
Bianchi, Eugene, and Rosemary Radford Ruether. 1992. "Introduction." Pages

7–13 in E. Bianchi and R. Ruether, eds. *A Democratic Catholic Church*. New York: Crossroad.

Blank, Josef. 1973. "The Person and Office of Peter in the New Testament." Pages 42–55 in Edward Schillebeeckx and Bas van Iersel, eds. *Truth and Certainty*. New York: Herder and Herder.

Bokenkotter, Thomas. 1990. *A Concise History of the Catholic Church*, third edition. New York: Doubleday.

Bork, Robert. 1996. *Slouching Toward Gomorrah: Modern Liberalism and American Decline*. New York: Regan Books.

Boswell, John. 1980. *Christianity, Social Tolerance, and Homosexuality: Gay People in Western Europe from the Beginning of the Christian Era to the Fourteenth Century*. Chicago: University of Chicago Press.

Boswell, John. 1994. *Same-Sex Unions in Premodern Europe*. New York: Villard Books.

Bourdieu, Pierre. 1984. *Distinction. A Social Critique of the Judgment of Taste*. Cambridge: Harvard University Press.

Bourque, Linda, and Eve Fielder. 1995. *How to Conduct Self Administered and Mail Surveys*. Thousand Oaks, Calif.: Sage.

Boyle, John. 1985. "The Academy and Church Teaching Authority: Current Issues." *CTSA Proceedings* 40: 172-180.

Bray, Gerald. 1994. "Review of *Same-Sex Unions in Premodern Europe* by John Boswell." *Christianity Today*, December 12, pp. 46–47.

Burns, Gene. 1992. *The Frontiers of Catholicism: The Politics of Ideology in a Liberal World*. Berkeley: University of California Press.

Burns, Gene. 1996. "Studying the Political Culture of American Catholicism." *Sociology of Religion* 57: 37-53.

Cahill, Lisa Sowle. 1996. *Sex, Gender, and Christian Ethics*. New York: Cambridge University Press.

Calhoun, Craig. 1995. *Critical Social Theory: Culture, History, and the Challenge of Difference*. Cambridge, Mass.: Blackwell.

Carroll, Michael. 1996. *Veiled Threats: The Logic of Popular Catholicism in Italy*. Baltimore: Johns Hopkins University Press.

Casanova, José. 1994. *Public Religions in the Modern World*. Chicago: University of Chicago Press.

Castells, Manuel. 1997. *The Power of Identity*. Cambridge, Mass.: Blackwell.

Catechism of the Catholic Church. 1994. Dublin: Veritas.

Catholic Theological Society of America (CTSA). 1997. "Women's Ordination 'Responsum.'" *Origins* 27 (June 19): 75–79.

Chaves, Mark. 1994. "Secularization as Declining Religious Authority." *Social Forces* 72: 49–774.

Cohen, Cathy. 1996. "Contested Membership: Black Gay Identities and the Politics of AIDS." Pages 362–394 in Steven Seidman, ed. *Queer Theory/Sociology*. Cambridge, Mass.: Blackwell.

Coleman, John. 1989. "Raison D'Eglise: Organizational Imperatives of the Church in the Political Order." Pages 252–275 in Jeffrey Hadden and Anson Shupe, eds. *Secularization and Fundamentalism Reconsidered*. New York: Paragon House.

Collins, Patricia Hill. 1990. *Black Feminist Thought*. Boston: Unwin Hyman.

Congar, Yves. 1957/1965. *Lay People in the Church*. Westminster, Md.: Newman Press.

Congar, Yves. 1967. *Tradition and Traditions. An Historical and Theological Essay*. New York: Macmillan.

Congregation for the Doctrine of the Faith (CDF). 1976. "Declaration on Sexual Ethics." *Origins* 5(January 22): 485, 487-494.

Congregation for the Doctrine of the Faith (CDF). 1977. "Vatican Declaration: Women in the Ministerial Priesthood." *Origins* 6 (February 3): 517, 519–531.

Congregation for the Doctrine of the Faith (CDF). 1986. "The Pastoral Care of Homosexual Persons." *Origins* 16 (November 13): 377, 379–382.

Congregation for the Doctrine of the Faith (CDF). 1990. "Instruction on the Ecclesial Vocation of the Theologian." *Origins* 20 (July 5): 117, 119–126.

Congregation for the Doctrine of the Faith (CDF). 1995. "Inadmissibility of Women to Ministerial Priesthood." *Origins* 25 (November 30): 401, 403–405.

Connery, John. 1977. *Abortion: The Development of the Roman Catholic Perspective*. Chicago: Loyola University Press.

Cook, Elizabeth, Ted Jelen, and Clyde Wilcox. 1992. *Between Two Absolutes: Public Opinion and the Politics of Abortion*. Boulder, Colo.: Westview Press.

Cuneo, Michael. 1997. *The Smoke of Satan: Conservative and Traditionalist Dissent in Contemporary American Catholicism*. New York: Oxford University Press.

Curran, Charles. 1992. *The Living Tradition of Catholic Moral Theology*. Notre Dame: University of Notre Dame Press.

Daly, Mary. 1996. "Sin Big." *The New Yorker*. (double issue) February 6 & March 4, pp. 76–84.

D'Antonio, William, James Davidson, Dean Hoge, and Ruth Wallace. 1989. *American Catholic Laity in a Changing Church*. Kansas City, Mo.: Sheed and Ward.

D'Antonio, William, James Davidson, Dean Hoge, and Ruth Wallace. 1996. *Laity, American and Catholic: Transforming the Church*. Kansas City, Mo.: Sheed and Ward.

Davidman, Lynn. 1991. *Tradition in a Rootless World: Women Turn to Orthodox Judaism*. Berkeley: University of California Press.

Davidson, James, Andrea Williams, Richard Lamanna, Jan Stenftenagel, Kathleen Weigert, William Whalen, and Patricia Wittberg. 1997. *The Search for Common Ground. What Unites and Divides American Catholics*. Huntington, Ind.: Our Sunday Visitor.

Davis, Nancy, and Robert Robinson. 1996a. "Religious Orthodoxy in American Society: The Myth of a Monolithic Camp." *Journal for the Scientific Study of Religion* 35: 229–245.

Davis, Nancy, and Robert Robinson. 1996b. "Are the Rumors of War Exaggerated?: Religious Orthodoxy and Moral Progressivism in America." *American Journal of Sociology* 102: 756–787.

Delanty, Gerard. 1997. "Habermas and Occidental Rationalism: The Politics of Identity, Social Learning, and the Cultural Limits of Moral Universalism." *Sociological Theory* 15: 30–59.

Demerath, N. J. III. 1997. "America's Culture Wars in Cross-Cultural Perspective."

In Rhys Williams, ed. *Cultural Wars in American Politics: Critical Reviews of a Popular Myth*. New York: Aldine de Gruyter.

Demerath, N. J., III, and Rhys Williams. 1992. *A Bridging of Faiths. Religion and Politics in a New England City*. Princeton: Princeton University Press.

Dillon, Michele. 1995. "Institutional Legitimation and Abortion: Monitoring the Catholic Church's Discourse." *Journal for the Scientific Study of Religion* 34: 141–151.

Dillon, Michele. 1996a. "Cultural Differences in the Abortion Discourse of the Catholic Church: Evidence from Four Countries." *Sociology of Religion* 57: 25–36

Dillon, Michele. 1996b. "The American Abortion Debate: Culture War or Normal Discourse?" In James Nolan, ed. *The American Culture Wars*. Charlottesville, Va.: University of Virginia Press.

Dillon, Michele. 1999. "The Catholic Church and Possible 'Organizational-Selves': The Implications for Institutional Change." *Journal for the Scientific Study of Religion* 38.

DiMaggio, Paul. 1986. "Cultural Entrepreneurship in Nineteenth Century Boston, Part II: The Classification and Framing of American Art." *Media, Culture, and Society* 4: 303–322.

DiMaggio, Paul, and Walter Powell. 1991. "Introduction." Pages 1–38 in Walter Powell and Paul DiMaggio, eds. *The New Institutionalism in Organizational Analysis*. Chicago: University of Chicago Press.

DiMaggio, Paul, John Evans, and Bethany Bryson. 1996. "Have Americans' Social Attitudes Become More Polarized?" *American Journal of Sociology* 102: 690–755.

Dolan, Jay. 1985. *The American Catholic Experience. A History from Colonial Times to the Present*. Garden City, N.Y.: Doubleday.

Donohue, William A. 1995. "The Politics of the Catholic League." *Catalyst. Journal of the Catholic League for Religious and Civil Rights* 22 (July-August) : 3.

Douglas, Ann. 1977. *The Feminization of American Culture*. New York: Avon Books.

Douglass, R. Bruce, and David Hollenbach, eds. 1994. *Catholicism and Liberalism: Contributions to American Public Philosophy*. New York: Cambridge University Press.

Dulles, Avery. 1976. "The Theologian and the Magisterium." *CTSA Proceedings* 31: 235–246.

Dulles, Avery. 1985. *The Catholicity of the Church*. Oxford: Clarendon Press.

Dulles, Avery. 1996. "Gender and Priesthood: Examining the Teaching." *Origins* 25 (May 2): 78–784.

Durkheim, Emile. 1912/1976. *The Elementary Forms of the Religious Life*. London: Allen and Unwin.

Ebaugh, Helen Rose. 1991. "Vatican II and the Revitalization Movement." Pages 3–19 in H. R. Ebaugh, ed. *Religion and the Social Order. Vatican II and U.S. Catholicism*. Greenwich, Conn.: JAI Press Inc.

Elton, G. R. 1963. *Reformation Europe*. London: Fontana.

Epstein, Cynthia Fuchs. 1988. *Deceptive Distinctions: Sex, Gender, and the Social Order*. New Haven: Yale University Press.

Epstein, Steven. 1987. "Gay Politics, Ethnic Identity: The Limits of Social Constructionism." *Socialist Review* 17: 9-54.

Etzioni, Amitai. 1996. "The Responsive Community: A Communitarian Perspective." *American Sociological Review* 61: 1–11.

Etzioni, Amitai. 1997. *The New Golden Rule*. New York: Basic Books.

Euart, Sharon. 1993. "Theologians and the Mandate to Teach." *Origins* 27 (December 16): 465, 467–472.

Fabrizio, McLaughlin, and Associates, Inc. 1995. *National Survey of Adult Catholics*. Alexandria, Va: Fabrizio, McLaughlin and Associates, Inc.

Farley, Margaret. 1995. "North American Bioethics: A Feminist Critique." Pages 131–147 in Michael Grodin, ed. *Meta Medical Ethics: The Philosophical Foundations of Bioethics*. Dordrecht/Boston/London: Kluwer Academic Publishers.

Fine, Gary Alan. 1995. "Public Narration and Group Culture: Discerning Discourse in Social Movements." Pages 127–143 in Hank Johnston and Bert Klandermans, eds. *Social Movements and Culture*. Minneapolis: University of Minnesota Press.

Finke, Roger, and Rodney Stark. 1992. *The Churching of America: Winners and Losers in Our Religious Economy*. New Brunswick, N.J.: Rutgers University Press.

Finke, Roger, Avery Guest, and Rodney Stark. 1996. "Mobilizing Local Religious Markets: Religious Pluralism in the Empire State, 1855 to 1865." *American Sociological Review* 61: 203–218.

Flax, Jane. 1990. *Thinking Fragments*. Berkeley: University of California Press.

Fligstein, Neil. 1991. "The Structural Transformation of American Industry." Pages 311–336 in Walter Powell and Paul DiMaggio, eds. *The New Institutionalism in Organizational Analysis*. Chicago: University of Chicago Press.

Fogerty, Gerald. 1985. *The Vatican and the American Hierarchy from 1870 to 1965*. Wilmington, Del.: Michael Glazier.

Foley, Nadine. 1976. "Who Are These Women?" Pages 3–7 in Anne Marie Gardiner, ed. *Women and Catholic Priesthood: An Expanded Vision*. New York: Paulist.

Foucault, Michel. 1977/1984. "Truth and Power." Pages 51–75 in Paul Rabinow, ed. *The Foucault Reader*. New York: Pantheon.

Foucault, Michel. 1978. *The History of Sexuality*, volume 1. New York: Vintage Books.

Foucault, Michel. 1981/1997. "Friendship as a Way of Life." Pages 135–140 in Paul Rabinow, ed. *Michel Foucault. Ethics. Subjectivity and Truth: The Essential Works of Foucault 1954–1984*, volume 1. New York: The New Press.

Foucault, Michel. 1982/1997. "Michel Foucault: An Interview by Stephen Riggins." Pages 121-133 in Paul Rabinow, ed. *Michel Foucault. Ethics. Subjectivity and Truth: The Essential Works of Foucault 1954–1984*, volume 1. New York: The New Press.

Foucault, Michel. 1984a/1997. "The Ethics of the Concern of the Self as a Practice of Freedom." Pages 281–301 in Paul Rabinow, ed. *Michel Foucault. Ethics. Subjectivity and Truth: The Essential Works of Foucault 1954–1984*, volume 1. New York: The New Press

Foucault, Michel. 1984b/1997. "Sex, Power, and the Politics of Identity." Pages 163–173 in Paul Rabinow, ed. *Michel Foucault. Ethics. Subjectivity and Truth: The Essential Works of Foucault 1954–1984*, volume 1. New York: The New Press.

Fraser, Nancy. 1992. "Rethinking the Public Sphere: A Contribution to the Critique of Actually Existing Democracy." Pages 109–142 in Craig Calhoun, ed. *Habermas and the Public Sphere*. Cambridge, Mass.: MIT Press.

Frazer, Elizabeth, and Nicola Lacey. 1993. *The Politics of Community: A Feminist Critique of the Liberal-Communitarian Debate*. Toronto: University of Toronto Press.

Freyne, Sean. 1996. "Infallible?" *The Furrow* 47: 44–46

Friedland, Roger, and Robert Alford. 1991. "Bringing Society Back In: Symbols, Practices and Institutional Contradictions." Pages 232–263 in Walter Powell and Paul DiMaggio, eds. *The New Institutionalism in Organizational Analysis*. Chicago: University of Chicago Press.

Fuss, Diana. 1989. *Essentially Speaking: Feminism, Nature, and Difference*. New York: Routledge.

Gale Research Company. 1995. *Encyclopedia of Associations*, volume 1. "National Organizations."

Gallup, George. 1994. *The Gallup Poll 1993*. Wilmington, Del.: Scholarly Resources Inc.

Gardiner, Anne Marie, ed. 1976. *Women and Catholic Priesthood: An Expanded Vision*. Proceedings of the Detroit Ordination Conference. New York: Paulist Press.

Gergen, Kenneth. 1991. *The Saturated Self: Dilemmas of Identity in Contemporary Life*. New York: Basic Books.

Giddens, Anthony. 1991. *Modernity and Self-Identity: Self and Society in the Late Modern Age*. Stanford: Stanford University Press.

Ginsburg, Faye. 1989. *Contested Lives: The Abortion Debate in an American Community*. Berkeley: University of California Press.

Glendon, Mary Ann. 1991. *Rights Talk*. New York: Free Press.

Goffman, Erving. 1963. *Stigma: Notes on the Management of Spoiled Identity*. Englewood Cliffs: Prentice Hall.

Goodstein, Laura, and Richard Morin. 1995. "Love the Messenger, Not His Message." *Washington Post* (national weekly edition) October 9–15, p. 37.

Gould, Carol. 1996. "Diversity and Democracy: Representing Difference." Pages 171–186 in Seyla Benhabib, ed. *Democracy and Difference. Contesting the Boundaries of the Political*. Princeton: Princeton University Press.

Gouldner, Alvin. 1976. *The Dialectic of Ideology and Technology*. New York: Oxford University Press.

Grant, Robert. 1970. *Augustus to Constantine. The Thrust of the Christian Movement into the Roman World*. New York: Harper and Row.

Greeley, Andrew. 1977. *The American Catholic: A Social Portrait*. New York: Basic Books.

Greeley, Andrew. 1985. *American Catholics since the Council*. Chicago: Thomas More Press.

Greeley, Andrew. 1989a. *Religious Change in America*. Cambridge, Mass.: Harvard University Press.

Greeley, Andrew. 1989b. "Protestant and Catholic: Is the Analogical Imagination Extinct?" *American Sociological Review* 54: 485–502.

Greeley, Andrew. 1995. *Religion as Poetry*. New Brunswick, N.J.: Transaction.

Greeley, Andrew, and Michael Hout. 1996. "Survey Finds Catholics Want More Say." *National Catholic Reporter*, June 14.

Habermas, Jürgen. 1975. *Legitimation Crisis*. Boston: Beacon Press.

Habermas, Jürgen. 1984. *The Theory of Communicative Action: Reason and the Rationalization of Society*. volume 1. Boston: Beacon Press.

Habermas, Jürgen. 1987. *The Theory of Communicative Action: Lifeworld and System*. volume 2. Boston: Beacon Press.

Habermas, Jürgen. 1991. *The Structural Transformation of the Public Sphere*, translated by Thomas Burger. Cambridge, Mass.: MIT Press.

Habermas, Jürgen. 1992. "Transcendence from Within, Transcendence in This World." Pages 226–250 in Don Browning and Francis Schüssler Fiorenza, eds. *Habermas, Modernity, and Public Theology*. New York: Crossroad.

Habermas, Jürgen. 1996. *Between Facts and Norms: Contributions to a Discourse Theory of Law and Democracy*. Cambridge, Mass.: MIT Press.

Haight, Roger. 1995. "Fifty Years of Theology." *CTSA Proceedings* 50: 1–14.

Hall, Stuart. 1973. "Encoding and Decoding in the Television Discourse." Birmingham: Center for Contemporary Cultural Studies. Mimeograph.

Hall, Stuart. 1992. "Cultural Identity and Diaspora." Pages 222–237 in Jonathan Rutherford, ed. *Identity: Community, Culture, Difference*. London: Lawrence and Wishart.

Hall, Stuart, and Tony Jefferson, eds. 1976. *Resistance Through Rituals: Youth Subcultures in Post-War Britain*. London: Hutchinson.

Hannan, Michael, and John Freeman. 1989. *Organizational Ecology*. Cambridge, Mass.: Harvard University Press.

Hannon, Patrick. 1992. *Church, State, Morality, and Law*. Dublin: Gill and Macmillan.

Harding, Sandra. 1991. *Whose Science? Whose Knowledge?* Ithaca: Cornell University Press.

Hart, Stephen. 1992. *What Does the Lord Require?* New York: Oxford University Press.

Hebdige, Dick. 1979. *Subculture: The Meaning of Style*. London: Methuen

Hellwig, Monika. 1987. "Who Is Truly a Catholic Theologian?" *CTSA Proceedings* 42: 91–100.

Hennesey, James. 1963. *The First Council of the Vatican: The American Experience*. New York: Herder and Herder.

Hennesey, J. J. 1967. "Vatican Council I." Pages 559–563 in *New Catholic Encyclopedia*, volume 14. New York: McGraw Hill.

Hirschman, Albert. 1970. *Exit, Voice and Loyalty: Responses to Decline in Firms, Organizations, and States*. Cambridge: Harvard University Press.

Hitchcock, Helen Hull. 1995. "Women for Faith and Family: Catholic Women Affirming Catholic Teaching." Pages 163–185 in Mary Jo Weaver and R. Scott Appleby, eds. *Being Right: Conservative Catholics in America*. Bloomington: Indiana University Press.

Hoge, Dean. 1976. *Division in the Protestant House*. Philadelphia: Westminster Press.

Hoge, Dean, Benton Johnson, and Donald Luidens. 1994. *Vanishing Boundaries: The Religion of Mainline Protestant Baby Boomers*. Louisville, Ky: Westminster/John Knox Press.

Hoge, Dean, Joseph Shields, and Douglas Griffin. 1995. "Changes in Satisfaction and Institutional Attitudes of Catholic Priests, 1970–1993." *Sociology of Religion* 56: 195–213.

Hollenbach, David. 1994. "Afterword: A Community of Freedom." Pages 323–343 in R. Bruce Douglass and David Hollenbach, eds. *Catholicism and Liberalism. Contributions to American Public Philosophy*. New York: Cambridge University Press.

Hollister, C. Warren. 1982. *Medieval Europe: A Short History*, fifth edition. New York: Knopf.

Hout, Michael, and Andrew Greeley. 1987. "The Center Doesn't Hold: Church Attendance in the United States, 1940–1984." *American Sociological Review* 52: 325–345.

Hunter, James 1991. *Culture Wars: The Struggle to Define America*. New York: Basic Books.

Hunter, James. 1994. *Before the Shooting Begins: Searching for Democracy in America's Culture War*. New York: Free Press.

Hunter, James. 1996. "Response to Davis and Robinson: Remembering Durkheim." *Journal for the Scientific Study of Religion* 35: 246–248.

Iannaccone, Laurence. 1991. "The Consequences of Religious Market Structure." *Rationality and Society* 3: 156–177.

Iannaccone, Laurence. 1992. "Sacrifice and Stigma: Reducing Free-riding in Cults, Communes, and Other Collectives." *Journal of Political Economy* 100: 271–291.

Iannaccone, Laurence. 1995a. "Risk, Rationality, and Religious Portfolios." *Economic Inquiry* 33: 285–295.

Iannaccone, Laurence. 1995b. "Voodoo Economics? Reviewing the Rational Choice Approach to Religion." *Journal for the Scientific Study of Religion* 34: 76–89.

Iannaccone, Laurence, Roger Finke, and Rodney Stark. 1997. "Deregulating Religion: The Economies of Church and State." *Economic Inquiry* 35: 350–364.

Inglehart, Ronald. 1990. *Culture Shift in Advanced Industrial Society*. Princeton: Princeton University Press.

Joas, Hans. 1993. *Pragmatism and Social Theory*. Chicago: University of Chicago Press.

John XXIII. 1961/1966. "Pope John Convokes the Council." Pages 703–709 in Walter Abbott, ed. *The Documents of Vatican II*. New York: Herder and Herder.

John XXIII. 1962/1966. "Pope John's Opening Speech to the Council." Pages 710–719 in Walter Abbott, ed. *The Documents of Vatican II*. New York: Herder and Herder.

John Paul II. 1993. "Veritatis Splendor." *Origins* 23 (October 14): 297, 299–334.

John Paul II. 1994. "Ordinatio Sacerdotalis." *Origins* 24 (June 9): 49–52.

John Paul II. 1995a. *Evangelium Vitae. The Gospel of Life. The Encyclical Letter on Abortion, Euthanasia, and the Death Penalty in Today's World*. New York: Random House.

John Paul II. 1995b. "Letter to Women." *Origins* 25 (July 27): 137, 139–143.

John Paul II. 1998. "Ad Tudendum Fidem." *Origins* 28 (July 16):113, 115–116.

Kennedy, Eugene. 1988. *Tomorrow's Catholics, Yesterday's Church: The Two Cultures of American Catholicism*. New York: Harper and Row.

Kenny, Michael. 1994. "Women's Ordination – Uneasy Questions." *America*, July 30, p. 16.

Komonchak, Joseph. 1985. "The Ecclesial and Cultural Roles of Theology." *CTSA Proceedings* 40: 15–32.

Kosnik, Anthony, William Carroll, Agnes Cunningham, Ronald Modras, and James Schulte. 1977. *Human Sexuality: New Directions in American Catholic Thought*. New York: Paulist Press.

Kowalewski, Mark. 1994. *All Things to All People: The Catholic Church Confronts the AIDS Crisis*. Albany: SUNY Press.

Kurtz, Lester. 1986. *The Politics of Heresy: The Modernist Crisis in Roman Catholicism*. Berkeley: University of California Press.

Lamont, Michele. 1992. *Money, Morals, and Manners*. Chicago: University of Chicago Press.

Langan, John, ed. 1993. *Catholic Universities in Church and Society: A Dialogue on Ex Corde Ecclesiae*. Washington, D.C.: Georgetown University Press.

Laurentin, Rene. 1973. "Peter as the Foundation Stone in the Present Uncertainty." Pages 95–113 in Edward Schillebeeckx and Bas van Iersel, eds. *Truth and Certainty*. New York: Herder and Herder.

Lichterman, Paul. 1995. "Beyond the Seesaw Model: Public Commitment in a Culture of Self-Fulfillment." *Sociological Theory* 13: 275–300.

Lindbeck, George. 1984. *The Nature of Doctrine: Religion and Theology in a Postliberal Age*. Philadelphia: Westminster.

Mannheim, Karl. 1936. *Ideology and Utopia: An Introduction to the Sociology of Knowledge*. San Diego: Harcourt Brace Jovanovich.

Mansbridge, Jane. 1993. "Feminism and Democratic Community." *Nomos* 35:339–395.

Mansbridge, Jane. 1996. "Using Power/Fighting Power: The Polity." Pages 46–66 in Seyla Benhabib, ed. *Democracy and Difference: Contesting the Boundaries of the Political*. Princeton: Princeton University Press.

McAvoy, Thomas. 1957. *The Great Crisis in American Catholicism*. Henry Regnery Company.

McBrien, Richard, ed. 1995. *The HarperCollins Encyclopedia of Catholicism*. San Francisco: Harper.

McCarthy, Thomas. 1984. "Translator's Introduction." Pages v–xxxvii in Jürgen Habermas. *The Theory of Communicative Action*, vol. 1. Boston: Beacon Press.

McCarthy, Thomas. 1991. *Ideals and Illusions: On Reconstruction and Deconstruction in Contemporary Critical Theory*. Cambridge, Mass.: MIT Press.

McCool, Gerald. 1977. *Catholic Theology in the Nineteenth Century: The Quest for a Unitary Method*. New York: Seabury Press.

McCormick, Richard. 1969. "The Teaching Role of the Magisterium and of Theologians." *CTSA Proceedings* 24: 239–254.

McCormick, Richard. 1994. "Some Early Reactions to Veritatis Splendor." *Theological Studies* 55: 481–506.

McCormick, Richard. 1995. "The Gospel of Life." *America*, April 29, pp. 10–17.

McDannell, Colleen. 1995. *Material Christianity*. New Haven: Yale University Press.

McNamara, Patrick. 1992. *Conscience First, Tradition Second: A Study of Young American Catholics*. Albany, N.Y.: SUNY Press.

McNeil, John. 1976. *The Church and the Homosexual*. Kansas City, Mo.: Sheed, Andrews, and McMeel Inc.

McSweeney, Bill. 1980. *Roman Catholicism: The Search for Relevance*. New York: St. Martin's Press.

Meyer, John, and Brian Rowan. 1977/1991. "Institutionalized Organizations: Formal Structure as Myth and Ceremony." Pages 41–62 in W. Powell and P. DiMaggio, eds. *The New Institutionalism in Organizational Analysis*. Chicago: University of Chicago Press.

Minkoff, Debra. 1995. *Organizing for Equality: The Evolution of Women's and Racial-Ethnic Organizations in America, 1955–1985*. New Brunswick, N.J.: Rutgers University Press.

Mouffe, Chantal. 1996. "Democracy, Power, and the 'Political.' " Pages 245–256 in Seyla Benhabib, ed. *Democracy and Difference. Contesting the Boundaries of the Political*. Princeton: Princeton University Press.

Neitz, Mary Jo. 1987. *Charisma and Community: A Study of Religious Commitment within the Charismatic Renewal*. New Brunswick, N.J.: Transaction.

Nicholson, Linda, and Steven Seidman. 1995. *Social Postmodernism: Beyond Identity Politics*. New York: Cambridge University Press.

Noonan, John. 1970. "An Almost Absolute Value in History". Pages 1–59 in John Noonan, ed. *The Morality of Abortion: Legal and Historical Perspectives*. Cambridge: Harvard University Press.

Noonan, John. 1993. "Development in Moral Doctrine." *Theological Studies* 54: 662–677.

Nugent, Robert, and Jeanine Gramick. 1992. *Building Bridges: Gay & Lesbian Reality and the Catholic Church*. Mystic, Conn.: Twenty-Third Publications.

O'Brien, David. 1989. *Public Catholicism*. New York: Macmillan.

Offe, Claus. 1984. *Contradictions of the Welfare State*. London: Hutchinson.

O'Malley, John. 1989. *Tradition and Transition: Historical Perspectives on Vatican II*. Wilmington, Del.: Michael Glazier.

Orsy, Ladislaus. 1996. "Lay Persons in Church Governance? A Disputed Question." *America*, April 6, pp. 10–13.

Paul VI. 1968/1983. *Humanae Vitae. Encyclical Letter of His Holiness Pope Paul VI*. San Francisco: Ignatius Press.

Paul VI. 1976. "Women: Balancing Rights and Duties." *Origins* 5 (February 19): 549, 551–552.

Perry, Troy, with Thomas Swicegood. 1990. *Don't Be Afraid Anymore: The Story of Reverend Troy Perry and the Metropolitan Community Churches*. New York: St. Martin's Press.

Pius XII. 1950. "Humani Generis." Pages 175–184 in Claudia Carlen, ed. *The Papal Encyclicals 1939-1958*. Raleigh, N.C.: McGrath Publishing.

Powell, Walter. 1987. "How the Past Informs the Present: The Uses and Liabilities of Organizational Memory." University of Arizona. Unpub. manuscript.

Powell, Walter. 1991. "Expanding the Scope of Institutional Analysis." Pages

183–203 in Walter Powell and Paul DiMaggio, eds. *The New Institutionalism in Organizational Analysis*. Chicago: University of Chicago Press.

Press, Andrea. 1991. *Women Watching Television*. Philadelphia: University of Pennsylvania Press.

Quinn, John. 1992. "Civil Rights of Gay and Lesbian Persons." *Origins* 22 (August 20): 204.

Quinn, John. 1996. "The Exercise of the Papacy: Facing the Cost of Christian Unity." *Commonweal*, July 12, pp. 11–20.

Radway, Janice. 1984. *Reading the Romance: Women, Patriarchy, and Popular Literature*. Chapel Hill, N.C.: University of North Carolina Press.

Ratzinger, Joseph. 1998. "Commentary on Profession of Faith's Concluding Paragraphs." *Origins*, 28 (July 16): 116–119.

Redmont, Jane. 1992. *Generous Lives: American Catholic Women Today*. New York: William Morrow.

Redmont, Jane. 1995. "The Women's Ordination Movement, Phase Two." *America*, December 9, pp. 16-19.

Reese, Thomas. 1996a. *Inside the Vatican: The Politics and Organization of the Catholic Church*. Cambridge, Mass.: Harvard University Press.

Reese, Thomas. 1996b. "Digging Into 'Common Ground.'" *America*, September 21, pp. 6–7.

Reynolds, Philip. 1995. "Review of *Same-Sex Unions in Premodern Europe* by John Boswell." *Christian Century*, January 18, pp. 49–54.

Roof, Wade Clark. 1993. *A Generation of Seekers: The Spiritual Journeys of the Baby Boomers*. San Francisco: Harper & Row.

Rosenau, Pauline. 1992. *Postmodernism and the Social Sciences*. Princeton: Princeton University Press.

Rude, George. 1964. *Revolutionary Europe, 1783–1815*. London: Fontana.

Ryan, Mary. 1992. "Gender and Public Access: Women's Politics in Nineteenth Century America." Pages 259–288 in Craig Calhoun, ed., *Habermas and the Public Sphere*. Cambridge, Mass.: MIT Press.

Said, Edward. 1978. *Orientalism*. New York: Random House.

Said, Edward. 1993. *Culture and Imperialism*. New York: Knopf.

Sanks, T. Howland. 1974. *Authority in the Church. A Study in Changing Paradigms*. Missoula, Mo.: Scholars' Press.

Sanks, T. Howland. 1993. "David Tracy's Theological Project: An Overview and Some Implications." *Theological Studies* 54: 698–727.

Schluchter, Wolfgang. 1990. "The Future of Religion." Pages 249–261 in Jeffrey Alexander and Steven Seidman, eds. *Culture and Society. Contemporary Debates*. New York: Cambridge University Press.

Schneiders, Sandra. 1991. *Beyond Patching: Faith and Feminism*. New York: Paulist Press.

Schudson, Michael. 1992. *Watergate in American Memory: How We Remember, Forget, and Reconstruct the Past*. New York: Basic Books.

Schüssler Fiorenza, Elisabeth. 1983/1994. *In Memory of Her: A Feminist Theological Reconstruction of Christian Origins*. New York: Crossroad.

Schüssler Fiorenza, Elisabeth. 1993. *Discipleship of Equals: A Critical Feminist Ekklesia-logy of Liberation*. New York: Crossroad.

Schüssler Fiorenza, Francis. 1991. "The Crisis of Hermeneutics and Christian

Theology." Pages 117–140 in Sheila Greeve Davaney, ed. *Theology and the End of Modernity*. Philadelphia: Trinity Press International.

Schüssler Fiorenza, Francis. 1992. "The Church as a Community of Interpretation: Political Theology between Discourse Ethics and Hermeneutical Reconstruction." Pages 66–91 in Don Browning and Francis Schüssler Fiorenza, eds. *Habermas, Modernity, and Public Theology*. New York: Crossroad.

Schüssler Fiorenza, Francis. 1994. "The Social Mission of Church." Pages 151–171 in Judith Dwyer, ed. *The New Dictionary of Catholic Social Thought*. Collegeville, Minn.: Liturgical Press.

Schwartz, Barry. 1996. "Memory as a Cultural System: Abraham Lincoln in World War II." *American Sociological Review* 61: 908–927.

Scott, Richard. 1991. "Unpacking Institutional Arguments." Pages 164–182 in Walter Powell and Paul DiMaggio, eds. *The New Institutionalism in Organizational Analysis*. Chicago: University of Chicago Press.

Seidler, John, and Katherine Meyer. 1989. *Conflict and Change in the Catholic Church*. New Brunswick, N.J.: Rutgers University Press.

Seidman, Steven. 1994. *Contested Knowledge. Social Theory in the Postmodern Era*. Cambridge, Mass.: Blackwell.

Sewell, William. 1990 "Collective Violence and Collective Loyalties in France: Why the French Revolution Made a Difference." *Politics and Society* 18: 527–551.

Sewell, William. 1992. "A Theory of Structure: Duality, Agency, and Transformation." *American Journal of Sociology* 98: 1–29.

Shannon, Thomas. 1995a. "A Scotistic Aside to the Ordination-of-Women Debate." *Theological Studies* 56: 353–354.

Shannon, Thomas. 1995b. "The Communitarian Perspective: Autonomy and the Common Good." Pages 61–76 in Michael Grodin, ed. *Meta Medical Ethics*. Dordrecht/Boston/London: Kluwer Academic Publishers.

Sheppard, Lancelot, ed. 1967. *The People Worship: A History of the Liturgical Movement*. New York: Hawthorn Books.

Smith, Dorothy. 1990a. *The Conceptual Practices of Power*. Boston: Northeastern University Press.

Smith, Dorothy. 1990b. *Texts, Facts, and Femininity*. London: Routledge.

Smith, Richard. 1994. *AIDS, Gays, and the American Catholic Church*. Cleveland: Pilgrim Press.

Spence, Donald. 1988. "Tough and Tender-Minded Hermeneutics." Pages 62–84 in Stanley Messer, Louis Sass, Robert Woolfolf eds. *Hermeneutics and Psychological Theory*. New Brunswick, N.J.: Rutgers University Press.

Stark, Rodney, and James McCann. 1993. "Market Forces and Catholic Commitment: Exploring the New Paradigm." *Journal for the Scientific Study of Religion* 32: 111–124.

Stein, Arlene. 1997. *Sex and Sensibility: Stories of a Lesbian Generation*. Berkeley: University of California Press.

Sullivan, Francis A. 1983. *Magisterium: Teaching Authority in the Catholic Church*. New York: Paulist Press.

Sullivan, Francis A. 1991. "The Theologian's Ecclesial Vocation and the 1990 CDF Instruction." *Theological Studies* 52: 51–68.

Sullivan, Francis A. 1995. "Guideposts from Catholic Tradition." *America*, December 9, pp. 5–6.

Sullivan, James. 1995. "Catholics United for the Faith: Dissent and the Laity." Pages 107–137 in Mary Jo Weaver & R. Scott Appleby, eds. *Being Right: Conservative Catholics in America*. Bloomington: Indiana University Press.

Surlis, Paul. 1996. "Theology Forum: The Ordination of Women." *The Furrow* 47: 42–44.

Swidler, Ann. 1986. "Culture in Action." *American Sociological Review* 51: 273–286.

Swidler, Ann. 1995. "Cultural Power and Social Movements." Pages 25–40 in Hank Johnston and Bert Klandermans, eds. *Social Movements and Culture*. Minneapolis: University of Minnesota Press.

Tajfel, Henry. 1978. *Differentiation Between Social Groups: Studies in the Social Psychology of Inter-group Relations*. London: Academic Press.

Thils, Gustave. 1973. "Truth and Verification at Vatican I." Pages 27–34 in Edward Schillebeeckx and Bas van Iersel, eds. *Truth and Certainty*. New York: Herder and Herder.

Thompson, John. 1990. *Ideology and Modern Culture*. Stanford: Stanford University Press.

Thumma, Scott. 1991. "Negotiating a Religious Identity: The Case of the Gay Evangelical." *Sociological Analysis* 52: 333–347.

Tierney, Brian. 1971. "Origins of Papal Infallibility." *Journal of Ecumenical Studies* 8: 841–864.

Tracy, David. 1981. *The Analogical Imagination: Christian Theology and the Culture of Pluralism*. New York: Crossroad.

Tracy, David. 1987. *Plurality and Ambiguity*. San Francisco: Harper and Row.

Tracy, David. 1994. "Catholic Classics in American Liberal Culture." Pages 196–213 in R. Bruce Douglass and David Hollenbach, eds. *Catholicism and Liberalism: Contributions to American Public Philosophy*. New York: Cambridge University Press.

Tripole, Martin. 1996. "The American Church in Jeopardy." *America*, September 28, pp. 9–15.

Turner, Mary Daniel. 1976. "Synthesis of Ordination Conference." Pages 135–140 in Anne Marie Gardiner, ed. *Women and Catholic Priesthood: An Expanded Vision*. New York: Paulist.

U.S. Bishops. 1988. "Partners in the Mystery of Christ." *Origins* 17 (April 21): 757, 759–788.

U.S. Bishops. 1989a. "Called to Compassion and Responsibility: A Response to the HIV/AIDS Crisis." *Origins* 19 (November 30): 421, 423–434.

U.S. Bishops. 1989b. "Resolution on Abortion." *Origins* 19: 395–396.

U.S. Bishops. 1992. "One in Christ Jesus. Ad hoc Committee Report/Women's Concerns." *Origins* 22 (December 31): 489–508.

U.S. Bishops. 1994. "Strengthening the Bonds of Peace." *Origins* 24 (December 1): 417, 419–422.

U.S. Bishops. 1996a. "Review Criticizes New Edition of Father McBrien's 'Catholicism.' " *Origins* 25 (April 18): 737, 739–744.

U.S. Bishops. 1996b. "Ex Corde Ecclesiae: An Application to the United States." *Origins* 26 (November 28): 381, 383–384.

U.S. Bishops. 1997. "Always Our Children" *Origins* 27 (October 9): 285, 287–291.

Vaillancourt, Jean-Guy. 1980. *Papal Power: A Study of Vatican Control over Lay Catholic Elites*. Berkeley: University of California Press.

Wagner, Walter. 1994. *After the Apostles: Christianity in the Second Century*. Minneapolis: Fortress Press.

Wallace, Ruth. 1991. "New Roles for Women in the Catholic Church, 1965–1990." Pages 123–136 in H.R. Ebaugh, ed. *Religion and the Social Order: Vatican II and U.S. Catholicism*. Greenwich, Conn.: JAI Press.

Wallace, Ruth. 1992. *They Call Her Pastor. A New Role for Catholic Women*. Albany: State University of New York Press.

Warner, R. Stephen. 1988. *New Wine in Old Wineskins: Evangelicals and Liberals in a Small-Town Church*. Berkeley: University of California Press.

Warner, R. Stephen. 1993. "Work in Progress toward a New Paradigm for the Sociological Study of Religion in the United States." *American Journal of Sociology* 98: 1044–1093.

Warner, R. Stephen. 1995. "The Metropolitan Community Churches and the Gay Agenda." *Religion and the Social Order* 5: 81–108.

Weakland, Rembert. 1994. "Bishops React to Ordinatio Sacerdotalis." *Origins 24* (June 9): 55–56.

Weaver, Mary Jo. 1985. *New Catholic Women: A Contemporary Challenge to Traditional Religious Authority*. Bloomington: Indiana University Press.

Weaver, Mary Jo, and R. Scott Appleby, eds. 1995. *Being Right: Conservative Catholics in America*. Bloomington: Indiana University Press.

Weber, Max. 1904-05/1976. *The Protestant Ethic and the Spirit of Capitalism*. London: Allen and Unwin.

Weber, Max. 1918–20/1978. *Economy and Society*, two volumes. Berkeley: University of California Press.

White, L. Michael. 1997. "House Church." Pages 546–547 in Everett Ferguson, ed. *Encyclopedia of Early Christianity*, volume 1. New York: Garland.

Wilken, Robert. 1994. "Review of *Same-Sex Unions in Premodern Europe* by John Boswell." *Commonweal*, September 9, pp. 24–26.

Williams, Rhys, ed. 1997. *Cultural Wars in American Politics: Critical Reviews of a Popular Myth*. New York: Aldine de Gruyter.

Wink, Paul. 1997. "Beyond Ethnic Differences: Contextualizing the Influence of Ethnicity on Individualism and Collectivism." *Journal of Social Issues* 53: 329–250.

Winter, Marie Therese, Adair Lummis, and Alison Stokes. 1994. *Defecting in Place. Women Claiming Responsibility for their Own Spiritual Lives*. New York: Crossroad.

Wood, James, and Jon Bloch. 1995. "The Role of Church Assemblies in Building a Civil Society: The Case of the United Methodist General Conference's Debate on Homosexuality." *Sociology of Religion* 56: 121–136.

Wuthnow, Robert. 1988. *The Restructuring of American Religion*. Princeton: Princeton University Press.

Wuthnow, Robert. 1989a. *The Struggle for America's Soul: Evangelicals, Liberals, and Secularism*. Grand Rapids, Mich.: Eerdmans.

Wuthnow, Robert. 1989b. *Communities of Discourse*. Cambridge, Mass.: Harvard University Press.

Wuthnow, Robert. 1992a. *Rediscovering the Sacred*. Grand Rapids, Mich.: Eerdmans.

Wuthnow, Robert. 1992b. "Introduction: New Directions in the Empirical Study of Cultural Codes." Pages 1–16 in R. Wuthnow, ed. *Vocabularies of Public Life: Empirical Essays in Symbolic Structure*. New York: Routledge.

Wuthnow, Robert. 1994a. *Producing the Sacred*. Grand Rapids, Mich.: Eerdmans.

Wuthnow, Robert. 1994b. *Sharing the Journey: Support Groups and America's New Quest for Community*. New York: Free Press.

Wuthnow, Robert. 1998. *After Heaven: Spirituality in America since the 1950s*. Berkeley: University of California Press.

Young, Iris Marion. 1990. *Justice and the Politics of Difference*. Princeton: Princeton University Press.

Young, Iris Marion. 1996. "Communication and the Other: Beyond Deliberative Democracy." Pages 120–135 in Seyla Benhabib, ed. *Democracy and Difference. Contesting the Boundaries of the Political*. Princeton: Princeton University Press.

Young, Michael. 1995. "Review of *Same-Sex Unions in Premodern Europe* by John Boswell." *The Historian* 58: 165–166.

Zald, Mayer. 1996. "Culture, Ideology, and Strategic Framing." Pages 261–274 in Doug McAdam, John McCarthy, and Mayer Zald, eds. *Comparative Perspectives on Social Movements*. New York: Cambridge University Press.

Zucker, Lynne. 1991. "The Role of Institutionalization in Cultural Persistence." Pages 83–107 in Walter Powell and Paul DiMaggio, eds. *The New Institutionalism in Organizational Analysis*. Chicago: University of Chicago Press.

Index